NAVIGATE
the SWIRL

ACTIVATE YOUR PURPOSE

ALIGN YOUR TEAM

ACHIEVE YOUR GOALS

NAVIGATE the SWIRL

7 CRUCIAL CONVERSATIONS for BUSINESS TRANSFORMATION

RICHARD S. HAWKES

FOUNDER, GROWTH RIVER

WILEY

Library of Congress Cataloging-in-Publication Data

Names: Hawkes, Richard S. (Change leadership expert), author.
Title: Navigate the Swirl : Seven Crucial Conversations
   for Business Transformation / Richard S. Hawkes.
Description: Hoboken, New Jersey : Wiley, [2022] | Includes index.
Identifiers: LCCN 2021059924 (print) | LCCN 2021059925 (ebook) | ISBN
   9781119868798 (cloth) | ISBN 9781119868811 (adobe pdf) | ISBN
   9781119868804 (epub)
Subjects: LCSH: Organizational change.
Classification: LCC HD58.8 .H389 2022 (print) | LCC HD58.8 (ebook) | DDC
   658.4/06—dc23/eng/20220113
LC record available at https://lccn.loc.gov/2021059924
LC ebook record available at https://lccn.loc.gov/2021059925

For Christina, the love of my life.

Contents

Foreword

by Penny Pennington, Managing Partner, Edward Jones

On January 1, 2019, I became the managing partner (as a private partnership, this is our corollary to a CEO) of Edward Jones—just the sixth one in our firm's 100-year history. The age and endurance of our firm is just one dimension of the moment we found ourselves in—we were a new leadership team, stewarding a storied company into the future.

Our firm was doing extremely well when I began my tenure. Edward Jones had experienced remarkable growth for decades. After starting with one financial advisor in 1922 and growing to 100 financial advisors in the early 1970s, the firm reached the milestone of 1,000 financial advisors in 1986, then added its 10,000th in 2008—and has nearly 19,000 financial advisors as I write this. In terms of number of financial advisors, we are one of the two or three largest firms today.

By almost any measure, the firm has been successful. Edward Jones is listed on the Fortune 500 and is the largest privately held financial services firm in the industry. We serve 7 million clients and care for $1.8 trillion of their assets as of the end of 2021. Our more than 50,000 associates consistently rate us highly as an employer, leading to 22 consecutive years on FORTUNE's "Best Companies to Work For" list.

At the same time, I was acutely aware of the fact that we are on the verge of unprecedented change—and it's change that was already underway before the COVID-19 pandemic began. The investors we meet with are often looking for more than traditional financial advice; what they're seeking looks more like advice about holistic financial wellness. They're interested in a very human-centered approach that is quite different from the way financial advisors have traditionally worked.

What this all means is that the role of the financial advisor must evolve—and the *value* of their role has changed. Clients are placing even more value on having a personal relationship with their financial advisor than ever before. Fortunately, at Edward Jones, that's been our competitive advantage from day one. We've always put our relationships with our clients at the center of what we do. But other firms have started to see the value in it, and they're working hard to close that gap.

In addition to these pressures, there are other elements of change creating great impacts for us. Regulatory changes are rightfully requiring us to serve our clients and their best interest. The economics of our business model are also under pressure—the transaction of purchasing securities has become a commodity and is nearly a free good. Competitive forces have lowered the breakpoint at which clients can purchase certain products. These pressures have an impact on revenue and compensation. Perhaps your business and model are undergoing the same kind of metamorphosis.

With all these factors in play, it was clear that our firm was at an inflection point. To me, it also meant that the conditions were ideal for transformation, and for putting conditions in place for our firm that would allow us to continuously improve over time. It's important in this context to recognize the difference between change and transformation. Change occurs in linear, predictable, and incremental ways—a change to a digitally enabled value proposition, for example. Transformation, on the other hand, is more vertical. It's often about multi-stakeholder (rather than single-stakeholder) impact, and it fundamentally impacts the purpose, culture, leadership, strategy, capabilities, and operating model of a company simultaneously. Transformation is riskier and more unpredictable than change.

Companies transform for one of two reasons. One, they're in a crisis; or two, because they get to—they see that the journey and the effort will be worth it, and they're excited by the possibilities. They recognize that transformational impact can improve not only the commercial enterprise, but also lives and possibilities. Edward Jones is firmly in the second camp. When you have a vision of the impact you want to have, you can either bring that vision down to fit your current reality or you can pull reality up to meet your vision as it was intended to be. Here again, we're in the latter group.

We're pulling reality up to our vision, and we're doing it from a position of strength. We began a change journey not as a discrete event with beginning and end points, but one that creates sustainable conditions for the firm to continuously improve and increase our impact over time—in fact, to quicken the pace of growth and innovation.

The Framework of Transformation

Every transformation must start somewhere—but it's not always easy to know where to start. We saw our initial challenge as identifying the future state we wanted for our firm, and the key competitive advantage that would endure through and beyond our transformation. As we began the work, we considered our purpose, culture, leadership, and capabilities, which helped us identify the gaps between where we were and where we aspired to be. We asked ourselves how we could future-proof our firm.

This exercise was, and is, a deeply human endeavor. We were considering the transformation of a beloved and impactful enterprise, one that tens of thousands of associates and millions of clients take very personally. Our mindset, our relationships, and the ways in which we collectively agreed to lead into the future, became fundamental to the work we were doing.

I believed strongly—and still do—that having a strong organizational purpose is the key to unlocking that organization's human potential. It provides a framework that everything else can be built upon. A worthy purpose unleashes the human spirit. It galvanizes people, and that's critically important, because the "how" of transforming from one thing to something else is hard. In fact, it flies right in the face of a deep human desire—to get good at something and stay good at it by relying on the things that helped you get good at it in the first place.

For a transformation to be successful, it needs to be purpose-driven, leader-led, and team-based. Those may sound like abstract or lofty words, but they become tangible and actionable when you put them to work in a large organization with a long history of working a certain way.

In our case, having some outside perspective proved to be very helpful—and confidence-boosting. We began working with Richard Hawkes and his team at Growth River to help us clarify the approach we wanted to align around in our multiyear journey. The Growth River

Operating System, and in particular the Seven Crucial Conversations, are all built upon a specific way of thinking about teams and organizations, a unique model for understanding businesses, and a particular perspective on how organizations grow and innovate in a team-based way. Richard and his team helped us understand these foundational concepts, which helped set the stage for our journey.

It's also important to note that the Growth River team helped us develop a common vernacular that's proven very helpful in how we approach situations. I've likened it to the language of accounting—everyone knows what a debit or credit is, for example, and we agree on what we're talking about when we use those words. I can't stress enough how important it is to establish a common language around transformation—it makes it easier for us to have meaningful conversations and ensure that we consistently understand each other.

In our case, we've developed a dialect that's unique to Edward Jones. It's connected to our culture and rooted in terminology we've used for a long time. We have added a language associated with a common understanding of how a high-performing team works in concert.

With this language in place, we can have conversations that build more trust with one another and can deeply engage on topics that are critical to our transformation. The language and behaviors of a high-performing team are not intended to make things easy—they exist to make challenging work more productive while unleashing the spirit of the terrifically talented people you have on your team. Richard's team helped us recognize the importance and power of our language and helped us establish a baseline for it. From there, it has become uniquely ours.

An Organization-Wide Approach

Growth River also helped us unlock the full potential of teams within our organization. The theory behind it is simple: we're able to do much more as a team than we can individually. Companies are not machines. They are social systems made up of individuals who themselves have a purpose and thirst to succeed and have impact. High-performing organizations are comprised of constellations of high-performing teams.

Teams are high-performing when they bring together all the necessary perspectives—in other words, the necessary elements to form a system of roles that enable a team to be in it together—to achieve the purpose of the enterprise, the business, and every person on the team. I've learned to never underestimate the power that this concept of role definition can provide in terms of clarity and focus. Defined roles unlock the human potential within teams and then across teams, ultimately lifting the entire organization.

Our leaders and associates lean into this philosophy, advocating for a particular set of priorities that are critical for our future success. They take ownership of that perspective because they know it will ultimately create the impact on our clients, colleagues, and communities that we want to have.

It's an approach that works because we are organized around a shared purpose. That purpose is to *partner for positive impact to improve the lives of our clients and colleagues, and together, better our communities and society.* It's a purpose that guides everything we do. Every decision is made, and every action is done, through the lens of our purpose. It's our "why." It reinforces the notion that our firm does not exist only to help people build wealth. We're more than that. We help people achieve things they might never have otherwise thought possible. We help them connect to their own purpose and bring it to life. Our purpose is the wellspring of our culture, leadership, business strategy, capabilities approach, and operating model. It demands that there be a logical connection among all those dimensions of our approach to growth and innovation.

For us to be able to serve our purpose throughout our second century in business as well as we did during our first, we must transform. Our purpose demands it.

It's equally important that our transformation be leader-led. Our leaders need to live and champion the mindsets needed for our transformation to succeed—their habits of thought and action need to always be in alignment with our goals and our desire to fulfill our purpose. But you don't just "tell" someone about this. Living it out, together, through shared experiences and a journey of discovery and learning, unleashes an ardor for the future that inspires leaders to engage others as they navigate the uncertainty of changing and learning. It's challenging, but it's worth it—the opportunity cost of *not* changing, of *not* adapting to the forces impacting our industry and our business, is too high.

How We're Transforming

As we build on our history and pivot toward the future, the conditions are right for our transformational journey. And we're once again working to stay ahead of the conditions of the stakeholders we seek to serve—the changing needs of investors, a new regulatory environment and pricing and competition pressures, the demands of talented associates, and the needs of our communities in order to be places where people can thrive.

Choosing not to change in our circumstances is also a fixed-mindset approach—and we're choosing to take a growth-mindset approach. That's critical to creating future innovation, staying relevant, and enhancing value to our clients, colleagues, and communities.

Exploring approaches like Agile, Lean, and Design Thinking has proven useful to us in our transformation, as these concepts have helped us recognize what vertical change might look like at the level of processes and operations. In that respect, they really can be quite powerful. The Seven Crucial Conversations referenced in this book, however, are designed to enact vertical change at the level of the social system itself. Resolving constraints at the social-system level is a unique and powerful type of transformation accelerator—the kind that has the potential to move an entire enterprise forward.

Perhaps the hardest part in any transformation is knowing where to start. It can feel like a daunting task, especially for a large, complex organization. It's too easy to start with the "whats" of change—what systems, what process, what talent, what technology. Importantly, Richard and the Growth River team helped us identify a strong starting point—with leadership and with culture, where a deeper understanding of and alignment around the need for transformation must take root and be shared. As Richard himself describes it, "Leadership and cultural agility are the launchpad for all successful transformational change journeys."

Once that learning culture is well established, then an organization and its leaders are able to move onto clarifying roles and identifying the capabilities the organization needs to develop—or not. Only at this stage can leaders begin the work of connecting the right people with the right work and giving them clear accountabilities and responsibilities.

From there, the transformation can progress to establishing strategies and building the right customer experience—which in turn accelerates the organization's ability to activate the operating system of developing, selling, and delivering its product or service within the context of the company's unique competitive advantage.

On paper, this all sounds straightforward, doesn't it? But believe me, in practice, it's not. The work of getting through this progression is the messy middle that requires equal parts IQ and EQ—knowledge and empathy—for the transformation to succeed. It also helps to have a good dose of stubborn determination to journey on through the learning.

In our case, we made significant changes to the structure and style of our leadership. We moved from a top-down directive leadership style to a distributed leadership approach in which we've spread decision-making out across a number of groups—seeking to put decisions closest to where value is created. This approach creates a team-based way of working that's supported by functional areas and is fueled by distributed intelligence and innovation.

Specifically, the most fundamental change we've made is to alter our leadership structure. Previously, we had two committees, an Executive Committee and a Management Committee, through which every major decision was funneled. Now we have a series of forums, each with their own clear roles. This revised structure allows us to move decision-making closer to those who are directly responsible for the work, and ultimately closer to our branch teams and clients.

In this new format, leadership is distributed; each forum comprises a group of leaders responsible for solving the complex challenges we face as an organization. And because different people are responsible for different aspects of our complexity, we have to trust each other. And we do. In that way, team-based leadership is clearly a journey into the interior of each leader, and the alignment of each of those humans to the worthy ambition of the entire enterprise.

Within these forums, the job of leadership is to create alignment— which is not the same as creating agreement. Alignment requires that all participants in the adaptive social system choose to move in the direction of growth. The key is being adaptive and always pointing to growth and innovation—not stagnating around yesterday's value, but discerning tomorrow's value and organizing to create it in sustainable ways that are fit for market.

The key for us will be to ensure that everyone in the Edward Jones organization—all 50,000 of our associates, including me—is going full-out in their role. Transformation is hard; it takes all of us pulling in the same direction. None of us has the luxury of sitting back and allowing "others" to do the heavy lifting. Each of us gets to be an active participant.

That approach is one that must take root at the senior leadership level first, and from there, it can make its way through the entire organization. Our leaders set the example and actively help others develop the mindsets and behaviors we all need to orient ourselves and enhance our ability to live out our shared purpose. We are the "lid" on our organization's success and growth. Whatever becomes available to us in our learning journey and our relationships becomes available to everyone else. It's how we lift the lid and enable our organization to achieve more. (The opposite is also true—if we can't build healthy, productive interdependencies among us in leadership, no one else should be expected to either.)

Growth River's Valuable Contribution

As we've embarked on our transformational journey, the Growth River team has played a fundamental role in the work we've done. I often refer to them as our Sherpas on our path to becoming a high-performing organization. That's because, while they guide us and provide much-needed expertise and perspective, the work is still ours to lead and to own. Richard and his team have consulted with us, but they have also deeply engaged with our teams, offering feedback and truly being in it with us.

Growth River's core tenet, that teams and organizations can achieve so much more than individuals can on their own, is one we fully believe in. The people of Edward Jones create more positive impact for our clients, colleagues, and communities when we're all pulling in the same direction. The Seven Crucial Conversations help us work in a social system and help us move with more agility and confidence as we continue to transform over time.

I consider Richard to be more than a consultant; he's a friend and a fellow traveler on the road to make businesses more useful to all our stakeholders. I'm honored that he asked me to share my thoughts about his approach. I hope his ideas are helpful to you as you consider your own steps toward transformation and work toward unleashing the potential of your organization—and of your greatest asset, your people—to benefit your own clients, colleagues, community, and society.

Enjoy the book!

Penny

Acknowledgments

This book is the product of decades of innovation, application, and reflection among a group of thoughtful, caring, and generous leaders. You know who you are. Please accept my gratitude for enabling me to capture our shared insights. My hope for this book is that you will be able to point to multiple places in it and say "I shaped that, and I know it is true and pragmatic."

To our clients—Alex, Amy, Andy, Bob, David, Gary, Joby, Josh, Julie, Kristen, Laura, Mary Ann, Mark, Marty, Michael, Nigel, Paul, Penny, Randy, Rich, Stacy, and Steve—thank you for giving me and my team the opportunity to create value with you and for you.

To my business partners—Robert, Everett, Deece, Bob, and Sri (in the United States), and Eb and Steffen (in Germany)—thank you for teaching me so much on our shared journey to unleash value in ourselves and others.

To my incredibly talented writing partners—Carter Phipps, Ellen Daly, and Joel Pitney—thank you for investing yourselves in translating the powerful ideas in this book into conversational language that is a pleasure to read.

To those of you who have contributed to the long and winding evolution of our company, Growth River—Marsha, Ted, Tom, Tim, Cristo, Sylvia, Steve, and Dan—thank you for the time together.

To those of you who contributed to my personal and professional learning journey—Ben, Mike, David, Bob, Sam, Howard, Klaus, Thom, Robin, and Jazmine—thank you for your support and coaching.

To Growth River associates—Andrea, Aya, Emma, Fran, Jeannine, Jenn, Louise, Nina, and Samta—thank you for helping us build a great team.

To animal friends—Adele, Blue, Brandy, Cinnamon, Gaspar, Katie, Lisa, Lyla, Muffin, Trinity, and Uxmal.

To my daughters, parents, siblings, and extended family—Emma, Isabelle, and Sophie; Dabby, Dudley; Andy, Jenny, and Tim; Abe, Amy,

Avery, Barbara, Bo, Benjamin, Cassie, Chaz, Chris, Genevieve, Hannah, Harry, Herb, Hildegard, Holly, Janet, Joby, John, Karl, Katrina, Lily, Lorraine, Lynn, Maisie, Mattie, Mary, Matty, Meg, Mimi, Phoebe, Reilly, Sam, Wade, and Zack—thank you for your steady love. I hope this book fuels your dreams and possibilities.

A Note to the Reader: How to Use This Book

The objective of this book is to plant seeds for a shared language, one that enables team members to work together in a deeply human way to evolve and grow companies. For these seeds to take root requires working through the three parts in this book in sequence. If your objective is to apply the Seven Crucial Conversations to plan a major transformational initiative, such as a breakthrough strategy, cultural transformation, or organizational redesign, use this book to create a context for key stakeholders to understand your plan.

This book has been many years in the making, and I'm delighted that it is finally in the hands of readers like you. It has been designed to share what I call the Growth River Operating System—a tightly integrated set of concepts, frameworks, and processes to guide teams and organizations on a transformational journey of growth. I use the term *operating system* because it is the best term that I've encountered to describe the systemic nature of this methodology—the way it provides a platform for ongoing growth and transformation in multiple dimensions of the organization. However, unlike a new OS on your computer, it's not just a package you can install with a click and a reboot. It is much more dynamic and requires ongoing engagement and participation. What I hope to provide you with in the pages that follow is a framework to understand the journey, and a shared language to describe the work you do, the potentials you see, and the challenges you face. I will highlight the key milestones on the journey to higher performance and offer processes for getting teams and businesses aligned. At the heart of this approach are the Seven Crucial Conversations referenced in the book's subtitle.

That being said, you might expect to turn the page and start with conversation 1. But that's not how this book is structured. Indeed, you might be surprised to find that the Seven Crucial Conversations don't appear until Part III. This is because those conversations are designed to take place within a particular framework. Parts I and II provide critical context for the conversations, inviting everyone—whether you are an enterprise leader, or a team member at any level of the organization—to take in the big picture, to step back and understand the broader journey of enterprise evolution.

I'll start with some fundamental questions that anyone serious about organizational change must grapple with. Part I: Framing the Conversation, asks: What is an organization? What is a business? And what does it mean for organizations and businesses to grow and transform? Considering these questions will provide critical shared language, models, and frameworks for the journey ahead.

Part II: The Evolution of an Enterprise, takes readers inside that journey from the perspective of the organization as a whole—starting with the formation of a business and moving through the four stages of enterprise evolution by which it can grow and transform into a large, complex, agile enterprise. In this journey, we zero in on the particular stage where many of today's companies get stuck, and analyze the confluence of factors that come together to create a transformational tipping point that I suspect will be familiar to many readers. I'll introduce new ways of thinking about roles, capabilities, business models, strategies, and teams that can help to anchor you in a higher stage of organizational evolution.

In Part III: The Seven Crucial Conversations, we will turn our attention to the building blocks of the organization—teams. The Seven Crucial Conversations are a transformational template for creating and sustaining a high-performing team—covering leadership, culture, roles, strategies, implementation, and more.

You may be tempted to jump right to Part III, but I'd encourage you to work through the book in sequence. No matter where you sit in your organization's system of roles, you'll benefit from taking in the big picture and considering the journey as a whole as well as engaging more deeply in your particular team and accelerating its journey to high performance. So let's begin! First, I'll invite you to consider an experience that may be all too familiar. I call it the Swirl . . .

Introduction: The Swirl

"We're failing and we don't know why."

"We seem to be succeeding, but we have no idea how."

"Our industry is changing so fast, we don't know how to keep up."

"We're doing the same things we've always done, but it's not working for us anymore."

"We're moving quickly, but we're not sure if we're going in the right direction."

"There are so many competing priorities, we can't seem to make decisions fast enough."

"Everyone is working hard but we're tripping over each other."

"We're stuck. We don't seem to be going anywhere."

D o these sentiments sound familiar? Most people in business are on intimate terms with some—or all—of these frustrating experiences. While they might sound like different, even contradictory, states, in fact they feel quite similar. And nothing captures that common feeling quite so well as one metaphor I hear again and again: *the Swirl*.

Imagine being lost in a churning river, thrown around by the rushing water. You might feel like you're being tumbled down dangerous rapids; you might feel like you're being spun around in a dizzying whirlpool; you might feel like you're entangled in rocks and roots and are hardly moving at all. There's a vague, uncomfortable feeling that a lot is happening around you, but it's hard to know if any of it is actually useful. The swirl is ongoing, but is anything getting clearer? Amidst all the sound and fury, is the team, the organization, or the business moving forward? And how would you know? A tremendous amount of energy is being expended, but to exactly what end?

Whatever the particulars, too many people I meet seem to live with a gnawing feeling that their team and indeed, their organizations as a whole, *could* and *should* run more smoothly, more purposefully, and more effectively. They long for a sense of direction and flow—like a broad, deep river flowing steadily toward the ocean, gaining momentum and power. They sense the potential, and many even have a vision of what's possible—a vision that inspires and motivates them. But they are unable to actualize it amidst the daily swirl. They have an aspiration to be part of a great company, populated with engaged, accountable, committed people doing meaningful work to serve the company's customers and other stakeholders. But they don't know exactly what changes they need to make to achieve this end. They may even have a sense of what needs to be done, but the task feels too daunting. Despite their positive aspiration, the gap between "here" and "there" is an uncomfortable chasm of confusion, and too often, at the bottom of that chasm lies a rusty wreckage of false starts. Elegant strategic plans. Expensive consultants. Inspiring off-sites. Complicated re-orgs. Their daily experience is not the buoyant current carrying them forward, it's the Swirl.

The Swirl is an absorbing state of organizational inertia. It draws our perspective in on itself, narrowing our vision. Our very consciousness runs aground in the muck of the everyday. There is always another problem to solve, pain point to acknowledge, issue to fix, turf battle to win, drama to ameliorate, or political challenge to overcome. And in the midst of it all, we lose track of the future. We forget that we're all on a journey together. Questions like "Where are we going?" and "How do we move forward together?" fade into the background as the endless demands of the everyday stifle our momentum like heavy weeds entangling the rudder of a boat.

I've been an organizational consultant for several decades, and have guided hundreds of organizations, large and small, as they have navigated the journey of growth. And what I've observed is that the Swirl isn't just an expression of organizational dysfunction. This all-too-common experience is a symptom of a much greater challenge. In fact, it might be described as the defining challenge facing organizations today. It's not just a sign that something's wrong with the way things are; it's a wake-up call that signals greater potentials ahead. It represents a critical inflection point in growth that most companies will encounter at a certain stage of their journeys—and that many are finding themselves in the midst of right now. There are a number of factors, both internal and external, that come together to create this frustrating experience. I'll explore these in more depth in the pages ahead, but it comes down to a few key issues.

Internally, it happens when the company reaches a point at which one leader or small top team, however good they may be, can no longer simply direct the company's operations and guide its growth. This may be a result of the company's size or the complexity of the business model; it may also be because the culture of the organization has started to chafe against traditional hierarchy and bureaucracy. Senior leaders and teams no longer have the bandwidth to be in the salient details of the business. They have become remote managers, dependent on others for key insights into business and operations. They are too far away from where the value is actually created.

Externally, it happens because the world around the company, the technologies available, and the markets in which it is operating are changing faster than the company is able to respond. In today's business world, that experience is heightened by circumstances like the Covid-19 pandemic, which has overturned the way we work, leaving organizations large and small frantically paddling, trying to figure out how to operate with a remote workforce while at the same time reinventing business models to meet new rules and more challenging market conditions. And there's no going back to business as usual. The questions we're asking now—How do we align a team and work interdependently when we're not in the same space? How do we make our business models more resilient? How do we win customers' loyalty so they'll stick with us during tough times?—will all continue to be relevant. And the underlying challenge for so many organizations today is this: How do we move from a hierarchical structure with one leader or executive team at the top to a more networked or team-based structure in which leadership is distributed throughout the organization? I call this the shift from directive leadership to distributed leadership.

I'm certainly not the first to broadly identify this as the critical organizational challenge of our time. Many distinguished business thinkers and leaders have addressed it, and many innovative solutions have been and continue to be proposed, developed, and adopted. Some focus on changing the way leaders lead; others focus on shifting corporate culture to be more inclusive and equitable. Some involve radical shifts in organizational structure to eliminate hierarchy or bureaucracy;

others rely on the implementation of operational processes and practices that create more agility and flexibility. I've come to believe that all these approaches have a role to play if an organization is to truly free itself from the Swirl and meet the challenges of the moment.

In 2007, with a group of talented business leaders, I founded Growth River, with the intention of bringing together everything I've learned and sharing it with teams and organizations that want to unleash higher performance. I call it the Growth River Operating System. It's based in my own experience and practice, but it also draws on and attempts to connect some of the best thinking in organizational development and business theory—including Lean, Agile, Theory of Constraints, and Operational Excellence (OpEx). I've also been influenced by other disciplines—complexity theory, evolutionary biology, systems theory, psychology, ontology, and integral philosophy. If that's starting to sound too high-minded, let me assure you that all my thinking and approach has been forged in the crucible of creating growth and delivering value. This is a rational, systematic, analytical, and results-driven approach that includes a comprehensive leadership and management toolbox. And front and center in this approach are people: messy, inspiring, unpredictable, creative, surprising human beings. After all, what is a business without people, for better and for worse?

Because people are front and center in this approach, the "social system" of an organization will get special attention in these pages. It's an essential aspect of the Growth River approach, culminating in the Seven Crucial Conversations. After all, the Swirl is an expression of a dysfunctional social system. Growth and high performance are the product of a social system intentionally created. The road to such a transformation must ultimately pass through individuals and teams, and the productive and purposeful conversations they engage in. Change driven at this level of the organization has the potential to reach all the way down to the ground, and take root.

This is not a theoretical supposition. My experience has shown me that there is a way out of the Swirl. There is a flow to the development of a team and the growth of a business. There is a steady current that can guide us from unproductive chaos to high performance, and that can carry a company from bogged-down and bureaucratic to agile and collaborative. And you don't have to figure it all out for yourself—you can chart your course by principles that are tested and proven.

That doesn't mean you'll always be able to see the way ahead, however—by its very nature this is a transformational journey, a form of fundamental change that reorganizes the whole system of roles and relationships that the organization is built around. How that might look and how it might feel is difficult if not impossible to imagine when you are on the front side of it.

I can't tell you that the journey will be easy. Transformational journeys aren't like that—at least not when they involve human beings. They offer too much to be proffered for so little. This journey will involve real work—reflective moments, honest conversations, hard-won insights, and difficult choices. It will include making important distinctions about team, business, and organizational life. And it will require courageous leadership.

If you're holding this book in your hands, I will consider you a leader, whether your job title confers that role officially or not. Anyone can be a leader on this transformational journey. Wherever you sit in your organization's system of roles, you have the opportunity to use the language, tools, and ideas in this book to create greater alignment and growth among your team. Whether that team is a small functional team responsible for a specific task or an executive team steering the company, its transformation will inspire and catalyze higher potentials in other teams. As teams become high performing, the organization becomes high performing. And as the organization becomes high performing, so, too, do its business models.

So, are you ready to break free of the Swirl? If you're failing, do you want to understand why, so you can change course? If you're succeeding, do you want to know how and be able to accelerate that success? If you're in a fast-changing industry, do you want to get ahead of the trends? If your old ways of doing things no longer work, are you open to trying something new? If you're moving fast, wouldn't you like to be sure you're headed in the right direction? If you're feeling stuck, are you ready to break free? There's never been a better moment to launch your team, your organization, and your business on the river of growth and transformation.

PART 1

Framing the Conversation

O rganization. Business. Growth. Transformation. If you've picked up this book, there's a very good chance that those words mean something to you. But what exactly do they mean? Have you ever stopped to think deeply about what those terms represent? And do they mean the same thing to you as they do to the other people you're working with? If you want to embark on a transformational journey together—to engage in crucial conversations that will carry you forward—it's essential to be aligned around the core concepts, frameworks, and ideas that will shape that journey.

What is an organization? What is a business? And what does it mean for organizations and businesses to grow and transform? Each of these questions opens up a rich set of meanings, metaphors, and models that can help a team or an organization get on the same page about what they are a part of and where they are going. These are questions to which I've given a great deal of thought and consideration. The Growth River Operating System and the Seven Crucial Conversations are all built upon a specific way of thinking about organizations, a unique model for understanding businesses, and a particular perspective on how they grow and develop. Understanding these foundational concepts will set the stage for the journey and frame the conversations to come.

Language is foundational, which is why I spend so much time in this book defining terms and explaining foundational ideas. The terms, models, and metaphors that we use to visualize systems and situations have a profound impact on how we approach them. They shape our expectations of what's possible and the solutions available to us. Languages are the building blocks of human systems, and our ability to collaborate and organize in sophisticated ways around a shared purpose depends entirely upon our ability to communicate. I always say, organizations evolve at the speed of conversation, but we can't even have a conversation—let alone engage deeply in crucial conversations that lead to transformation—if we don't speak the same language. And too often, we may think we're speaking the same language, but actually have very different ideas about what the words we're using mean. That's a major contributor to the frustrating experience of the Swirl.

Throughout this book, you'll see the Growth River definitions of terms called out, with precise interpretations of words and phrases you may never have stopped to think closely about before. (A compendium of terms is also included in the Glossary.) But certain foundational ideas require deeper consideration and discussion: Organization. Business. Growth. Transformation. That's what we'll be doing in this part of the book. As leaders take the time to be more deliberate about how they use these terms, they bring much-needed clarity and direction to the organization's journey, creating a shared narrative. As team members begin to have a truly common language that describes their interactions and endeavors, as well as revealing new possibilities, they find themselves more easily able to align around their shared purpose and direction. So let's take the time to ask these questions: What is an organization? What is a business? And what does it mean for organizations and businesses to grow and transform?

CHAPTER 1

Understanding Organizations

Social Systems, Not Machines

A company is a multidimensional system capable of growth, expansion, and self-regulation. It is, therefore, not a thing but a set of interacting forces. Any theory of organization must be capable of reflecting a company's many facets, its dynamism, and its basic orderliness. When company organization is reviewed, or when reorganizing a company, it must be looked upon as a whole, as a total system.

—Albert Low Zen and Creative Management

"If you to want truly to understand something, try to change it," the psychologist and organizational development pioneer Kurt Lewin is said to have declared. Over the course of the past few decades, my colleagues and I have tried to change numerous organizations—from small startups to well-established mid-sized businesses to massive multinational enterprises.

In the process, I have indeed come to understand a thing or two about these strange beasts. It's not the most elegant way to learn, especially when starting out, since the true nature of an entity is often revealed as it resists efforts at transformation. It's only when you start trying to move the pieces that you see how they're all connected, what keeps them in place, and what animates them. And more often than not, what you discover forces you to rethink your approach. I'm still learning, to this day, but what I can say with confidence is that the more I've learned about what an organization is, the more effective I've become as an agent of change. It is my hope that this learned knowledge may enable me to reverse that quotation for my readers and help you to avoid at least some of the trial and error. *If you want to truly change something, try to understand it first.* Otherwise, you won't get very far. At this point in this book, I invite you to pause and consider the question, *What is an organization?*

Many leaders think an organization is just a business, and their job is simply to run it. If only it were so simple. In fact, the strictly "business" part of an enterprise—the shared work we do to develop, sell, and deliver a product or service to customers—is only part of the endeavor. (That doesn't mean it's not critical—we'll come back to this definition of a business and how to optimize it in Chapter 2, when we introduce the Business Triangle®.) If you're a one-person company doing everything yourself, the business may be all you need to focus on. But the minute you want to grow or scale your company, you have to do something else. You have to deal with people. You must persuade people to join you and motivate them to come along on the journey with you. You must figure out how to inspire people to cooperate, to collaborate, and to become leaders in their own right. And, newsflash: people can be messy, complicated, and difficult—especially when you're dealing with groups of them. There is no getting around this truth.

But along with all of that messiness comes incredible potential. That's why, when we want to achieve things that matter, we form organizations: because we know that we can do so much more together than we could ever do alone. And not just by bending others to our will, but by working to unleash their creativity and intelligence. People can be difficult but they can also be original, innovative, caring, and independent. They can be complicated, but they can surprise you with their commitment and capabilities. Which brings us to the question that has spawned a thousand books about leadership: How do we get from messy, complicated, and dispersed to capable, creative, and aligned? If an organization is much more than a business, what's the best approach to managing it, leading it, and growing it? The answer starts with how we *see* it.

Metaphors matter. As storytelling creatures, when confronted with a complicated, multidimensional, somewhat abstract entity like an organization, we tend to look for images that help us to describe it and make sense of it. We need something we can visualize. And these metaphors we choose will inevitably shape not just the way we talk about our organizations, but how we respond to them and how we lead them.

For example, it's common for leaders and change-management experts today to talk about organizations as if they were machines or computers. Machines have parts, which either work or break down, in which case they need to be repaired or replaced. They have inputs and outputs. Sometimes, they need tune-ups, new engines, or software updates. It's a convenient metaphor, pleasingly concrete. There's just one problem: actual organizations don't work like machines. Businesses are not body shops. And people don't respond well to being treated like parts that either function well or are deficient. If you think simply replacing all your dysfunctional parts or installing the latest trendy management theory like a software update is the answer to building a high-performing organization, you will be in for a long, difficult journey.

One of the central shortcomings of the mechanistic approach is that it sees the whole as being simply the sum of the parts, and the parts as being essentially predictable and self-contained. As anyone who's tried to lead a team of people knows, this could not be farther from the truth. An organization is much more than the sum of the people involved—that's what makes it powerful, but also challenging to manage. And those people are anything but predictable, while being profoundly interconnected. In this sense, as in many others, the machine metaphor is a poor fit and gives rise to leadership approaches that are limited at best. And yet this metaphor—and the perspective and management methods it spawns—is surprisingly persistent in the business community today.

Metaphors matter. How we frame problems and opportunities in our organizations creates the expectations, solution-sets, and "possibility space" in which we operate. A limited metaphor tends to limit our thinking. So, if organizations are not machines, how might we understand them better? What metaphors or images might we adopt to help us describe and guide them? I've come to the conclusion that that best way to see—and lead—an organization is as a *system*. More specifically, as *a complex, adaptive social system.*

That may not be as conveniently concrete as a machine or a computer, but it's a more accurate and therefore more powerful way to understand the human dynamics involved. Organizations are not machines subject to immutable laws of physics, they are human systems subject to the more complex social dynamics of relationships. I've found that this shift of metaphor works with leaders and teams to release and make visible their mental frameworks and consequently opens the door for them to envision and lead transformations that otherwise might have seemed impossible. Leaders and team members must become *systems thinkers*—able to visualize and model the ways in which the elements of the system interact and transform. The Growth River approach to creating high-performing teams and companies is based on this fundamental premise: teams and organizations are complex, adaptive, social systems.

"Complex adaptive system" is a term that comes out of the science of complexity theory. It refers to any system—whether in the natural world, in technology, or in human culture—in which the behavior of the system as a whole cannot be explained simply by looking at the individual parts. It is a system that has something called swarm intelligence—a population of decentralized agents that interact with each other to self-organize around shared purpose and aligned behaviors. For example, think about an ecosystem, an ant colony, the flow of urban traffic, an economy, a language, the human immune system, the Internet, a cell, a nation. In each of these diverse examples, the system has its own properties that cannot always be predicted by understanding the parts. It exhibits self-organizing, or emergent, behavior. You could study an individual bee for years and never fully understand the behavior of a hive. You could analyze a single blood cell from every conceivable angle and not come close to grasping the functioning of the circulatory system. You could memorize every word of an unfamiliar language yet have no ability to use it to communicate.

Complex adaptive systems occur in the natural world and in the human world, but when it comes to human systems, we add the term *social.* In such systems, the complexity is increased by the fact that the system is made up of individual people, each possessing a degree of agency—the ability to choose, adapt, surprise, change direction, as well as create and collaborate in new and interesting ways. Each agent in this system has a unique mental and emotional universe, an interior, subjective world that influences their choices in ways that are hard, if not impossible, to predict or control. At times, that can make everything immensely more difficult and confusing, and yet, the good news is that it makes so much more possible.

> A **system** is a set of things that work together in a way that produces certain outcomes.
>
> **Systems thinking** is when you seek to identify and model the set of things within a system and the relationships between them so that you can accurately plan or produce target outcomes and identify performance improvement opportunities.
>
> A **complex adaptive social system** is a network of individuals that exhibits self-organizing properties and can adapt behavior purposefully, both individually and collectively, in response to changing circumstances.

One of the most remarkable things about human beings is our ability to intentionally *organize* around a shared goal or purpose and in so doing, to achieve things we could never do alone. You might be a brilliant medical scientist who invents a powerful new drug to cure cancer, but if it's just you in your lab, you won't save many lives. You need others to help you manufacture the drug, test it and ensure it's safe, sell it, distribute it, and so on. Or perhaps you're passionate about combating climate change and you come up with a way to generate more efficient energy from solar panels. If you only install it on your own roof, you aren't going to make much of a difference to net carbon emissions. But if you can create an organization to manufacture, sell, and promote your product to tens of thousands of households, you could have a significant impact.

Complex adaptive social systems include all manner of human groupings, from tribes, political parties, sports teams, and religious communities to terrorist groups, gangs, and cults. The term is fittingly applied to business organizations as well. A human organization does not behave like a collection of molecules interacting to create a cell. It doesn't pattern itself like a colony of bacteria, or even the complex interactions of plants, animals, insects, and climate that make up an ecosystem. Although it may have a lot in common with all these systems, the human element adds another dimension to the mix.

When people talk about complex adaptive social systems in complexity theory, they often refer to ants. Ants are a favorite of scientists, in part because of their unique organizing capabilities. They get so much done! They constantly toil, build, and expand their colonies. They exhibit self-organization, division of labor, and can adapt to changing circumstances. And they do it all with only a few types of ants fulfilling a few roles and with brains the size of a microliter (albeit quite large relative to their size). Like ants, humans have the ability to organize, solve problems as a group, and exhibit remarkable feats of collective intelligence. But we do it on a completely different scale of complexity. But it's not only the brain size that makes a difference; it's the balance between our individual agency and our social natures. Humans can collectively organize in large groups, while retaining a high degree of individual capacity for creativity and agency. Indeed, with all due respect to the remarkable feats of our insect friends, human potential for dynamic, creative, collective intelligence is off the charts.

You might think that's obvious, but there are many organizational approaches that assume people are not that different to ants—that we are merely Pavlovian creatures of instinct and incentive. Of course, humans certainly do respond to incentives, and are partially driven by instinct, but that is not all that is going on. And if we want to reach the full potential of organizational life, it's important to recognize that truth. A business is a complex adaptive social system because it is more than the sum of its parts, but also because its parts are people—unruly, innovative, unpredictable, irrational, responsible, empathetic, intentional, creative, surprising people.

In fact, one of the things I love about business is that it represents the cutting edge of our capacity as human beings to join together, engage our best efforts, and improve our lives both individually and collectively. Business, as a shared endeavor, is a kind of evolutionary forefront in our cultural capacity to organize. Of course, humans are tribal creatures and we have always naturally come together and cooperated in small bands, and over the last several thousand years gathered together in larger cities. But larger organizational efforts have been more limited. Indeed, there was a time when the most dramatic and impressive examples of humans banding together in large collectives only happened in rare circumstances, usually through intensive government effort, religious solidarity, or out of military necessity. But over the past few hundred years, something remarkable has happened. Humans have begun to band together in an historically unprecedented way—to accomplish things through the domain of business. These extended tribes have arisen to accomplish all kinds of things together— to create and innovate, to build and scale, to produce and sell. Today's organizational entities go beyond business of course—there are many other examples of large and impressive organizations today, like non-profits or educational institutions. But even so, business has truly been at the leading edge, and sometimes bleeding edge, of learning how to make human organization adaptive and dynamic even as it grows larger and more complex. Indeed, understanding how to make large organizations work in a dynamic way is still a relatively new science, and there is so much to learn. But make no mistake, our ability to solve tomorrow's great challenges will, in no small way, depend on our ability to effectively organize and accomplish things together at scale, in complex adaptive social systems.

In my experience, many business leaders don't think about any of this when they start a company, or even take over an established one. They focus their attention on creating or refining their value proposition, developing their product or services, finding customers, marketing, sales, and so forth. Then one day, they wake up and realize that they are in charge of much more than profit and loss statements. It dawns on them that they are holding the reins of a strange, unpredictable beast that has its own ideas, its own seeming agency, and can be quite resistant to outside input and to demands for change. Occasionally, the necessary leadership skills come naturally, and an entrepreneur or executive manages to navigate this task with instinct and intuition. But even the best instincts in the world only get you so far when it comes to something as complex as human systems.

I remember one painful situation in which thinking of teams and companies as mechanical systems, rather than social systems, led to a near disaster for a company, and a professional setback for me personally. The context was a recent merger of three large consumer products companies. The opportunity, as envisioned by the board of directors who had engineered the merger, was to increase the market potential of the enterprise and to reduce its overall costs by combining and streamlining the sales capabilities across the three companies.

After the transaction had been completed, they moved quickly to change the organizational structure, so that all the sales capabilities from across the three companies now reported to a single functional leader. I remember they gave that person the title of "Global Head of Sales" and he was appointed as the new enterprise leader. The board then directed the three former CEOs, who still had their CEO titles, and the new Global Head of Sales, to work as a team and align on a path forward for the company. As you might imagine, it easily turned into a battle zone, as the three CEOs competed for access to sales resources.

The board had been approaching the issue in mechanical terms, not social system ones. Thinking they could plug and play various leaders from a distance, they'd given little thought to what would make the social system of the combined businesses thrive. And in my role as consultant, I was tasked with aligning this team. Unfortunately, I had not yet embraced a deeper view of organizational life, nor fully understood the nature of the system I was working with. I wasn't yet approaching these issues from a social systems perspective. So I tried to simply convince the competing CEOs that I had a great plan. They resisted. I failed to recognize the social dynamics that were setting them on a path of conflict, and even more importantly, I failed to work with them to build relationships, understand their needs, and co-develop an organic path forward that could actually achieve alignment from the inside out. I was offering a monologue when a deeper dialogue was needed. But in those days, I didn't yet appreciate the transformative power of authentic conversations to influence social systems. As a result, I lost influence, and failed in my mission.

I've seen many business leaders reach the point when they begin to realize that leading an organizational social system is much more complex and difficult than they had bargained for. At that point, they sometimes start wishing that they could simply replace their team. Hire a new group of super-talented, easy-to-manage, uncomplicated team members who already work perfectly well together, and all the problems will simply vanish! But of course, that's not possible. Sometimes bringing in new blood is helpful, but the idea that the problems are rooted in having the wrong people as opposed to inadequate leadership and a dysfunctional organizational regime is the unfortunate root of many problems in today's workplace. I promise you, there is no perfect team out there on LinkedIn waiting to answer your email. Sooner or later, every successful leader has to grapple with a terrible but liberating truth—they can't solve their problems through hiring and firing. They have to find ways to develop their own leadership intelligence, which will then allow them to develop their team and ultimately influence their company. Thus begins the journey, and the real work of organizational transformation.

In most cases, the unpredictability of a complex adaptive social system only reveals itself under the pressures of change. The company may have been ticking along just fine for its first couple of years—small but profitable. It has systems and structures in place; established ways of working; and a well-developed business model for delivering its services. The team is tight, and they've been together since the beginning. They know how things work, and they know who has power and influence. They've learned how to get what they need to do their jobs. But then, one day, everything has to change.

The pressure of change can take many forms. Sometimes, it's good news, like a new market opportunity. Demand for the company's products or services takes off, and it suddenly needs to grow from a quirky startup into a larger enterprise. Sometimes, it's bad news. Competitive pressures in the industry render an existing business model ineffective, and the company realizes it needs to innovate new offerings or risk going out of business. Perhaps it acquires another company or is acquired. As the company begins to grapple with the demand for dramatic transformation, it quickly becomes clear that its old ways of doing things are not going to get it where it needs to go.

The particulars can vary, but it begins to become clear that the existing culture of the organization is faltering. Changes are needed, but aren't happening. Strategic shifts seem impossible. Cultural confusion escalates. People start acting strangely. They seem to agree with what's said in the meeting but then go away and do something different than what was agreed. The Swirl accelerates even as the need to transcend it becomes acute. Frustration grows. Indeed, it can feel as if the system itself is resisting the change. And the leader needs to figure out how to lead the system itself on the journey to higher performance.

Leadership is the art and the science of inspiring and guiding groups of people in a complex adaptive social system to align and navigate the uncertainty of changing and learning together, toward a shared purpose.

Making the type of changes that can lead the organization out of the Swirl is never quick and easy. But here is the good news. It's not just about escaping what's wrong; it's also about discovering what's possible. And this requires a deeper understanding of how we view the organization we're trying to change. Indeed, if you truly want your business to reach its higher potentials, you're going to need to learn how to wield influence not just over individuals but over complex adaptive social systems. Change, in a complex adaptive social system, cannot really be "managed," whatever consultants would like you to believe. It must be led, first through the development of team and company leaders, and then through the development of teams. But leadership of a social system is not a one-way street. As I learned with those three companies in the merger I mentioned earlier, it requires much more than a monologue, however uplifting or inspiring. It's a dialogue, a conversation—in fact, it requires a series of ongoing intentional conversations that have the power to align, reimagine, and consciously upgrade the social system. I've worked hard to refine these conversations into a series of Seven Crucial Conversations, a Growth River methodology that is essential to this upgrade and to building high-performing teams. They also inspired the title of this book. But before exploring these conversations in the second half of the book, there is much I need to convey about social systems, the nature of a business, growth and transformation, the evolutionary stages of an enterprise, and the latent potentials that are embedded in organizational social systems, even those that are mired in the Swirl.

I used the word *consciously* earlier, and it's an important term to pause and reflect on. There comes a point in the evolution of an enterprise when change must be consciously engaged. And that requires leadership. Otherwise, the inertia, good or bad, of the existing culture dominates. Indeed, one way to think about the culture is that it's *what people do when no one is telling them what to do*. That's unconscious or natural culture—the natural pattern of the social system when it is undirected, when people are filling the void and choosing how to behave in the absence of leadership. That may be positive, negative, or otherwise, but when you reach a point where you need to upgrade, shift, or evolve the complex adaptive social system of your organizations, make no mistake, leadership will be essential. It takes leadership to create a more conscious or intentional culture, one in which the ways of thinking and acting are purposefully aligned at a higher level of performance.

Leading Social Systems versus Leading Mechanical Systems

Again, a leadership style is shaped by how the leader sees the system they are working in. If you view your organization as a mechanical system made up of parts, inputs, and outputs, you'll lead it one way. If you view it as a social system composed of people playing their roles, forming relationships with others, exercising their agency to negotiate shared purpose and ways of working in the context of those relationships, you'll lead it another way. The social systems view includes the process flow of inputs and outputs between roles in the system but goes beyond it to take into consideration the human aspect of those interdependencies as well.

In the mechanical systems view, solutions are designed top-down and team members are expected to follow the directives set forth as tasks, processes, and project plans. In this view, some roles are assigned strategic planning responsibilities, and others are expected to execute. Conversely, when operating from the social systems view, all roles are expected to engage and contribute their perspective to the overall strategy. Solutions may still be designed top-down but validated and updated based on bottom-up feedback, and in the context of aligning purpose, roles, and ways of working. In this view, all players are empowered to exercise their agency and choice, and leaders need to align team members around their decisions through communication and consultation.

Although both perspectives have their advantages, the journey of growth and transformation that I'm describing in these pages can only occur if all team members fully embrace the implications of a social systems perspective, as a necessary condition for reaching higher levels of team and organizational performance.

The following are a few key characteristics of the social system mindset as contrasted with the mechanical system mindset:

- **Interpersonal, not impersonal:** Leaders focus on influencing others and creating alignment through conversation, rather than relying on the weight of hierarchical authority.

- **Relational, not transactional:** Leaders focus on building and maintaining strong mutual relationships, rather than supervising outputs.

- **Inclusive, not exclusive:** Leaders focus on ensuring everyone on the team has agency and choice and is fully engaged in the transformation process.

The Art of Alignment

Let's return to that swirling, tumbling river we were navigating earlier in these pages. As you steer your team and organizational watercraft through the rapids of changing markets, around your competitors, avoiding the rocks, and riding the currents, the last thing you need is for all the people on board to be rowing in different directions. You need them to be aligned. You need them to be working for a common purpose, pointing in the same direction—the direction of growth and higher performance.

If the river is calm and the current steady, it can feel like it is less important for everyone to work in a closely aligned way. Some might be rowing faster, some slower. Some might be taking a break and watching the scenery pass by. A few strong arms can keep the boat on course. But as the river gets rougher, with more obstacles, rapids, and eddies, you need all hands on deck. The more complex a system becomes, the more critical alignment is. In any system, there are multiple parts that are in motion, and the overall success of the system is the sum total of those parts aligning in the same direction. In a simple system with just a few parts, some semblance of alignment might be achieved with top-down authority, but it's really just compliance. Once the system grows in complexity, that simply doesn't work. A top-down controlled system will never be able to adapt quickly enough to the changing environment, nor will it harness the creativity and potential that is inherent in its many parts. You're treating people like parts in a machine, and the best that mechanical parts can do is not break down. They can't transform, evolve, or innovate. But if you respect that the parts are free-thinking, creative human beings who make their own choices about how to use their time and energy, you have to take a different approach. Sure, you could enforce compliance, but you recognize that that will never add up to truly high performance. The job of leadership is to create alignment, which is different than creating agreement. That difference is critical. Alignment requires that the individuals *choose* to move in the direction of growth. People can agree, disagree, or anything in between, but they can still independently align and move forward, and that makes all the difference. They don't simply go through the motions; they actively contribute. People who are merely complying feel victimized, and that state of mind is never conducive to high performance. Alignment is a free choice that liberates innovation and intelligence. See Figure 1.1.

> *"Every person in your company is a vector.*
> *Your progress is determined by the sum of your vectors."*
> — *Elon Musk*

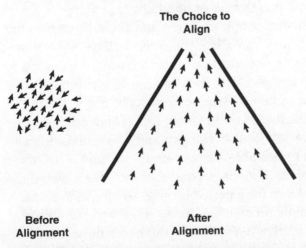

The Choice to Align

Before Alignment   **After Alignment**

FIGURE 1.1   The Art of Aligning People as Vectors

Alignment occurs in a social system, like a team or company, when the individuals come together and adopt shared ways of working toward a common goal. It is not necessary for each person to agree, but they must choose to align out of a recognition that it is for the common good of the team or organization.

To achieve alignment in a complex adaptive social system, leaders must become skilled at breaking complex issues down to the key choice points. These are the moments when people need to consciously choose to come along on the journey together, and the leader's job is to initiate the conversations that lead to those choices. These are the seven "crucial conversations" that we will delve into more deeply in the third section of this book. They are an essential part of the Growth River Operating System. Out of these conversations, people can come to a choice about what's right for the team and decide upon and implement shared ways of working. There is no subterfuge or sleight of hand involved in obtaining alignment. That would defeat the purpose. These are conversations that are held transparently and openly. Suffice to say again that we're not talking about requiring every individual to perfectly agree with or even like the decisions that are made, but we are talking about every individual recognizing those decisions to be in the best interests of the team or organization. Therefore, they'll choose to put that above their own preferences or opinions.

Unless a leader respects people's agency, and skillfully creates the choice points at which they can align, the result will never be transformation in the team or organization. But this way of thinking is counterintuitive. People often think that they can grow faster if they drive choice out of the system. When you're caught in the Swirl, the last thing you feel like doing is inviting more input, opinions, and perspectives into the conversation. That brings about a level of complexity that some leaders find unbearable. They want to "nail and scale" their business models and their systems, so that they run like a well-oiled machine. It may even work for a period of time, so long as the waters are calm and the currents predictable. It may even be appropriate at certain points in the organization's journey. But here's the issue. Without knowing it, they have created a culture with so little tolerance for diversity that it can't handle complexity. As soon as they hit a certain level of complexity, or unexpected events throw them off balance, it becomes difficult to function. By driving choice and agency out of the system for all but the top leadership, they have lowered their own potential as an organization to adapt, to be creative, to pivot, and ultimately to grow and thrive over the long term. If you want to get out of the Swirl, you don't do so by shutting down the conversation; you do so by accelerating the clarity of the conversation, which means getting to alignment.

That is what the Growth River Operating System allows you to do—create alignment and lead transformation in complex adaptive social systems. "Operating System" may sound like it's straight out of the old machine metaphor I've just advised you to leave behind. But it's not software I'm talking about; it's "social-ware." *social-ware* means a system for working together in a social system that enables higher performance. It is an upgrade for the human system in the same way that software can be an upgrade for a computer system. Again, it's not simple, because human systems are not simple. It's not a quick fix, because adaptation and evolution doesn't happen quickly. But it is elegant, creative, uplifting, and powerful, because at their best, human systems are all of those things.

CHAPTER 2

Understanding Businesses

The Business Triangle

If you can't describe what you're doing as a process, you don't know what you are doing.

—W. Edwards Deming

What is a business? And what does it mean to be in business together?

Sometimes in workshops, I lead a simple exercise: I ask people to jot down on a piece of paper their best definition of a business. It's revealing. The answers that people give tend to be strongly influenced by the roles that they play in the company. So, for example, a marketing person might say "a business is a system for winning in the marketplace," whereas a product designer might say "a business is an engine for innovation." People naturally tend to be focused on the deliverables, metrics, and priorities that are their responsibilities. As a result, to borrow an oft-used phrase coined by Michael Gerber, they're used to working *in the business* but they're unable to work *on the business*—because they can't even see the business as a whole. Too often, team members don't have a clear picture of the relationships between different aspects of the business and the way they all fit together. In their minds, it is as if the organization is just a big collection of people with different jobs, all working alongside each other—a giant blob of activity and intersecting objectives.

That's not really a helpful way to think. Organizations may be social systems, but in a business context, they're more than just communities of people. A business organization exists for a purpose: *to create value for customers*. That's what connects the people in the organization and the activities they enact. But when I ask people to describe that overall value creation process—the shared work they are in together with their team and their organization—too often, they come up short. If the people working in a business do not have a shared definition and model of what a business is, is it any wonder that they struggle to align as they go about doing their jobs?

Unless we can visualize our shared work, it is inevitable that we will fall into difficult decision-making, unhelpful politics, unclear roles, redundancies, and inefficiencies. And unless we have a common way to understand the business we're in, we can't work on, improve, optimize, and grow that business together.

The Importance of Visualizing Shared Work

If you work in a manufacturing context—in a production line, for example—it may not be that difficult to visualize the shared work of the team or company. You may be responsible for just one step in the process, but the production line itself is a physical representation of all the stages through which the work flows, and the order in which it must be enacted. You wouldn't try to pick up a widget from one end of the assembly line and move it somewhere else, and you're not worried that someone further down the line is going to start trying to do your job.

These days, however, most people don't work in production lines. In today's flat digital work world, most of us are *"knowledge workers,"* a term coined in 1959 by business writer and consultant Peter Drucker to refer to any person whose job involves handling or using information. According to research firm Gartner, there are now more than a billion knowledge workers globally.[1] And the core challenge for the knowledge worker is finding a way to optimize and streamline their shared work when the processes and products of that work are no longer physical objects being moved from one place to another. So much confusion in organizations comes down to these issues. Things fall through the cracks because no one feels responsible for them. Two people realize they're both doing the same thing. This person isn't talking to that person. No one knows who has the authority to make certain decisions. Or too many people have the authority to make certain decisions. Leaders try to move people around or redesign their org charts to fix these problems, but they don't really drill down to see the system or process that underlie those human roles, responsibilities, and relationships. That system *is* the business, and unless we get clarity on the business, our best attempts to organize around it will still be scattershot. As Drucker pointed out, in order to be productive and effective, teams engaged in knowledge work must invest the time and resources to visualize shared processes and ways of working, because how else will they be able to easily plan, start, stop, track, troubleshoot, and optimize shared work together?

The challenge of visualizing business processes has preoccupied some of the brightest minds over the past century, and you're probably familiar with concepts like value chains, value streams, Lean, Six Sigma, and so on. All these systems—which represented breakthroughs in management and organizational development—are approaches to mapping and optimizing business processes and workflows. However, many of them come out of a mechanistic, manufacturing mindset. They're top-down methods that a leader or consultant can apply to a system to reduce inefficiencies and increase throughput, but they're not really designed for a knowledge work environment in which team members need to be actively, ongoingly engaged in negotiating and optimizing their shared work. They describe a business workflow, but not the set of relationships and the nature of the relationships that have to be enacted for that workflow to happen smoothly. That's the

[1]Craig Roth, "2019: When We Exceeded 1 Billion Knowledge Workers," Gartner blog post, December 11, 2019, https://blogs.gartner.com/craig-roth/2019/12/11/2019-exceeded-1-billion-knowledge-workers/.

question that preoccupied me, from my early days as a consultant. Even with my limited experience at that time, I could begin to see how the lack of shared clarity on what people were "in together" caused numerous problems. I was wrestling with this conundrum when I showed up for a consulting engagement one day—and stumbled upon an insight that would lead me to an answer so elegant that it became a staple of my own work and a foundational element of Growth River for well over a decade now. The story of how I came to it is worth sharing, since it highlights important distinctions. It all started out with the sides of a conference table.

The Business Triangle

I was working with a small business that day, trying to help them understand their workflow so they could get more clarity about who was doing what and how they needed to work together. After discussing their issues for much of the day, it occurred to me that it might help to give them a visual experience of their workflow. The first image that came to mind was the one right in front of me: the conference table. I went around the table and explained each person's respective place in the workflow, from developing their product to delivering it to the customer. The scientist was critical to developing the product but had little interaction with the customer; the salesperson was down the line a bit, ensuring that relationships with customers were value-based and effective; the operations person was further downstream; and on and on. I showed how their business flowed around the table, from role to role, through these various activities. Each was essential and each played a different part.

That session was helpful, and it inspired me to think more deeply about what it means to be in a business together. My conference table brainstorm helped to clarify some of the confusion about roles in the company and it set me on the path to capturing the ways of working that made up that dynamic business system. I asked myself: Is the flow I'm seeing specific to this company? Or is it something more universal? After all, every business had a product or service—be it software, hardware, clothing, food, energy, entertainment, education, and so on. They all have to *develop*, *sell*, and *deliver* that product or service. They each have to manage processes through those sets of activities to deliver value to the customer. And every business has *support* functions that make it all possible, such as accounting, IT, HR, and so on.

These activities each rely on human beings, of course, but they also include resources, processes, technologies, and so on, so I use the term *capabilities* to describe them, and I group capabilities into four types of business capabilities: Develop, Sell, Deliver, Support. A capability is a strategic factor critical to creating value in a business or for a customer. It can be almost any kind of key factor or point of leverage including an activity, a skill, an expertise, a resource, a process, a product, a way of working, or a type of culture. This distinguishes capabilities from *roles*, which are the groupings of responsibilities we assign to particular people in order to enact those capabilities.

Based on my initial insights, I started to create a simple model. On one side was Develop and Sell. On the other was Support and Deliver. The people on one side developed the products or services and sold them. The people on the other side delivered the products and provided customer support. It was basic, but it broke out the essential elements of the business in such a way that anyone could understand the workflow. I worked with this model for a time, and it was very helpful for a number of small businesses. It provided clarity about roles and gave leaders a workflow map that made it easier to diagnose bottlenecks, identify gaps, and untangle overlapping responsibilities. I also noticed something else: When I would speak about this model with leaders and team members, it got them focused on the business as a whole, visualizing it as a complex social system. *It seemed to give them permission to work on the business together, not just in the business*—to rise above the operational trees and see the forest, so to speak. So, I was pleased with the basic tool. Soon, however, I hit a wall—in the form of a large enterprise.

I was scheduled to give a presentation to the executive team of this company, a national clothing retailer, during which I planned to use my model. While preparing, however, I began to realize that the version I had been working with up until now was inadequate to represent their workflow. A large enterprise like this was a different beast compared to the small companies that I'd been applying this model with so far.

In order to help them design a better system of roles that would eliminate many of the problems they were having in their operations, we needed to be able to effectively visualize their business as a system. And my model simply wasn't good enough. I was worried it would create more confusion than clarity. Sitting in my hotel room, the night before the session, I found myself undergoing a mild panic at the recognition that in a matter of hours, I'd be standing in a room full of executives with a blank slide unless I could figure out how to fix it.

I didn't give up. I considered the issues, examined their existing organizational structure, and compared it to the model I had developed. Eventually, late that night, I had a breakthrough. I needed to separate Develop and Sell as well as Support and Deliver. In fact, Develop, Sell, and Deliver each formed a discrete part of a workflow process. Further, there were feedback loops between Develop and Sell, Sell and Deliver, and Deliver and Develop. So was it a circle? No, because circles don't clearly distinguish one part from the other. It was more like a triangle, with three clearly differentiated but connected sides. I sketched out my makeshift triangle on a piece of paper and went to sleep.

In the morning, bleary-eyed and more than a little insecure about my nocturnal breakthrough, I presented the model to the CEO (Figure 2.1). He glanced at it briefly, and then exclaimed, "That's exactly right! It describes us perfectly." Later that day, I led a four-hour discussion using this newly created business triangle with the

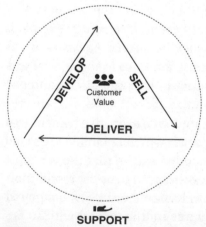

FIGURE 2.1 The Four Business Capabilities Around the Business Triangle

company's executive team. Since that day, my colleagues and I have used the Business Triangle hundreds if not thousands of times with countless companies. It's become one of the foundational pieces of the Growth River approach to unleashing transformation to grow and scale teams and companies.

Develop-Sell-Deliver—three sides of any business activity. Together, those capabilities make up the basic elements of any workflow. *Support*, I realized, was something else entirely. Functions like accounting, IT, or HR, are not directly responsible for the customer experience. Rather, they are responsible for economies of scale within the business. In that sense, they "support" the business, and are best represented as a circle around the triangle.

Business refers to a system of capabilities and roles designed and managed to develop, sell, deliver, and support products and services to target customers toward competitive advantage. The Business Triangle is a way to visualize this definition.

Business capabilities are strategic factors critical to creating value in a business or for a customer. Capabilities answer the question, "What do we need to have in place to execute our strategy?"

Role refers to the function, responsibilities, and accountabilities assumed by a person or a team in a particular situation, scenario, or system.

The Business Triangle provides business teams with an approach to visualize and discuss operating models and organizational structures, which are the place where most company transformations fail. When you visualize and map processes with your team, and use those visualizations to define and organize shared work, you are creating shared language. And, that shared language will enable you and your teammates to accelerate crucial conversations, which will enable your team and company to become high performing. People are able to negotiate how, why, and for what purpose they will interact. We should never underestimate, in business or in life, the power of creating an authentic sense that "we're in this together."

The **Business Triangle** is applied by business teams to visualize the business social system, which includes the flow and interdependencies of capabilities and roles in companies that constitute a business. In Figure 2.2, you can see a simplified example. The capabilities and roles are roughly in sequence of the flow of value around the sides—a discussion that often generates insights. Next to each capability is the name of the business team member who is playing that role, and as such, is responsible for managing and continuously improving those capabilities. Of course, each business will vary a little when it comes to the specific capabilities and roles that populate each side of the triangle.

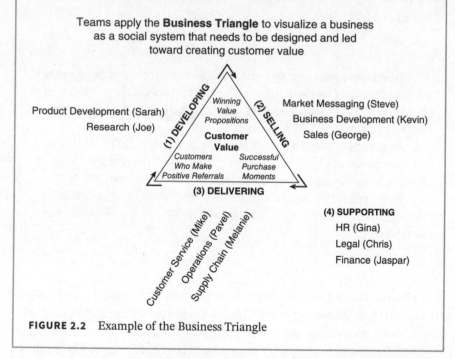

FIGURE 2.2 Example of the Business Triangle

In the Business Triangle for a startup company, the leader's name may show up multiple times against capabilities and roles, because they essentially do everything—develop, sell, deliver, and support! But as the business grows, this changes. In a small to medium-sized business, there may be several people working on each side of the triangle. In a large business, there are likely to be multiple triangles, representing the many business segments or models within the enterprise.

Kairos and Chronos Balance—Time to Work *In* and *On*

In high-performing business teams, members plan and make time to work both *in* and *on* the team and business. They are good at focusing on tasks to be done but are also good at taking time to step back and reflect on progress. They manage a good balance between *Chronos* and *Kairos* time.

We can describe two types of conversations and meeting agendas, using the two Greek words for time: *Chronos* and *Kairos* (see Figure 2.3).

Two Conceptions of Time
that drive different meeting agendas

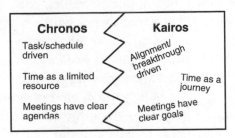

FIGURE 2.3 Chronos and Kairos

Chronos refers to thinking about time as a limited resource that is allocated to tasks and constrained by resources. Chronos meetings have clear agendas and a tight schedule so that everything can be covered.

Kairos, on the other hand, is what happens when we immerse ourselves in crucial conversations around goals and realities. Participants work together, helping each other process complex topics and accelerate thinking. They study, listen, sense, design, choose, align, all following the conversational landscape together. Complex topics can require multiple Kairos meetings, with breaks between, to arrive at a breakthrough, reach a decision, and align a commitment.

Every team needs a healthy balance between Chronos and Kairos. If you spend too much time on Chronos, you'll never grow and scale a company. On the other hand, if you spend too much time in Kairos, you'll never grow and scale a company.

The Engine of a Business

I have been amazed to see the power of the Business Triangle to effectively cut through the seeming complexity of a large enterprise, clarifying the confusion of roles, sorting out overlapping responsibilities, and revealing essential interdependencies. This, in turn, helps catalyze the right conversations to create clarity and alignment. Over time, I've only come to appreciate the power of this model more deeply—in small, medium, and large organizations. In later chapters, I will show how the natural creative tensions between the different sides of the triangle, often a source of crippling conflict, can be leveraged as a source of innovation. It's rare that I work with a business with which, sooner or later, there isn't a significant "aha" moment when the business team realizes how truly tangled its system of capabilities and roles is, which is fueling the Swirl and stymying growth.

The Business Triangle is like the engine of a business. It works best when everything is flowing smoothly around the various functions from Develop to Sell to Deliver without major blockages or confusion. Value creation flows from the original conception and creation of the product or service all the way to the customer, and then there is a feedback chain, coming back from the customer into the Develop part of the business. And around the triangle we go (see Figure 2.4). Meanwhile, our support functions are doing just that—supporting. And the customer is always in sight.

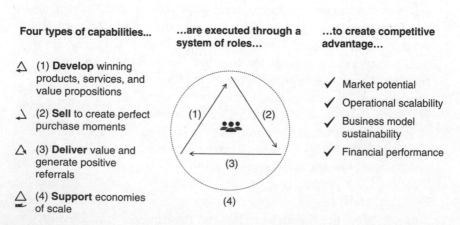

Four types of capabilities...

△ (1) **Develop** winning products, services, and value propositions

△ (2) **Sell** to create perfect purchase moments

△ (3) **Deliver** value and generate positive referrals

△ (4) **Support** economies of scale

...are executed through a system of roles...

(1)   (2)

(3)

(4)

...to create competitive advantage...

✓ Market potential

✓ Operational scalability

✓ Business model sustainability

✓ Financial performance

FIGURE 2.4   The Business Triangle in Action

Indeed, the Business Triangle provides a model of the business that always keeps serving the target customer's needs as a core objective, and aligning the business social system to work interdependently as the solution path. It sounds simple, but in practice, most organizations struggle to identify problems and resolve gaps in their system of roles fast enough to keep up with the needs of an evolving business. When we have the Business Triangle as a simple, shared language with which to discuss who the target customer is for each type of business capability, and what roles are going to own those capabilities, it becomes so much easier to shorten the distance between a problem or a breakdown and an elegant solution and resolution.

And, perhaps most importantly, the Business Triangle provides a model for organizing and growing a business that engages the social system and respects people's natural agency. It doesn't try to slot people into a mechanistic process; it allows them to see what they are in together and negotiate their roles within that system. This is essential for successfully navigating the difficult org structure conversations that come up in (and too often derail) any transformational journey. It provides an empowering and liberating shared language that clarifies priorities and reveals possibilities for optimizing how your business creates value as a team. It's visually clarifying. It boils the essential elements of your business down to a system of capabilities and roles, which then sets the stage for mapping and managing all the critical activities in a business through clear accountabilities. In sum, it allows us to model the seeming complexity of everything that goes on in a business. Throughout the journey of growth that we'll be exploring in this book, this model will be an essential tool. It doesn't capture everything about the nature of an organization or enterprise but it is a critical element in the shared language we are developing. As we bring clarity and transparency to the social system of an organization, the confusion of the Swirl recedes, and we set the stage for the crucial conversations that follow.

Now that we've unpacked and modeled the definition of a business, let's turn to a final framing question: What is growth? In terms of the model I've just shared, there's a simple answer: *business growth is an acceleration in the velocity of value created around the Business Triangle.* Indeed, the throughput around the triangle from Develop, to Sell, to Deliver will determine the speed of growth—for the business or businesses. However, as I've defined it in these pages, an organization is also much more than a business, and one organization can contain many businesses. So if an organization is a complex, adaptive social system and can contain one or more businesses, what does it mean for all of that to grow? And just as important, what might prevent it from doing so?

CHAPTER 3

Understanding Growth

Dynamics of Organizational Development

One can choose to go back toward safety or forward toward growth. Growth must be chosen again and again; fear must be overcome again and again.

—Abraham Maslow

W hat does *growth* mean? In business, the term is used in many different ways. Broadly speaking, it means the business is expanding and improving—perhaps in terms of revenue or profit, perhaps in its number of employees or customers, perhaps in its physical footprint, perhaps in its range of products or services, perhaps in its value as a company. All these are metrics that businesses use to define and quantify growth. Growth can be slow and steady, or it can come in a sudden surge. Sometimes, if growth happens too fast, it proves to be unsustainable. As we've discussed, a business is more than its physical metrics, and if growth is to be sustained, it must become established in the social system. For an organization to grow and thrive, we must consider what "growth" means for that whole system, and how it can be skillfully led.

To take a simple analogy, think of the organization as a child. If you're a parent, you want that child to grow up in the healthiest way possible—to progress in physical, emotional, and intellectual maturity. And most of us, whether we're parents ourselves or not, have a sense of what a child needs at various points in the life cycle. We intuitively know that certain conditions are nurturing and supportive, whereas others might be destabilizing and even damaging. Of course, parenting is far from a perfect science, and growth is not a linear or simple process—it's an interwoven, unfolding set of dynamics with all kinds of complexities involved. But the more a parent understands and recognizes those, the more they can guide, encourage, and support the child's growth. In the same way, the leader of a growing company needs to understand the dynamics of organizational growth, the stages through which it passes, the different needs and challenges of each stage, the constraints it might encounter, and so on.

Growth in an organization—just like growth in a child—has a natural pathway and order. Don't fight that flow. Part of the job of a leader is to understand it better, and in so doing find ways to support and encourage it. You don't need to reengineer the child; you just need to give them optimal conditions, support, and protection. And one of the most important accelerators of growth is that simple awareness: when everyone in an organization, from the leader on down, begins to understand the dynamics of development and to *think developmentally*—about their own roles and about the organization as a whole.

Over the years, I've watched hundreds of organizations, large and small, navigate the journey of growth—from tech startups to national retail chains, from wealth management firms to healthcare systems. In many ways, each journey is unique—the people are different, the customers vary, the products and services are specific to each market. Some are public companies; some are private. Some are for-profit and some are nonprofit. Some are complex enterprises with numerous business lines; others are streamlined specialists with a single offering. But as I observed, and participated in, these disparate journeys, what caught my attention were not the differences but the remarkable similarities. While many aspects of the growth journey are particular to the business involved, the overall trajectory is in fact quite consistent. If you step back from the details of each organization, the path they follow has the same general structure. It includes the same fundamental milestones; it encounters similar breakdowns and breakthroughs; and it leads to the same general destination. Indeed, amidst all of the tremendous variation in the business landscape, there is a game-changing truth that is easy to miss: *The journey of organizational growth and scale passes through a series of stages that are common to every traveler.*

Growth Moves Through Stages

To help illustrate what I mean by "stages," let's continue with the childhood analogy—since it's a journey that you've certainly experienced personally and may also have observed up close if you're a parent. Every human baby embarks on a journey of growth and development—from infant to toddler to child to adolescent and finally to adulthood. Most people would agree that in this process, children pass through recognizable stages that they then outgrow, moving on to the next. Life stage transitions are not only predictable—they are predicted. This doesn't mean all children are the same, or that they all move through the stages of maturation at the same speed. Indeed, any parent will tell you that no two children develop in exactly the same way, and that the ages at which they reach certain milestones like talking, walking, or puberty may differ quite widely, even within a family. But nevertheless, the stages through which they pass are clearly identifiable. They follow an inexorable developmental logic.

This probably seems obvious to most, but it wasn't always recognized clearly. In fact, before the early twentieth century, there was a general tendency to think of children as simply having less knowledge than adults. Their bodies were obviously growing and changing, but it wasn't understood that their psychology, their ways of organizing reality, and their capacities to process their experiences were also developing. It was the pioneering psychologist James Mark Baldwin who first proposed, after observing his own daughter, that children pass through a specific series of developmental stages on their journey to adulthood. This idea was further advanced by the great developmental psychologist Jean Piaget, and today it's become so widely accepted that many of us don't even realize that human beings ever thought differently.

I'd suggest that this is as true when it comes to organizations as to people. Just as a child is not simply a little adult, a startup is not just a smaller company than a global enterprise. It's a *less developed* company. And the journey from one to the other doesn't just involve increasing headcount, square footage, assets, production levels, or revenue. It involves developing and maturing through a series of essential stages that are as predictable and consistent as infancy, toddlerhood, and adolescence. At each change, the organization must fundamentally reinvent how it sees itself, how it organizes itself, and how it interacts with its stakeholders. In Part II of this book, I'll give an overview of what I call the four stages of enterprise evolution, and then we'll take a journey inside the evolutionary process as a company moves through each. But first, there are a few more fundamentals to be covered about the dynamics of organizational growth.

Growth Happens in Three Domains

When you're trying to effectuate growth, the question inevitably arises: what exactly needs to change? No doubt, you'll come up with a list of dozens of things, large and small. Is it the structure of the organization? Its leadership? Its focus? Its operational processes? Its business model? Perhaps it's all the above, and more. Moving your organization to a new stage in its development will likely involve multiple shifts—just as a child moving from infancy into toddlerhood develops in body, mind, heart, and soul. Remember, what's growing is not an object like a machine, but a system—a complex adaptive social system that has formed to create value through one or more Business Triangles. So very quickly, you have a new question: What needs to change *first*? You may know that you want to grow, to transform your team and your organization, but where should you start? It's important to have a method for discerning the right sequence for implementing changes—for knowing which breakthroughs to aim for, in what order, and being intentional about it. Some years ago, I visited the Inca temples in Peru, and it struck me how the bottom of each wall was made up of great big blocks, which got smaller as they moved up the wall. It seemed an apt analogy for the process of organizational change. Which are the big blocks that have to go on the bottom? If you start with all the little ones and then try to balance the big one on top, your wall is likely to fall down. You risk destabilizing the system, creating waste, and causing confusion and resistance. The right sequence will unlock the potential for growth of the business as a social system, the potential for people to fully engage together, whereas the wrong sequence might give you the short-term deliverables that you seek but not the growth potential. I refer to this as a natural developmental path. As a general rule, I've come to recognize that successful change initiatives that move an organization to a new stage need to unfold through three domains of change, in the sequence shown in Figure 3.1.

The transformation begins with **Leadership and Culture**, where a deeper understanding needs to take root and be shared. Leadership and cultural agility are the launch pad for all successful transformational change journeys. High-performing teams and organizations work to get leadership and culture right before diving into the content of roles, strategies, tactics, and execution. The old business adage "culture eats strategy for breakfast" speaks directly to this point. Put another way, a great strategy in an ineffective culture is worth less than a mediocre strategy in a learning culture.

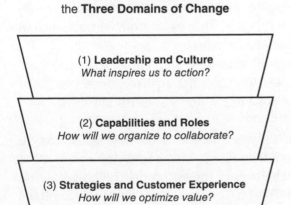

In Teams and Companies
Transformational Change
unfolds in the direction of
the **Three Domains of Change**

(1) **Leadership and Culture**
What inspires us to action?

(2) **Capabilities and Roles**
How will we organize to collaborate?

(3) **Strategies and Customer Experience**
How will we optimize value?

FIGURE 3.1   Transformational Change and the Three Domains of Change

Once the change is established in the domain of Leadership and Culture, it can unfold into **Capabilities and Roles**, playing out in the behaviors of each individual as they relate to the collective. Capabilities and Roles essentially means that it is critical to get the right people doing the right jobs with the right visibility, responsibility, and accountability. And once these are in place, the change can spill over into **Strategies and Customer Experience**, accelerating the company's ability to develop, sell, and deliver its product or service and increasing its competitive advantage. It sounds simple, and in a sense, it is. But, actually enacting this cascade of transformation though these domains of change takes great skill and awareness.

> **A natural developmental path** is the best sequence for you to drive performance improvements in a complex system for maximum impact, and minimum resistance.

Change management initiatives that try to bypass this natural order of unfolding are rarely successful. If you jump straight to strategy before the new forms of leadership and culture are established, you'll lose people's trust very quickly, creating a veneer of compliance but not real engagement. Ultimately, such initiatives lead to change fatigue. Remember, these are human systems, not machines. Human beings have agency. It's a game of choice, not compliance. That doesn't mean everything must be run by consensus, but it does mean that people need to be offered choices, and incentives, to align with the overall direction of growth and high performance.

Likewise, if you jump to strategies and customer experience before you have fully implemented a functional workable system of capabilities and roles, you will likely find those initiatives stymied and undercut.

In Part II of this book, as we explore how the journey of growth looks and feels in more detail, you'll see change playing out in all of these three domains at each stage in the enterprise's evolution. And when we turn to the Seven Crucial Conversations in Part III, you'll see that they are specifically designed to guide a team through these three domains, in sequence. Of course, transformation is not as simple as one-two-three-and-done, because organizations are layered and complex. But in broad strokes, at each level, whether it be a single team, a small business, or a large enterprise, you'll see how the natural path of transformation flows from leadership and culture, through capabilities and roles, and on into strategies and customer experience. Following this sequence unlocks the potential for long-term, sustainable growth in the entire social system.

What Limits Growth? Understanding Constraints

The analogy between organizational growth and childhood development is helpful, but it only goes so far. When it comes to organizations, the fact that stages of development exist does not mean they are inevitable. Indeed, unlike the biological and psychological journey of babies growing into adults, an organization's evolutionary journey cannot be taken for granted. All organizations may encounter the same pressures and problems sooner or later, but as complex adaptive social systems, they have to *choose* and *align* to take the next step.

Yes, I believe that the stages represent a natural developmental path. In other words, they are not a system we impose on an organization or a senior leadership team so much as a pattern that emerges organically as an organization evolves, once constraints to its growth are removed. They involve a series of challenges and breakthroughs that companies can be expected to experience as they develop. In many companies, these stages will unfold all by themselves, over years or even decades. However, progress through these stages isn't a given. It is all too easy for arrested development to occur. An organization can get stuck at one stage or fail to see the potential that awaits it on the other side of an entrenched status quo.

Why do organizations get stuck? Growth occurs naturally in most systems, when the conditions are right. If growth stops, it's because something is blocking its path, like a logjam in the river. When debris piles up, the forward-rushing flow of water may be reduced to a trickle. Stagnant pools form, and things settle into stasis. The same happens in an organizational system. Growth is happening, production lines are flowing, customers are buying, revenue is increasing, the organization scales up in response, and then at some point, it slows, or stagnates. Sometimes, the reason is obvious. Changes in the competitive landscape. Location issues. Infrastructure. Personnel. Other times, it can be hard to pinpoint where exactly things got stuck.

In the business world, the sticking point in a system is often called a *constraint*. The term comes from the work of Dr. Eliyahu Goldratt, who shared it in a hugely popular 1984 business novel entitled *The Goal*. The essential insight of constraint theory is that in any given system there will be one key limiting factor that stands in the way of the system growing, improving, and achieving its goals. This is known as the primary constraint. Sometimes the constraint is obvious; other times it's hidden. Sometimes it's unchangeable, in which case all you can do is optimize around it. However, if you can identify and remove or resolve the primary constraint, a system will transform and move to a higher level of growth. Figure 3.2 shows a system resolve its primary constraints and break through to higher performance levels.

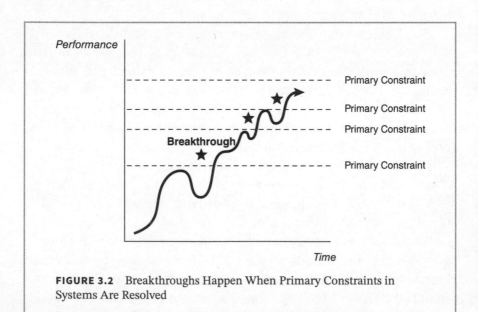

FIGURE 3.2 Breakthroughs Happen When Primary Constraints in Systems Are Resolved

Goldratt used a manufacturing scenario to illustrate this idea, showing how removing bottlenecks in a production process increases efficiency and throughput (see Figure 3.3). But it is equally true in any system. "Since the strength of the chain is determined by the weakest link, then the first step to improve an organization must be to identify the weakest link," he writes.[1]

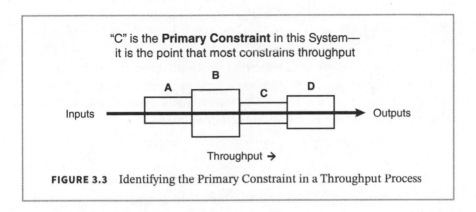

FIGURE 3.3   Identifying the Primary Constraint in a Throughput Process

A simple example of a primary constraint in a manufacturing environment might be a certain type of machine. If the machine is only capable of producing 10 items every hour, that will always limit your capacity to deliver your products. You might try to change other things—hiring more people to speed up other parts of the system, moving your factory to a better location, improving your delivery processes to ensure fast delivery to customers. These changes will make some difference, but the essential bottleneck remains in place. But if you can increase the capacity of that machine by, for example, purchasing more machines or getting a better machine, you could resolve the primary constraint in the system, and the business could grow exponentially.

---

[1]Eliyahu M. Goldratt, *The Goal: A Process of Ongoing Improvement*, 3rd ed. (Great Barrington, MA: North Rover Press, 2004).

A **system** refers to a group of things or parts that interact to create outputs or outcomes. To apply primary constraint thinking, you must visualize the system, describing its parts and how they interact.

A **primary constraint** is the one key condition that currently most limits higher sustainable throughput or performance in the system. When it is resolved, another will emerge to take its place. Actions that optimize a primary constraint, or resolve it have the highest potential impact. All systems will have a single primary constraint.

Throughput refers to the capacity of the system to create intended value within a given timeframe.

A **breakthrough** is an event that resolves a primary constraint in a system, thereby making performance jump up. High-performing teams and companies grow and scale by intentionally creating and leading breakthroughs, which requires constraint thinking.

The Theory of Constraints, as Goldratt initially conceived it, was aimed primarily at optimizing manufacturing processes, not transforming organizations as a whole. But it is also a powerful way to think about growing and scaling companies because it can focus leadership teams on the the highest leverage point for transformation. Identifying and resolving constraints is the fastest path to high performance. You can change and optimize all kinds of factors in a system and not fundamentally impact its potential for growth. But if you can identify and resolve the primary constraint, growth will occur, even if there are many other areas that could still use improvement. This is what we call a breakthrough, because it moves the whole system to a sustainable higher level of performance. When a primary constraint is resolved, sooner or later another will reveal itself. At that point, the higher level has become a plateau, and to go to the next level, you need a different approach than whatever led to your last.

Some years ago, I was brought in to consult with the leadership team at a national women's clothing retail chain. The company had been founded in the early 1980s in a small gallery on a Gulf Coast Island that was popular with tourists. The founder worked in close collaboration with his vendors and channel partners to create a winning customer experience. They sold unique pieces designed and curated

The team at the Woman's Clothing Company created
a **Business Triangle** that was something like this one...

Clothing and Accessory Design and Curation
Consumer and Marketing Research

Market Messaging and Branding
Real Estate and Store Construction

FIGURE 3.4   Example Capabilities Mapping Around the Business Triangle

to inspire women to feel good (no matter their age) and to help them express their personality and individuality with confidence. He had nailed his value proposition and the next step was to scale it, which he did, building a business team to fill out the capabilities around the Business Triangle. Figure 3.4 shows a simplified example of how that looked.

Their aim was simple: to open and support as many retail stores as possible, capitalizing on the winning customer experience. Their primary constraint was on the Sell side of the triangle: it was the speed at which they could open those stores. Put another way, the company could grow as fast as it could open stores to sell and deliver.

And it did. It went public and scaled over the next couple of decades to have over a thousand stores. It hired the best lawyers and real estate experts and effectively removed that constraint to growth. It was so successful that at one time it had the highest sales per square foot of retail space in the industry. But by the time I arrived to work with the enterprise team, things weren't looking so bright. Same-store sales had been declining week-over-week for almost a year, and the company's stock price was in a tailspin.

At our first offsite meeting, I introduced the Business Triangle, and in short order it was clear that the primary constraint had shifted. It was no longer on the Sell side—opening new stores faster wouldn't help them grow. It was on the Develop side. They needed to make significant changes to their value proposition, rethinking the store concept in light of changing fashion trends and changing consumer behavior and increased competition.

As I looked into team members' eyes, I could tell this was not new news. They already knew that their primary constraint had shifted. So, why were they stuck? The challenge, I learned, was that no one on the senior leadership team, not even the CEO, had a license to make significant changes to the founder's original formula. The founder was the majority shareholder, he controlled the board of directors, he had chosen the current CEO, and he had not given him the authority to make those kinds of changes.

Over the next day and a half, the team openly discussed various dimensions of the challenge. They made commitments to stick it out together. And they reached initial alignment on a plan. This was a smart and experienced group of business leaders that was pulling together to do whatever they needed to do to win as a team. The CEO agreed to meet with the founder and make the case for having the decision rights that he needed to lead the transformation. Other team members would draft the plan for rethinking the core brand experience. In private back-channel discussions between the CEO, the CFO, and me, the CEO framed out how he might want to reconfigure the membership of his enterprise team, adding more representation from the Develop side. He thought that one particular person should be promoted to enterprise team. In addition, he warned, the company would likely need to pause plans for opening new stores, at least until same-store sales could be aimed in a positive direction. After a day and a half of intense work, the team atmosphere still felt a little nervous but also much more hopeful.

Unfortunately, though we had identified the new constraint and a way forward, the existing social system would prove intransigent. We had agreed to meet again in a month, but the meeting got postponed, and then postponed again. Finally, when two months had passed, I arrived for our session, only to discover that no progress had been made toward resolving the constraint. The founder had remained adamant that his formula was not to be changed. What had they been doing for two whole months, I wondered? Well, it turned out they'd been doing something: they'd opened more than 50 new stores! They'd reverted to doing what they were good at, unable to deal with the fact that the constraint had moved and something different was required if they were to grow.

Constraints theory is a powerful tool for revealing what needs to happen in a business to reach the next level of performance and growth. But organizations, as we've seen, are not machines or even assembly lines. To resolve the constraint in such a way that propelled them to a high level of growth, the company would have needed to engage with the difficult human dynamics embedded in its social system. I worked with the team for a few more months, but the writing was on the wall. Not much later the CEO and other senior leaders began to leave the company.

Two Types of Performance Improvement: Horizontal and Vertical

Understanding constraints leads us to one final distinction that is critical to understanding the dynamics of growth. There are fundamentally two different ways to think about performance improvement in any kind of system: *horizontal and vertical*. Put simply, horizontal improvement means that you optimize within the constraints of the current system. You don't try to remove or resolve the primary constraint, but you do everything you can to perform better with the constraint in place. Vertical performance improvement occurs when you resolve a primary constraint. A breakthrough occurs where you find yourself in a different landscape. It's the domain of innovation and transformation.

Horizontal improvement refers to improving the performance of a system by managing or optimizing conditions at the present limiting constraint while not resolving the constraint itself (see Figure 3.5).

Vertical improvement refers to improving the performance of a system by resolving or removing the limiting constraint, leading to a breakthrough that allows the system to gain a new higher sustainable level of performance (see Figure 3.6).

(continued)

(continued)

Horizontal Improvement—optimizing the System
within current constraints and perfecting the System

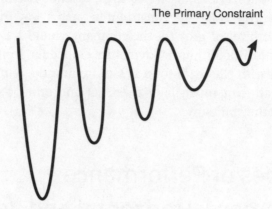

FIGURE 3.5 Horizontal Improvement

Vertical Improvement—resolving Primary
Constraints and transforming the System

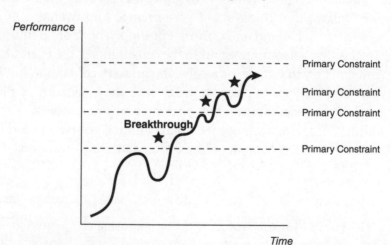

FIGURE 3.6 Vertical Improvement

Successful innovation always includes both vertical and horizontal shifts.

A classic example of the two perspectives is a railway company. Horizontal improvement is about having the trains run more on time—cutting costs, improving processes, streamlining operations. You know the rails you're running on, but you can make the train more efficient and predictable. Vertical improvement, on the other hand, is like laying new tracks that take your train to a new destination.

All that being said, both horizontal and vertical are important modes of change. Both are necessary for a company to thrive. It's not an either/or situation; nor is one better than the other. Transformational growth in an organizational system requires both. If you only focus on horizontal change, sooner or later your system will stagnate. You'll eliminate all the inefficiencies from the system, but because you're not tackling the primary constraint, sooner or later you'll reach the limits of optimization. You see this often in companies that are really good at one thing—for example, maybe they have a sophisticated production process, or a great marketing team—but they have little capacity to innovate beyond that singular strength. Horizontal change is rarely adequate to meet the demands of long-term development and growth. However, it is necessary. If you focus only on vertical change, you'll neglect the important work of stabilizing your processes, becoming more efficient, and keeping costs down. Entrepreneurs are often likely to err on this side of the equation, because their natural inclination is to innovate, not to manage.

Managing the delicate balance of vertical and horizontal is a task every leader must embrace. And it's not possible unless you know where the constraints lie in your system. Sometimes, once you recognize a constraint, you might decide it's a positive check on the system. I'm part owner of a baked goods company that makes vegan minimuffins. We've created a very efficient production system, but the speed at which we can produce our minimuffins is constrained by how fast we can mix the batter. The mixing bowls are our primary constraint—and we've decided that's a good thing. It gives us a point of control in the system, which helps us to ensure quality and control work in progress.

When it comes to horizontal change, there's plenty of great advice to be found and systems you can adopt. Approaches like Six Sigma and OpEx can help you optimize within the limits of your current system. When it comes to vertical change, that's a greater challenge. Approaches like Agile, Lean, or Design Thinking can help you consider what vertical change might look like at the level of processes and operations. In that respect, they can be quite powerful. Growth River and the Seven Crucial Conversations are designed to enact vertical change at the level of the social system itself. Upgrading the "social-ware" of an organization—resolving constraints at that level—is a unique and powerful type of transformation. It can move your entire organization—its leadership and culture; its capabilities and roles; its strategies and implementation—to a new developmental stage, reflected in a new structure and operating model that tell a whole new story about who you are and why you exist. Are you ready to experience the four-stage journey of enterprise evolution? Let's begin . . .

PART 2

The Evolution of an Enterprise

Organizations evolve. And not only do they evolve, they do so through a predictable series of four evolutionary stages. In this part of the book, I'll be introducing those stages and then inviting you on a journey inside the process of enterprise evolution. Each stage, as you'll see, represents a greater capacity to manage complexity, enact transformation, and respond to changing conditions with agility. At each stage, the organization goes through a multidimensional transformation that embraces each of the three domains of change: leadership and culture, capabilities and roles, strategies and customer experience. From a 10,000-foot vantage point, we can look down and see the contours of the journey. This is powerful because it allows us to see where we are and where we are going—to orient ourselves in the midst of change.

In the chapters that follow, I'll start with that big picture overview of the evolutionary stages, and then take a slower approach to each stage, guided by questions such as these: What does each stage look like and feel like on the ground? How do companies make the transition from one stage to another? What pressures push them forward? What potentials begin to be revealed? What kind of leadership is required to make the leap? And what conditions are necessary to sustain it? In this journey, we'll pay particular attention to the critical transition that faces more and more companies today: the transition from stage 2 to stage 3, from directive leadership to distributed leadership.

In this part of the book I've chosen to use a fictional company—Radiant Love, Inc.—to illustrate the journey through the early stages of enterprise evolution. Although the challenges our heroes face and the lessons they learn are all based on very real challenges faced and lessons learned in countless companies I've worked with, the particular situations and characters in this story are fictional, and any resemblance to a real company or real persons is entirely accidental.

The attributes of this fictional company are intentional. I wanted the purpose of Radiant Love to be profoundly important to its founders and customers. I also wanted to portray a fragile purpose that could be easily be corrupted through unconscious or unintentional leadership. It needed to be a company that would be challenging to grow and scale with integrity of purpose. And that is how my team invented the Radiant Love Café: a place where people looking for true love and hopefully finding "the one."

CHAPTER 4

The Four Stages of Enterprise Evolution

Every structure is to be thought of as a particular form of equilibrium, more or less stable within its restricted field and losing its stability on reaching the limits of the field.

—Jean Piaget, *The Psychology of Intelligence*

So, what are the four stages of enterprise evolution? Let's begin with a quick overview, so you can see the trajectory of the journey. In the chapters that follow, we'll take a slower approach, following our fictional company, Radiant Love LLC, through the stages and exploring the dynamics of transformation from one stage to the next.

Obviously, any given organization is unique in many ways; each will have its own culture and business focus. Each will require certain skillsets, attract specific types of employees, serve different markets, thrive in different locations, and so on. But if you go a step deeper, beyond the surface specificities, you will see deeper structural patterns and ways of working that will be similar, even across widely different sectors. This model has been validated through direct application in hundreds of companies across different industries, countries, and cultures over decades.

The first stage, which could be compared to the organization's infancy, is what I call **Independent Contributors**. This is the early formation stage, where an entrepreneur or group of founders get together to turn an idea into a business. The social system is just beginning to form and has little formal structure. There isn't a single governing business strategy yet but there is a strong willingness to pool resources and figure out how to deliver value. The organization does whatever needs to be done to get its products or services to market.

The second stage, which represents the beginning of a more mature organization, is what I call **Directive Leadership**. The organization has naturally grown to a point where it can't just function in a haphazard way anymore if it is to effectively scale. Someone needs to take charge and create more structure and order. The senior team needs to have a single business and team leader responsible for higher performance. From here, the organization can "nail and scale" its business model—for a while.

But eventually the social system becomes too complex for a single leader to manage and competitive advantage erodes. There are many reasons why this happens, as we will see, but in the process companies can easily get caught in the Swirl of bureaucracy, internal politics, power struggles, and constant re-orgs. For some organizations, the solution to declining competitive advantage is to double down and refocus on scaling a single business segment led by a single business leadership team. However, for others, the solution is to broaden the scope of products and services in order serve new markets—becoming an enterprise with several business lines. For those organizations, the way through the Swirl is to mature into the third stage, which I call **Distributed Leadership**.

This stage reveals a new level of effective leadership and a team-based, matrix structure that can innovate and bring to market an ongoing portfolio of business lines, supported by cross-organization functionality, and fueled by distributed intelligence and innovation. From here, the organization can expand and grow into multiple compatible business segments in parallel—for a while. But eventually, the pool of business leadership talent in these organizations becomes overstretched. At this point, some organizations mature into the fourth stage, which I call **Leaders Leading Leaders**.

Organizations in this fourth stage invest to mature in two ways. First, they invest to systematize and scale the work of leaders and managers, so that team leaders can delegate to team members. Second, they invest to systematize and resource workflows at key points of interdependency between teams, building cross-functional teams and capabilities. See Figure 4.1.

Their goal is to create the conditions to sustain a flat agile team-based organization, in which a relatively small pool of senior leaders is able to operate from a strategic perspective, above the details, and to leverage a focused leadership mechanism across portfolios of self-managing teams.

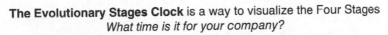

The Evolutionary Stages Clock is a way to visualize the Four Stages
What time is it for your company?

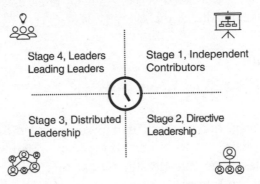

Stage 4, Leaders
Leading Leaders

Stage 1, Independent
Contributors

Stage 3, Distributed
Leadership

Stage 2, Directive
Leadership

FIGURE 4.1　The Evolutionary Stages Clock Is a Visualization of the Four Stages of Enterprise Evolution

Stage 1: Independent Contributors. 0:01—A loose confederation of allies has joined forces, and a nascent business is born. The goal of the group is to pool resources, but it is not necessarily to align as a single business. Aligned leadership in the group is based on consensus.

Stage 2: Directive Leadership. 3:01—A single intact business leadership team leads the organization with the goal of nailing and scaling one business model. Functional capabilities are organized to support this business model. Aligned leadership is based on autocratic decision-making by the leader of the business and team, as required.

Stage 3: Distributed Leadership. 6:01—The organization is a portfolio of capabilities that serve multiple business models and segments. It has been restructured into a team-based matrix, based on intact high-performance teams (HPTs). Aligned leadership is driven mostly by consultative decision-making, direct conflict resolution, and other HPT ways of working. Decisions are only rarely escalated for autocratic decision-making by the enterprise leader.

(continued)

(continued)

> **Stage 4: Leaders Leading Leaders.** 9:01—The enterprise has developed the systems needed to charter and support agile self-managing teams, at the level below intact teams that are required at senior enterprise, business, and functional capability levels. The organizational structure is flat, with the fewest required intact teams at the top and self-managing teams reporting into those teams. Aligned leadership is driven by consultative decision-making, direct conflict resolution, and other HPT ways of working. Decisions are only rarely escalated for autocratic decision-making by the enterprise leader.

Stages of How, Not What

These are not stages of *what* a company does, but of *how* it does it. Critical to this picture is the mode of leadership, which is why many of the stages are described in leadership terms. But there is much more to each stage than just leadership.

It's important to understand that these stages don't represent a hierarchy of purpose or virtue, nor do they correlate with levels of sophistication in products or services. You could have a stage 1 company offering a state-of-the-art product or performing a critical service to the community. And you could have a stage 4 company that's making very mundane products.

That being said, because higher stages are able to manage more complexity, higher-stage companies can be expected to have a significantly greater potential for value creation and performance than lower stage companies. They will be more agile, innovative, and scalable and as a result, able to identify and capitalize on opportunities faster. Higher-stage companies will also require access to significantly greater pools of capital and talent to sustain higher performance. However, it's important not to simply equate "higher" with "better." We don't say that an adult is better than a child, even though we acknowledge that they are more developed and have greater capacities. Lower-stage companies may be perfectly suited for their particular goals, challenges, and opportunities at a given moment—and some companies will be very successful without ever progressing beyond stage 2. Every stage in the journey has its own intrinsic value and should be honored, even as we recognize that over time, the movement toward higher levels of performance will necessitate a move up the stages.

Nor can these stages simply be equated with increasing size. Does size matter? "Not really" is the simple answer. Any size organization can be highly developed, just as any size can be simpler. The evolutionary stages are not just about an organization getting bigger, although sometimes there is a correlation.

What the stages really track is the evolution of our ways of organizing—our ability to align a social system and optimize the capabilities and roles through which we work together to create value for a customer.

As a business grows, the need for a workable, functional system of capabilities and roles matters more and more. As an organization journeys through the stages of enterprise evolution, its capabilities and roles evolve at each stage, reflected in a more sophisticated leadership mechanism, more intentional culture, and a more complex but also integrated structure.

Organizational structure refers to how organizations divide roles, authority, and reporting relationships. This is typically envisioned as a top-down approach that can be more about compliance than exercising individual agency.

System of capabilities and roles refers to a dynamic way in which teams or organizations design, distribute, and align roles and interdependencies to create value. This is both a top-down and a bottom-up conversation that encourages individual agency, ensures strategic alignment, and creates the conditions to leverage distributed leadership.

Systems of capabilities and roles and organizational structures are much more than just a set of job descriptions. They are the platform that determines how the social system aligns and organizes itself to create value. One could say that this system or structure is a reflection of the mindset and consciousness of the organization—reflecting how the organization sees itself, and also the people who work for it.

Consider the difference between an organization that is structured like a pyramid, with a leader at the top and successive layers of management below, and a company that is structured like a circle, with equal power-sharing among partners. I'm not saying one is good and one is bad, or one is better than the other. But they do tell very different stories. Have you ever asked yourself the question: What story does your organizational structure tell? What narrative does it reflect—about its role in the market, it's products and services, the quality of its people, it's confidence and maturity?

When I go into any company, there is always a story that the leaders will tell me about why it's succeeding or failing, why it needs to change, where it's come from, where it's going, and so forth. That's all well and good, but I'm also interested in the stories that are more deeply embedded in the very design of an organization. What narrative does the org chart tell? What story is embedded in the balance sheet and budget? Does the system or structure of the organization match the story of its leaders? Does it reflect the organization's future, or its past?

Organizations are holders and carriers of a tremendous amount of human energy and purpose dedicated to a specific end. If, for whatever reason, the organizational system or structure is problematic or dysfunctional, or mismatched with the mission, things break down. All of that positive human energy, instead of being focused, amplified, and concentrated on the purpose of the enterprise, dissipates or gets trapped internally. Bureaucratic wrangling and inertia, internal politics, competing goals and priorities, disconnection with the marketplace—these are each ways in which that human energy becomes stuck. Ineffective or mismatched organizational systems or structures sap human energy, trap it in unproductive organizational loops or bureaucratic whirlpools, and prevent it from a more natural outflow of purposeful activity. Such energetic blocks also prevent easy information out of and back into an organization. In other words, they prevent healthy external feedback. Instead of information entering the organization and getting quickly and properly funneled through it, natural feedback from the market gets lost and bogs down as it travels through layers of bureaucracy. It is unable to provide the role of supporting and empowering a nimble, adaptive response. Sooner or later, that is reflected in the success of the mission, not to mention the bottom line.

I'm not saying that systems of capabilities and roles and organizational structures are the be-all and end-all of business activity. No structure, leadership mechanism, or system of roles on its own can unleash human potential. But it can certainly hold it back. Usually, it is a reflection of the mindset of leadership. But there are times when that mindset goes through positive changes, yet the organizational system or structure stagnates. Trying to send fresh, new energetic engagement through a crusty, old structure can be like trying to send electricity through a medium that carries it poorly. You get some semblance of a charge, but the result underwhelms.

As we journey through the stages of growth, you'll see examples of how transforming a company's leadership mechanism, system of roles, and structure can optimize the flow of human energy and creativity, and can unleash the power inherent in the social system.

Each of the evolutionary stages looks and feels completely different on the inside of the business, and also has very different results on the outside. Each stage has its own constraints and limitations, and the desire to solve these is what propels the company forward. The key change that happens at the transition points is a change in the ways of thinking and acting of leaders and team members. These changes then ripple out to the leadership, culture, strategies, customer experience, and other aspects of the business.

In the chapters ahead, we will take a deep dive into each stage, focusing on how an organization grows from one stage to the next— the critical pressure points that propel that growth, the potential roadblocks it may encounter, and the ways in which leaders can encourage and streamline this natural journey. In particular, we'll focus on the critical transition from stage 2 to stage 3, because that is where most organizations find themselves caught in the Swirl. But before we do that, let's take a moment to appreciate the simple but powerful insight that there is a series of consistent stages through which organizational growth and development occurs when the conditions are right.

Why is this important? Because knowing what the organizational journey looks like and being able to pinpoint where you are on that journey can mean the difference between effective, targeted change leadership and multiple, expensive, ineffective re-orgs. If you know where you are and where you're going, you can institute smart policies that grow the business and make every team member more satisfied and productive and avoid pouring time and money into change efforts that leave you with nothing to show for it.

Perspective is everything. Without understanding the journey, a leader is like a mouse trying to find its way through a maze without a map to the piece of cheese waiting in the middle. They run into a wall of problems, and they make a turn toward daylight, trying to forge a better direction. Sometimes they wonder if they're covering ground they've already traversed, or whether they're going forward at all. When the leader understands the journey of growth, however, it's as if the mouse is lifted above the maze. Suddenly it can see the twists and turns from above, and it can discern the path that will take it where it wants to go. Not only can it see the milestones ahead; it can also see possible shortcuts and ways to accelerate the journey.

Understanding the evolutionary stages model and the current transition you are facing as a company—knowing what "time it is on the clock"—is essential to understanding your team's journey and the desired future you're trying to achieve together. The model provides insight into the challenges and opportunities that companies face at each stage. Knowing this enables companies to accelerate their performance journey.

The journey may not follow a straight line, but it moves in the general direction of growth and higher performance. Challenges and problems may still arise, but they can be anticipated and skillfully navigated. There may be a long way to go, but the destination awaits. No matter where you find yourself on the journey of growth, seeing the journey as a whole gives confidence and courage to forge ahead.

CHAPTER 5

A Business Is Born

Stage 1, Independent Contributors

An entrepreneur's life is really a continuous journey.

—Kiran Mazumdar Shaw, founder, Biocon Ltd

Strega Regio knew a thing or two about love. In fact, her matchmaking skills were nothing short of legendary in the small Midwestern town where she'd settled after a long journey from the "old country" when she was just a teenager. Some said she'd learned her secrets from her Italian *nonna*. Some speculated that she possessed psychic powers. Some claimed she'd single-handedly been responsible for as many as a hundred happy marriages, including that of the town's mayor. Whatever the case, as she celebrated her seventy-ninth birthday, surrounded by her children and grandchildren, Strega was enjoying a comfortable retirement. But her grandson Paul, who was seated beside her during the festivities, couldn't help marveling at how many people approached her to ask for dating advice or introductions.

Fresh out of business school, Paul knew an opportunity when he saw one. His grandmother was already helping a surprising number of people—but what if they could turn her skill into a business where many more lonely singles could find a chance at love? When he pitched his grandmother on his idea, Strega was secretly thrilled to have a reason to get out of the house every day. They met at a local coffee house, sipped espresso, and began to plan. The setting for these early conversations found its way into the business plan, and in 1995, their shared vision became reality with the launch of the Radiant Love Café: a place where people looking for true love could connect over coffee and hopefully find "the one."

The café was an instant success, drawing crowds of hopeful singles and creating a vibrant community. They came up with creative ways to encourage long-term connections—like offering two-for-one specials for people who met at the café and came back for a second date, and coffee on the house for any couple who made it to 10 dates. The space was designed to invite people to linger and settle in, and each table was set up with getting-to-know-you question cards that quickly had strangers laughing together. A "missed connections" corkboard allowed guests to leave notes if they'd lost someone's phone number or been too shy to say hello in person. Special events provided opportunities to mix and mingle, and guests could sign up for singles adventures led by various local businesses. Paul set up a limited liabilities corporation (LLC), opened bank accounts, negotiated with suppliers, and did the books himself. He was the first one there every morning, and the last to close up at night. Strega herself showed up almost every day, to the delight of guests, and the wall behind the bar soon filled with smiling photos of couples whose love stories had begun right there.

Early-stage businesses, like the Radiant Love Café, are often delightfully unique. Indeed, part of what makes a new business successful is some degree of novelty, along with a healthy dash of personality that helps it catch the attention of its first customers. There are endless beginnings in the entrepreneurial imagination, but when those seed ideas go from mental conception to physical and social reality, they have more in common than you might think. Just as all babies have unique genetic makeups and distinct personalities, yet are also all clearly babies; enterprises in the first stage of their development are both distinctive and possessed of a particular set of identifiable characteristics.

The first steps in the formation of a business are usually tentative, fumbling, even idiosyncratic. Early stage ventures are often barely even structured. At Radiant Love, they didn't have an org chart. Paul ran the business stuff because he had the MBA, while Strega was in charge of the look and feel of the place—as well as occasionally serving cappuccinos herself with a dose of romantic wisdom on the side. They hired a couple of high school kids to work behind the counter and clean up, and struck up an ad-hoc partnership with a local coffee roaster to provide fresh beans and give the place an artisan vibe. When one of their regulars mentioned that she'd once been a pastry chef at a fancy New York restaurant, they worked out a deal to buy pastries and pies to serve with the coffee. Eventually, a couple of other partners came on board, including a local event planner.

This is the stage of enterprise evolution that I call Independent Contributors. There is no fully formed organizational structure with established roles and job titles, no star-studded venture capital firm issuing directives, no board of directors raising money. Think of two or more consultants who share an office and one day decide to go into business together. They slowly form a partnership, hire employees, share clients, work their networks, and try to build back-end infrastructure. Or a couple starting a web design business out of their living room. Or two friends tinkering with electronics in their garage and creating something they think they can sell. Or three scientists working in a lab, deciding to go all-in on an early-stage medical device company. Who does what? How do they handle development? Sales? Ownership shares? The initial stage of a business is often filled with uncertain alliances and partnerships, unpredictable growth, lots of twists and turns, and a struggle just to build out the necessary infrastructure to sustain their emerging organization. You wear any hat that needs wearing. The recipe for success at stage 1 is usually expressed in terms like this: *We, the partners, are better off together than separately.*

Stage 1: Independent Contributors. *A loose confederation of partners, each with its own business approach. Central leadership is based on achieving consensus among senior partners.*

Entrepreneurs or founders at this early stage—and I have worked with a lot of them—often feel like they are in the middle of an unfamiliar river, just trying to do whatever they have to do in order to keep the company afloat. If you talk to them, they will tell you a story that goes something like this: They're treading water, trying to find something to hang onto in order to get the organization to function. Little by little, pieces of flotsam float by and they grab every piece they can. Eventually, through great effort, they manage to create a makeshift raft. They use just about anything available to make that raft hold together. They cut any deal, work with who they need to work with, create whatever alliances they need in order to get their craft to float on the water. Everything is up for negotiation to achieve the goal.

In a stage 1 organization, and especially in a fast-growing one, it takes a tremendous amount of effort, intention, and resourcefulness to get things to stabilize. The raft may not be pretty, it may not be elegant, it may not be efficient—but it floats! It's even able to navigate the river in some rudimentary way. And that's better than sinking. Through great individual effort by each of the people involved, you have built an organization that actually functions. The result is one or several independent rafts, heroically built and captained by highly resourceful independent contributors with MacGyver-esque capabilities, each struggling to float and maneuver on the rushing river. Decisions are usually made by consensus among the various founders or team members, and the ability to manage any kind of complexity beyond day-to-day operations is limited. Such is the nature of stage 1. And that's okay—when a company is just getting started, it doesn't need to be bogged down in bureaucratic systems, nor do the founders have time to be designing org charts and writing job descriptions. They just need to get the job done!

Occasionally, companies skip stage 1 altogether. Today, we hear about powerful, venture-funded startups emerging fully formed out of the forge of a technology incubator, with five-year business plans and clearly designated roles and responsibilities, right off the bat. Such companies are essentially going straight to stage 2. With the right resources, it's possible for a company to bypass the early, messy era of growth. But that's the exception, not the rule. For the most part, early-stage businesses in their infancy have little in common with the well-funded Silicon Valley unicorns. Instead, they muddle through, doing the best they can to stay afloat and attain some stability. Slowly, a customer base is built, cash flow increases, patterns are established, and the raft begins to pick up a little momentum as it moves down the river. It only works for so long, however. If a company is to have a future, it will need to leave this independent contributor era behind.

Like the coffee beans they ground freshly every day, Radiant Love grew organically. It wasn't always a smooth ride, by any means. Paul had plenty of days when he wondered why on earth he'd thought this was a good idea. As he tinkered with a cash flow spreadsheet while simultaneously trying to fix the malfunctioning espresso machine and field calls from a pair of newly engaged customers who wanted Strega to officiate at their wedding, he thought longingly of what life would have been like had he turned his MBA into a cushy consulting job. But there were plenty more days when his heart swelled with pride to see his grandmother's superpower turned into such a thriving business. The original café was so popular that they soon outgrew their small location and moved into a larger space in a busy downtown plaza, with outdoor seating and a small stage for live music. They hired more baristas and got an accountant so Paul didn't have to do the books himself. Strega mentored a few aspiring matchmakers who became known as the "love coaches." Eventually, they hired a manager to oversee the operations on the ground. The Radiant Love raft had become a river-worthy vessel. When the coffee roaster proposed creating a second location near the university, Paul didn't hesitate, and the new café quickly proved to be a hit with students.

Two years after their launch, Paul got an email from a journalist who'd heard about this unusual matchmaking venue and wanted to feature the café in a story for the *New York Times* magazine. The day after the story went to press, the phone wouldn't stop ringing. Café owners across the country wanted to copy the Radiant Love model. "Can you teach us how to do it?" they asked. "Can we partner with you? We'd like to use your branding and model ourselves on your success." Paul's entrepreneurial instincts told him they were onto something. His business savvy also told him that there was no way they were ready for this.

Radiant Love had been doing quite well for a small local business. It was profitable—not something many early-stage businesses can boast. It had basic systems and structures in place, and the team trusted each other and knew how to work together. But how were they to respond to the sudden opportunity that had landed at their feet? They didn't have a business model that could easily be replicated in multiple locations. They didn't even do things the same way at their two cafés. To meet the new opportunities the market was offering, they needed to become more than a quirky, beloved local business. They needed to create a brand identity that could be rolled out nationally. If they didn't want to just run all the new locations themselves, they would have to become a franchising body and create a certification and training arm of the company. And as they began to grapple with that dramatic transformation, it quickly became clear that their old ways of doing things were not going to get them where they needed to go. They weren't even clear who should be making the decisions, much less what decisions they should be making. They needed to make a shift—and it wasn't just about getting bigger. It was about moving to a new stage in their evolution as an organization.

In the evolution of an enterprise, the catalyst for a shift from stage 1 to stage 2 is sometimes an unexpected opportunity, as in the case of Radiant Love. Perhaps it's an influx of investment, or an unsought celebrity endorsement on Instagram. Other times, it's a crisis. Perhaps the complexity of the company reaches a point at which it is simply too difficult to steer all these independent rafts in the same direction. Sometimes, with organizations at this stage, it's not even clear who is steering. There is often no single governing vision, but rather, a system of complicated alliances and power-sharing agreements. The need to decide by consensus gets more and more cumbersome as the business grows. So, the realization dawns that *someone has to lead*. Someone has to take charge, in order to simply get everyone pointing in the same direction. The organization needs a clear vision, a more deliberate structure, and a strategy for clear execution. And it needs one person to drive that. Otherwise, chaos reigns and sooner or later the business will flounder. Whoever becomes that leader has to figure out how to wrest control of the company from a bunch of independent contributors, take the helm of the newly redesigned ship, and captain it more intentionally.

Paul knew that the writing was on the wall. People were naturally looking to him for leadership—after all, he was the one with the MBA. He kept trying to bring everyone into the decision-making process, but it was slowing things down. He could feel the tensions rising as the company struggled to re-create itself. He tried to seek counsel from Strega, but her relational wisdom was more suited to romantic partnerships than the challenge of structuring a fast-growing national enterprise. Finally, he realized that he needed to be CEO: "If we're going to do this without completely losing control of our vision, I need to be in charge of the whole company." Strega was more than happy to agree, as were the other partners. None of them felt qualified to lead the company where it was going, and quite frankly, none of them wanted to.

The shift to directive leadership often involves renegotiating the original agreements and partnerships that formed the business. That can be easy or painful, but it needs to be done to give the business the best chance at success. Otherwise, there's little chance it will survive, much less thrive, as the river swells and you encounter rapids.

Whatever the catalyst that brings the principals in the business to the realization that it's time for a single leader, it's generally something everyone can recognize. Sometimes the impetus is internal, with the founders simply reaching a breaking point. Other times, it takes an outsider like a new executive, a consultant, or a board member to come along and look at the makeshift raft with fresh eyes. "This doesn't make any sense!" they declare. "Why would you put things together this way? It's completely inefficient. There are much, much better ways to do this!"

Indeed, there are. But that's not an indictment of the founders who built the raft. Remember, at stage 1, the point was just to get the raft to float, whatever it took! Never blame people for succeeding under the conditions they've been given. They're doing the best they can with what they have, even if the eventual goal is to change those conditions and discover new ways to thrive. But when the new ways become visible—indeed, when they become unavoidable—there's no sense in hanging on to that rickety old raft. It's time to get better organized. It's time to bring some semblance of sanity, functionality, and efficiency to the business. The organization is ready to embark on stage 2 of its developmental journey, which is called Directive Leadership.

CHAPTER 6

A Leader Steps Up

Stage 2, Directive Leadership

Your first and foremost job as a leader is to take charge of your own energy and then help to orchestrate the energy of those around you.

—Peter F. Drucker

In a chaotic organization that is growing fast, the move to directive leadership can be a sweet relief. The chaos of stage 1 abates. Decisions are made more quickly, strategies become consistent, clarity is established, and the company is able to align and move forward. It no longer feels like everyone is just muddling through and trying to stay afloat.

For an organization or a business that has been toiling in stage 1, clear direction is like manna from heaven. Everyone can focus on developing, selling, delivering, supporting, or whatever their particular job may be. Directive leadership is the natural answer to the confusion of stage 1, which is why it is the next step forward in the journey of enterprise evolution.

Stage 2 is the most common of the four stages of enterprise evolution. In terms of sheer numbers, stage 1 companies may be prolific but they are often short-lived. By some estimates, more than 50 percent of companies fail within the first five years. Successful stage 2 companies have made it through the rough waters of their infancy, become established, and started to scale. The transition to stage 2 represents the moment when venture capital might step in, once the value proposition is established and the business needs an infusion of funding to scale. Companies at this stage generally have a single business model and a boss or leadership team directing operations. Most small to medium-sized companies fit this description. Decision-making falls to that single business leader or team whose job is to drive everything forward. They will be responsible for purpose, focus, strategies, roles, and incentives. Leaders provide directives and consequences, and compliance is expected. The recipe for success at stage 2 is usually expressed in terms like this: *We, the executive business team, have to nail and scale our business model.*

Stage 2: Directive Leadership. *A single intact business leadership team leads the organization with the goal of nailing and scaling one business model. Functional capabilities are organized to support this business model.*

We often hear the phrase "command and control" when people talk about old-school models of leadership. This military-style method tends to be unfavorably contrasted with more enlightened, distributed models of authority. It's important to be clear, however, that the stage of organizational evolution we're calling the directive leadership stage is not just command and control. Or at least, it doesn't have to be. Directive leadership is not just an assertion of authority, an imposition of one person's will on everyone around them. It isn't about controlling people. It's about clear direction and execution. Directive leadership is usually a very positive step forward in the evolution of a business. It's appropriate for a certain stage of development. It's a significant part of how you grow a business! In fact, that reorganization of the social system around a new leadership model and organizational priority is what supports a new level of growth and success.

One of the early challenges in stage 2 is that a newly appointed CEO or leader often has to learn how to fulfill the requirements of that position. If they've been brought in from outside, having played the role before, this might not be hard. But if, as is more common, they're an entrepreneurial founder emerging out of stage 1, suddenly they have to learn how to be directive. They have to be willing to make the final call—on incentives, compensation, strategic priorities, and on who plays what role. For any new leader, this can be a serious hurdle, but it has to be done. Of course, I'm not talking about some kind of autocratic takeover. In a directive leadership context, the leader needs help from all sides, and seeks input, advice, and strategic guidance. One person or one team is not expected to have all the answers. But that person or leadership team is expected to have a consistent, clear set of strategic priorities that they execute with efficiency. That makes a huge difference. It brings everything into alignment.

Whenever I think of stage 2 leadership, a quote by Elon Musk comes to mind: "Every person in your company is a vector. Your progress is determined by the sum of all vectors." That may sound abstract, but it's a great way to think about directive leadership. It's an emanation of energy, intention, and direction from a central source—the CEO or the executive team—directed through the organization, aligning everyone and pointing them in the direction of the company's priorities. In a sense, the employees in such organizations become like the arms, legs, hands, and feet of the overall organizational body, delivering on the strategic directives of the brain. In stage 2, everyone knows the business they're in, they know the plan, they know where they're going— they just have to nail it and scale it! Yes, there will be changes and adjustments along the way. But the path is clear.

Once Paul stepped up to be CEO of Radiant Love, the national rollout began to gain momentum. Investors were eager to get in on this promising company, and with the influx of capital, Radiant Love was able to select key locations for new cafés in cities across the country and hire managers to run them. Paul sought out local partners to provide coffee and baked goods for the new cafés. Knowing that his ability to oversee multiple locations was limited, he also brought in experts to help him create a franchise model, with support services for the franchise owners. He hired consultants to refine and standardize the brand identity. As the company grew, he found himself needing to assert clearer guidelines for everything—from the way the cafés looked to the people they hired to the marketing materials they used. At the root of much of it, he realized, was language.

Shared language was something the team had never really thought about when they were sharing the same small café space every day. That is, unless Strega started whispering conspiratorially in Italian to the young barista, and the manager demanded to know what she was saying! But when they decided to expand, language became absolutely critical. One person's idea of a "cozy, welcoming coffeehouse" was another person's idea of a rather sleazy looking bar. One franchise owner seemed genuinely puzzled that the skimpy uniforms he'd designed for the girls serving coffee were not quite what the company meant by "warm and informal." One love coach's idea of frequently checking in with clients via text was seen as overprotective handholding by others. Paul, Strega, and their leadership team quickly realized they had to reach for a much greater degree of clarity and be more assertive in setting rules for their café managers and franchise owners if they were to preserve what made their brand and culture special as the company rapidly grew.

Avoiding Stage 2 Bottlenecks

Directive leadership doesn't mean the leader or executive team has to do everything. In fact, companies that take this approach quickly get a lesson in the Theory of Constraints (see "What Limits Growth? Understanding Constraints" in Chapter 3). Radiant Love had plenty of eager café operators who wanted to become franchise owners, but at first, setting up each new franchise required Paul to fly there himself and ensure that the space was suitable and the brand was being honored. He had to train the staff personally and spend considerable time on the ground. Even if he did nothing else, he was still a bottleneck. His time became the company's primary constraint, and without resolving that constraint, its growth would be stymied. Paul tried hard to be more efficient—delegating all his other responsibilities, spending so much time on the road that his wife and kids began to complain—but he still couldn't keep up with demand. Finally, his mentor—an old professor from business school—sat him down and said, "Paul, you've got to stop. Focus your energies on standardizing your protocols and values. Then, train people who can go out in your place and help set up the cafés." Paul took the advice, hired and trained a team of regional managers, and the company's primary constraint was resolved. Over the years that followed, dozens of new franchises were able to get up and running, and Paul missed fewer of his kids' baseball games.

For a while, Paul was so caught up in the company's rapid expansion that he didn't notice that Strega was fading. It just seemed like occasional absent-mindedness and general fatigue, but it soon became unavoidably clear that the demands of being involved with the business were simply too much for her. At the urging of her family, she stopped her daily visits to the original café, but not before she sat down with Paul over cappuccinos and confided in him that she was worried about the growing business. She didn't want the cafés to just become a casual meeting place and lose their focus on creating long-term love matches for their target market of "serious singles." The managers Paul had hired were good at keeping the cafés profitable, but did they understand the human heart? Paul took his grandmother's concerns seriously and they agreed that the Radiant Love Certified Coach program needed to be robust and true to Strega's approach and principles in order to support the cafés.

In 2000, Strega passed away peacefully at home, surrounded by her loving family, and leaving her fast-growing and fast-transforming company in the capable hands of her grandson, who was proving himself to be a strong but fair-minded leader.

With a good leader in place, many companies find their groove at stage 2 and spend the majority of their lifetimes there. They keep optimizing—solving constraints and bottlenecks and getting more efficient at what they do without fundamentally changing the model. There is nothing wrong with that. It can be a perfectly functional way of organizing and serve all of the needs of the business. Let's take a software company that has developed a popular and successful app to fill a need that hasn't been met before. The company spent several years designing, iterating, and getting the product right, but now, it works great. There will still be regular upgrades to roll out, but the main job of the company is to "nail and scale"—to find and serve more customers. Directive leadership is an ideal model for that company. Or let's consider a different industry. Perhaps an enterprising chef has developed a restaurant concept that is perfectly positioned for the urban market. She started out in one city, opened several locations, and built an enthusiastic following. Now, the company's job is to scale up that restaurant chain by opening a hundred more identical restaurants in similar locations across the country. Yes, there may be adjustments and refinements along the way. But the concept works, the business model is established, and the main thing to do is replicate it. That's a job for directive leadership. A great business concept often has a long runway for growth, and harvesting the potential of that type of business takes a smart leadership team.

However, there are many situations in which directive leadership starts to become dysfunctional as an organizing structure for the company. The frustrating experience we've been calling the Swirl starts to consume people's energy, creativity, and focus. That dysfunction is a sign—it lets us know that we have outgrown this particular model and the company is ready for stage 3. On the evolutionary stages clock (Figure 4.1), it's that point right around 5:30—an appropriate point for a wake-up call! *It's time to evolve.* The evolutionary pressures the company is encountering, both internally and externally, are setting the stage for the next transition, from directive leadership to distributed leadership. And it's no small step for an organization to take. Indeed, this is the developmental challenge that constantly confounds even the best and brightest in our executive ranks. If there is anything we've learned about organizations over the past couple of decades, it's that in a fast-moving information age, directive leadership has its limits. And the bureaucracy that often replaces it is ineffective. This is the context in which Growth River's social-ware upgrade becomes mission critical.

CHAPTER 7

A 5:30 Wake-Up Call

The Transition to Stage 3, Distributed Leadership

I hope you will abandon the urge to simplify everything,
to look for formulas and easy answers, and begin to think
multidimensionally, to glory in the mystery and paradoxes of life,
not to be dismayed by the multitude of causes and consequences
that are inherent in each experience—to appreciate the fact that
life is complex.

—M. Scott Peck, *The Road Less Traveled*

Beep ... beep ... beep ...beep ... When the wake-up call comes, telling us it's time to transition to stage 3, it's unavoidable. Of course, "beep" sounds different, depending on the company and circumstances. You might hear things like, "The market is changing too fast," "We can't innovate," or "We're falling behind our competition." You might hear, "We're disconnected from our customer," or "We're not responsive," or "The technology has all changed *again* and we just got through the last big upgrade!" The successes of the past are no longer translating in the present. People will ask, "Are all big organizations as dysfunctional as we are?"

The challenges aren't just in the marketplace; they're also internal. "I spend all my time in meetings! When am I supposed to get my work done?" is a common complaint that you start hearing from team members when that wake-up call gets louder. The Swirl is sapping their energy and creativity, and they don't know how to break free of it. They have gone from having a direct line to the customer to being encumbered by a new sense of bureaucracy and stagnation. There is a "way to do things" that just doesn't seem to get the job done anymore. People have good ideas, but they don't seem to make an impact.

Meanwhile, the senior leadership team, with which all the power once resided, is now too far away from the operational details to be effective—and too far away from the customer. One way or the other, it becomes clear to all those who are paying close attention that management has lost its tactile feel for the market. The capacity of the organization to learn, grow, and pivot is severely impacted. Leaders in this position will say, "I feel out of touch with the company. I can't keep track of it all." The more self-aware leaders will worry that they are becoming bottlenecks and wish they could empower more people. Some simply experience burnout as a result of the overwhelming pressure they feel to continue to direct an organization that's become too large and too complex for them to handle.

This is especially true when a company reaches a point at which its original value proposition is growing stale, and leadership recognizes that it needs to diversify its offerings into multiple business lines. Directive leadership works great when you're all working together on a single Business Triangle. But when that company grows into an enterprise with multiple Business Triangles, products, or services; various markets and customer demographics; and functional teams that are suddenly required to support them all; the organization's structure needs to evolve.

To some extent, all this is an inevitable consequence of growth. Growth, in a complex, adaptive social system tends to bring with it an increase in complexity. That means more people, and an exponentially greater number of relationships between people. It may mean more teams that need to work together and coordinate. The more people and teams you have, the more interdependencies are created. There is an increase in connectivity and communication. To work effectively, with cross-functional teams serving multiple business lines, a team-based matrix-like structure is required. But if the company's functions are siloed, and the people filling those roles continue to make independent and sometimes unpredictable or misaligned choices, performance will inevitably suffer.

The predictable breaking point for a stage 2 directive leadership business is an overwhelming sense that the organization's leadership model, structure, and system of capabilities and roles is no longer a fit for the strategic challenges of the enterprise. It doesn't have to just be about size—the company becoming too big; rather, the key factor is usually complexity. That is where business leaders can learn a critical lesson from an unlikely source: an embattled general in the Iraqi desert.

"To Win We Had to Change"

When General Stanley McChrystal took over American forces in Iraq in 2005, the army was struggling to keep up with its adversary. Al Qaida's religious philosophy may have been stuck in the dark ages, but its organizational structure was decidedly more innovative. Small, distributed groups of fighters attacked quickly and dispersed almost as fast. It was as unorthodox, in a military sense, as it was effective. As the general wrote in his memoir about that era, "In place of a traditional hierarchy, [al Qaida] took the form of a dispersed network that proved devastatingly effective against our objectively more qualified force."[1] More qualified or not, the US military response was taken aback to be confronted with a combat theater that was much more complex and disruptive than what the military in previous eras had faced. The organizational structure was ill-fitted for the mission, and the general, to his credit, didn't just call for more weapons or more troops. He recognized that what

---

[1]General Stanley McChrystal with Tantum Collins, David Silverman, and Chris Fussell, *Team of Teams: New Rules of Engagement for a Complex World* (New York: Portfolio/Penguin, 2015), p. 32.

he was facing was a more fundamental structural challenge. Reflecting on it later, he writes:

> *AQI's unorthodox structure allowed it to thrive in an operating environment that diverged radically from what we had traditionally faced: the twenty-first century is more connected, faster paced, and less predictable than previous eras. Though we encountered this shift on the battlefield similar changes are affecting almost every sector of society.*
>
> *To win we had to change. Surprisingly, that change was less about tactics or new technology than it was about the internal architecture and culture of our force—in other words, our approach to management.*

McChrystal's strategic response involved building a new team-focused organizational structure that allowed a different level of adaptivity, information-sharing, and transparency. This transformation was critical to turning the tide of the conflict, at least in the short run, and it involved a significant overhaul of the military's traditional organizational structure. The force in Iraq was, in a sense, facing a 5:30 wake-up call, and McChrystal was able to guide them to the next stage in their organizational evolution. The shift they made was akin to transforming a company's culture and system of roles from stage 2 Directive Leadership to stage 3 Distributed Leadership (see Figure 7.1).

Today's companies are in general not dealing with daily life-and-death challenges, but many of the lessons McChrystal emphasizes—distributed teams, information-sharing, deeper trust across the organization, and a much less hands-on approach to leadership—are central to organizations making the stage 2 to 3 transition. Like McChrystal's army, these companies are too bureaucratic, too siloed, and too reliant on command and control. Competitors are more nimble and closer to the customer. Senior leadership is not innovating fast enough. And the enterprise is unable to compete well on multiple fronts. Like the soldiers in the desert, the leaders of these organizations hearing an urgent wake-up call telling them: *to win we have to change.*

Bureaucracy Is Not the Answer

Not all business leaders are as ready to change as McChrystal was. When the limits of a stage 2 leadership model begin to rear their heads, some directive leaders feel the need to control the chaos through instituting more rules, often accompanied by more managers. This leads to the kind of unwieldy bureaucracy that is all too common in large organizations. And once functional silos and bureaucracy set in, it can be very difficult to break out. As management expert Gary Hamel, who argues passionately for liberating our organizations from this stranglehold, points out, "Bureaucracy is a massive, role-playing game. If you're an advanced player, you know how to deflect blame, defend turf, manage up, hoard resources, trade favors, negotiate targets and avoid scrutiny. Unsurprisingly, those who excel at the game are unenthusiastic about changing it."[2]

Recently, I was working with a new CEO of a large, complex stage 2 firm, in the financial advisory industry, with almost 20,000

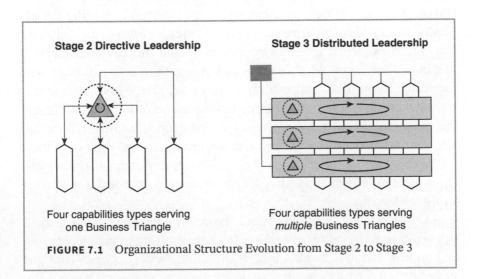

FIGURE 7.1 Organizational Structure Evolution from Stage 2 to Stage 3

[2]Gary Hamel and Michele Zanini, "Busting Bureaucracy," blog post, http://www
.garyhamel.com/blog/busting-bureaucracy.

retail locations. In an effort to get a handle on the state of the business and the organization, she shadowed one of the most successful leaders in the field with financial advisors and clients. This provided her with invaluable "intel," and she came away with a list of important priorities, issues to be addressed, and questions to pursue. But as she considered her next steps, she realized that there was simply no one individual to hand that priority list to. There was no single executive or functional team that could be trusted to pursue it, and not to get mired in the conflicting interests or bureaucratic wrangling—in essence, the Swirl. This is a classic sign of a 5:30 organization. The way the organization had scaled had created independent silos. Leaders and teams were proficient at and rewarded for working within silos and not across. Indeed, these silos had become so independent from each other that the ability to efficiently learn and adapt across them had stagnated such that even the best ideas struggled to be implemented cross-functionally. Her list of priorities, in all likelihood, would have suffered a slow death on the bureaucratic vine.

The most difficult challenge in such situations can often be that the company doesn't even seem to have the internal capability to talk about, much less implement, effective interventions. Not only are they falling short in some form; they also lack the key structures to ask questions about why. Leaders and teams that aspire to high performance know that a transition is necessary. They just don't know exactly how to go about it. They can glimpse the other side and imagine the possibilities, but the river seems too deep, the canyon too wide, the changes too unknown, the risk too great. Often, they can list a withering backlog of priorities but can't figure out how to navigate them sequentially because they lack a structured approach for distributing leadership.

Another of the common characteristics of a business at late stage 2 is a sense that the culture itself has become limiting to people's potential or, at least, it is headed in that direction. Whereas once it might have brimmed with new energy and fresh takes on leadership and the market, it now feels more set in its ways. A strong culture, even an entrenched one, in and of itself, is not a bad thing. All businesses have cultures, and good ones often develop exceptionally strong cultures. But in any organization, as the culture has become more and more institutionalized, it will develop deeper and deeper layers. Sometimes those can take on an almost cultlike character, with rituals and internal narratives that reinforce a particular way of doing things. There are all kinds of overt and subtle ways in which cultural norms are acknowledged and reinforced. Again, these have their place, and often their beauty, but when an organization reaches that inflection point toward the end of stage 2, the power of these cultural narratives, and people's loyalty to them, can inhibit the capacity to reinvent what is necessary to reach the next stage of organizational development. Why? Well, many of these narratives become a way of signaling loyalty to the stage 2 leadership model. They're often connected to the origin story of the company that, once upon a time, helped provide the clear direction and mindset to move everyone forward. It is the code for how people advanced as leaders that is often hardwired into rewards and punishments. Often, for a long time, the code worked, but it doesn't work anymore. It was successful, but no longer. It was once the secret sauce, but now the sauce is souring. It needs modification, change, and evolution. And that modification and transformation inevitably runs counter to the established rhythms of the culture. It will disrupt all those "ways of doing things." And when it does, the stage 2 antibodies will wake up and tend to resist change.

It was around 2012 that Radiant Love LLC began to hear the "Beep, beep, beep." The company had come a long way under Paul's leadership. It now had a couple of hundred locations across the country, the majority of which were franchised. The Certified Love Coach program had trained many coaches that were successfully supporting the cafés and events. With the birth of the Internet, certified coaches could work with individuals and couples online, not relying on the physical locations of the cafes. As more and more singles began to use the Internet as a starting point in their search for loving relationships, it made sense for the coaches to offer virtual services. And as these coaches began to work with young clients who shared their adventures in the newly booming world of online dating, they sent a consistent message back to management: "We should provide our own dating app." But Paul resisted. He was already trying to learn about running café franchises. What did he know about dating apps—or any apps for that matter? He still missed his BlackBerry, and his kids teased him about how uncomfortable he was with his smartphone. He didn't need to translate that discomfort into his company. Some days, he thought longingly back to when his biggest problem was fixing the espresso machine. And he often wondered, "What would Strega think?" How could the impersonal algorithm of an app capture the secrets of his grandmother's matchmaking wisdom? And how could the company keep its focus on "serious singles" looking for long-term love if they ventured into the kind of platform that he believed was more suitable for facilitating casual hookups? Strega would have turned in her grave to see her company turning into Tinder.

At first, Paul did what many directive leaders do when things start to spiral into the Swirl: he hired more managers and instituted more checks and balances. He was stretched too thin to seek input and collaboration from his people; instead, he increasingly tried to run the company by issuing directives. It's a common, and understandable way that leaders respond in such moments; it's also a critical error. The last thing Paul felt like doing was inviting more opinions and perspectives into the conversation. The level of complexity was already unbearable. Years and years of directive leadership deliberately driving choice and agency out of the system for all but the top team had lowered the potential of the organization to adapt, to be creative, to pivot, and ultimately to grow and thrive over the long term. And the loyal team members who'd been with the company for years felt slighted that he wasn't asking for their input. Wasn't this a moment when he could have invited them to step up? Didn't they deserve a say in how the organization was evolving?

Increasingly, Paul began to feel as if he was out of his depth as a leader. He could see the potential for where the company could go— and even grudgingly acknowledged that it might include an app—but he wasn't sure he was the person to get it there. He was good at doing things a certain way, and at this stage in his life and career, the idea of learning a different leadership style was daunting. Plus, he was in his mid-fifties. He'd made plenty of money and the idea of an early retirement was appealing. Among his executive team was a woman he sensed had just the capacities needed to take Radiant Love to the next level. She was young, and some might be surprised to see her tapped for the top job. But she was flexible, open-minded, and excelled at collaboration. In 2015, Paul announced his retirement, and Sarah Stevenson took over as CEO.

When directive leadership begins to fail, it doesn't always mean that the leader has personally fallen short. Some leaders stay with their companies through the 5:30 swirl and make the transition to a different model and a different leadership style. But it's not uncommon for a stage transition to coincide with a leadership transition. Either way, when "nail and scale" has run its course, when a business finds itself bogged down in bureaucracy, when culture becomes entrenched and stagnant, when problems arise that seem strangely impervious to existing solution-sets, the time has come for a momentous shift.

Some companies delay the inevitable by launching a re-org or bringing in a new, better directive leader. There is nothing inherently wrong with that. Sometimes a fresh injection of directive leadership breathes new life into an organizational framework, getting everyone on the same page, moving in the same direction, at least for a time, and resulting in a temporary boost in performance. The culture resets and performance improves. This is what most organizational turnarounds are all about. You get new energy, and a better business. But you won't get stage 3 potential. You won't get transformational capabilities built into the system itself. You won't get the sustained, adaptive, strategic intelligence throughout the organizational system. You might get a new level of allegiance, but you won't get a high degree of empowerment. You might get focus, but you won't get surprising creativity. You might get temporary clarity, but you won't get a greater ability to deal with complexity. For all that, you have to go beyond a top-down design, however elegant. You have to go beyond a directive leader, however capable. To open up the marvelous vistas of stage 3 and stage 4 organizational performance, you need to start distributing, not just power and authority, but a transformational template that reaches all the way to the ground of your organization. See Figure 7.2.

Most organizations that have reached that point in their life cycle when they begin to contemplate the deeper, transformative organizational change to a distributed leadership model come to the conclusion that there is simply no other viable way forward. The journey must be undertaken; the task can no longer be postponed. The need for and attachment (even addiction) to directive leadership has run its course. There is no version of that form of leadership that will satisfy—no reinvigoration of the executive team, no doubling down on an old formula, no new top-down strategies that will effectively move

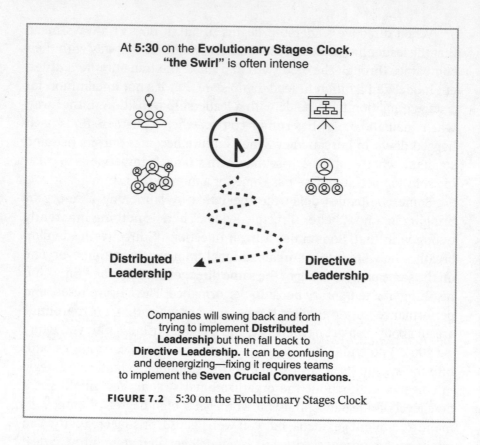

At **5:30** on the **Evolutionary Stages Clock**, **"the Swirl"** is often intense

Distributed Leadership

Directive Leadership

Companies will swing back and forth trying to implement **Distributed Leadership** but then fall back to **Directive Leadership.** It can be confusing and deenergizing—fixing it requires teams to implement the **Seven Crucial Conversations.**

FIGURE 7.2   5:30 on the Evolutionary Stages Clock

things forward. Usually, all the above have been tried and found wanting. It's always tempting to search for some snazzy new scheme that will promise results without the confusion of passing through a period of uncertainty that always accompanies transformation. Such temptations protect us from the unknown. But the inevitable uncertainty that comes with deep, transformational change is part of the initiation phase at 5:30. It can be uncomfortable, but ideally, the organizational leadership is not pretending any more. They're facing the challenge directly.

When the leadership of the organization has decided that they are committed to making the necessary changes, whatever the short-term pain or organizational resistance, something very important happens. Leadership stops trying to run from the growing organizational complexity, and starts trying to actually embrace it, engage it, learn how to live with it, and develop systems that bring it to a higher level of integration.

CHAPTER 8

A Complete System of Roles

Stage 3, Distributed Leadership

Leadership is a distributed or collective capacity in a system, not just something that individuals do. Leadership is about the capacity of the whole system to sense and actualize the future that wants to emerge.

—Otto Scharmer

I t's a big step to recognize that your organization needs to change— to face that truth, to accept it, even embrace it. But for those leaders who do, it's another thing altogether to successfully manage that shift. As IBM pointed out in a recent report on organizations struggling with the complex challenges of change management driven by disruptive forces in the marketplace, "The gap between the magnitude of change and the ability of organizations to manage it continues to widen."[1] In other words, more and more companies know they need to shift from stage 2 to stage 3, but they have no idea how to do it.

---

[1]Hans-Henrik Jorgensen, Oliver Bruehl, and Neele Franke, "Making Change Work . . . While the Work Keeps Changing," IBM Institute for Business Value, 2014, https://www.ibm.com/downloads/cas/WA3NR3NM.

To start with, even the idea of "change management" may be a misnomer. Change and transformation in today's, and tomorrow's, world cannot simply be managed from the executive suite. Sure, you can go through a complex re-org that temporarily updates your entire structure, but by the time you're done, the world will have gotten ahead of you again. The clock starts ticking on its viability. The ossification timeline begins, as does the countdown to the next needed overhaul. That's why we need something more than occasional change efforts. We need a social system that can continue to adapt and develop without waiting for top-down directives. To keep up with the pace of change today, *the capacity to transform must be built into the organization, embedded in its social-ware.* That's the essence of stage 3, Distributed Leadership. As change management expert Gary Hamel puts it, "I believe that in the future, every change program will need to be socially constructed. Change programs need to roll up, not down. Change programs that cascade down are too slow. They're too incremental. They're not sufficiently nuanced—they don't take account of local subtleties. They feel imposed, and therefore illegitimate. This is why 70% of change programs fail."[2]

"Socially constructed," in an organization, means that the capacity to change needs to be distributed throughout the system of roles, capabilities, and strategies that make up the organization's social system. That's what stage 3, Distributed Leadership, is all about. The question leaders should be asking isn't, "How do we manage this change process?" Rather, it is: "How do we build an organization that has the capacity to continuously transform—one that has the ability to adapt and change built into its DNA?"

Stage 3: Distributed Leadership. The organization is a portfolio of capabilities that serve multiple business models and segments. It has been restructured into a team-based matrix, based on intact high-performing teams (HPTs). Aligned leadership is driven mostly by consultative

---

[2]Gary Hamel, "Hacking the Management Model: Q+A with Dr. Gary Hamel (Part 2)," Workhuman, February 19, 2016, https://www.workhuman.com/resources/globoforce-blog/hacking-the-management-model-q-a-with-dr-gary-hamel-part-2.

decision-making, direct conflict resolution, and other HPT ways of working. Decisions are only rarely escalated for autocratic decision-making by the enterprise leader.

Organizational systems that can effectively distribute authority, adaptability, and intelligence in this way are sometimes called flat or matrix organizations. There are a number of popular, new organizational systems today designed to achieve this end. They promise less management, less bureaucracy, more speed, flatter hierarchies, and better responsiveness. Some are successful, several have innovative contributions, and others descend into decision-making paralysis, directionless chaos, or even something resembling anarchy. Whatever the outcome, I think the continued popularity of these new systems points to the real pain point being felt out there across the corporate world. I see it every day. It's demanding solutions—and the old consulting guard with its outdated solution-set has struggled to provide them. So, I welcome the experimentation. By all means, let a thousand flowers bloom. But for my money, and from my experience, the ones that truly succeed embrace transformation at the ground level. It's not reserved for leadership; it's baked into the company's DNA in some form.

Growth River, unlike many organizational development systems, doesn't avoid the human and social side of organizational life, and the messiness that comes with it. Organizational life is highly complex—we embrace it. Organizational team members have their own ideas about how the business should unfold—we accept it. Human beings are social animals, highly influenced by and involved with those around them—we encourage it. We've made the decision not to avoid the massive complexity of the organization, but to find our way through it, to implement solutions that take all of it into account. At stage 3, an important truth is discovered: Complex organizations will not reach their full potential until and unless they take advantage of the creativity, agency, and collaborative skills of their people. I'm reminded of the words of legendary Visa CEO Dee Hock, who once lamented that, "The most abundant, least expensive, and most constantly abused resource in the world is human ingenuity."

At the transition point between stages 2 and 3, this truth looms large. When we decide to take this next step in our organizational journey, we aren't avoiding the human and social side of things. We're tacking into the wind, and eventually, as we get better and better at doing so, eventually, the headwind becomes a massive tailwind.

On the other side of this transformation is a renewed, reinvigorated, empowered organization with distributed, strategic intelligence replacing the stagnant bureaucracy. At stage 3, we discover a new level of effective leadership, cross-organization functionality, distributed intelligence and innovation. This stage, like the problems it responds to, is complex and multidimensional. In this chapter, we'll focus on the major elements—the matrix structure, the changing leadership mechanism; the critical task of redesigning the system of capabilities and roles and the new approach to strategy that arises when you do so. In the next two chapters, I'll focus in on how to further optimize a stage 3 organization, through *leveraging creative tensions* and *creating high-performing teams*.

A Matrix Structure

Structurally, the shift to a stage 3 distributed leadership model means that an organization moves from being one business to being an enterprise—a portfolio of business units and shared capabilities. Like a fleet of ships sailing in formation, each with its own captain and crew, led by an admiral, this new structure is a matrix. Functional teams provide shared services across business units. Why does an organization make this shift? Primarily, to make the CEO role scalable, distributing the leadership function between multiple business leaders. This gives each key business segment the capacity to act independently, while still aligning with the larger organizational direction. In this stage, business unit leaders will typically report directly to a single enterprise leader, usually the CEO. Organizations that are structured like this are able to be more agile and nimble, to respond to market opportunities with speed. They can manage multiple business lines with efficiency. They accelerate the ability for people within teams—and across teams—to sustain higher performance. Achieving this speed and agility without sacrificing size and reach is one of the competitive challenges of the information age.

  Business leader or team refers to type of role in an enterprise that is responsible for leading and managing a business segment or Business Triangle toward competitive advantage. This ideally includes responsibility for the financial profit and loss (P&L) performance of the business.

  Function refers to a type of role in an enterprise that is responsible for execution. The term can be applied with different levels of strategic sophistication. In less strategically mature organizations, a function is simply a moniker for a nonexecutive role, job, or team with an area of expertise, such as marketing, sales, or quality. However, in companies with greater strategic sophistication, in which teams analyze capabilities, a function is a label for a cluster of closely related capabilities. So, for example, the marketing function will be responsible for managing and improving capabilities including market research, customer experience, market messaging, and so forth.

  Functional leader refers to the leader of a function, a functional team, or a capabilities leadership team.

To illustrate this shift, let's return to the team at Radiant Love (see Figure 8.1). Paul had recently retired, and Sarah, the new CEO, was overseeing the development of their new dating app, in addition to the existing café business. The app was being developed by the IT team, under the purview of Lily, the head of IT, but Sarah recognized that it made no sense to have this essential development opportunity tucked away inside a support team. The app, she realized, was not just another project—it represented a whole new business segment for the company, one that was fundamentally different from their café business. In addition, offering an app meant significant changes to almost every function in the company. What it would take to develop, sell, deliver, and support an app was completely different to what it took to develop, sell, deliver, and support their cafés. Some functions might serve both, others would be independent. It was time to rethink the company's structure around two distinct Business Triangles.

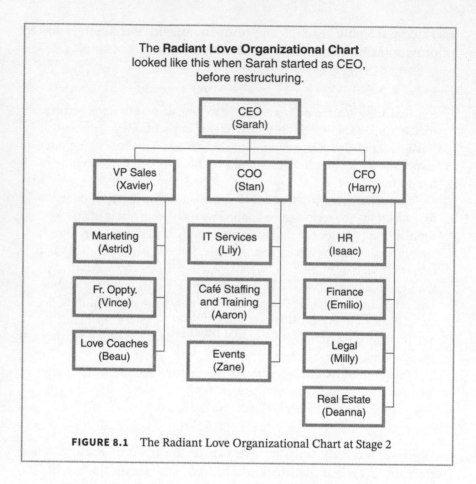

FIGURE 8.1   The Radiant Love Organizational Chart at Stage 2

Sarah led the Radiant Love team through the process of mapping the organization's current capabilities, organizing people by their functional roles around the Business Triangle—Develop, Sell, Deliver, and Support—and identifying gaps (we'll talk through this process in more detail when we get to Crucial Conversation 4, Specifying Capabilities and Roles). She and the leadership team also sketched out a new Business Triangle for the digital business segment, and this showed her the key roles that needed to be filled, including the all-important role of a business leader for that segment.

In this process, several other issues became clear. It wasn't just the new digital business segment that lacked a business leader. The café business segment also lacked a business leader, because Paul, as CEO, had played that role himself. That had worked fine when the cafés were the only business the company was in. But if Sarah was to stay above the fray as enterprise leader, she needed to assign a leader to each of the two business segments.

Xavier, VP of sales, who was also responsible for the Love Coaches team and events planning, was concerned that the development of the app should really be driven by his team, since they were the ones who knew the matchmaking secrets passed down by Strega. Part of Radiant Love for over 15 years, he felt passionately about honoring Strega's legacy, and didn't trust that a bunch of programmers would do it justice. Plus, he argued, Lily and the IT team were spending so much time on the app that they weren't responsive to requests for support from the other teams. He was right that it didn't belong in IT. But Sarah recognized that Xavier's role as a functional leader in sales meant that he needed to serve both businesses, not lead one of them. That would have created a conflict of interest and added to the tangled spaghetti.

The end result of Radiant Love's restructuring was an enterprise with two triangles, each with its own business leader (see Figure 8.2). Paula, a savvy entrepreneur, was hired to lead the virtual business

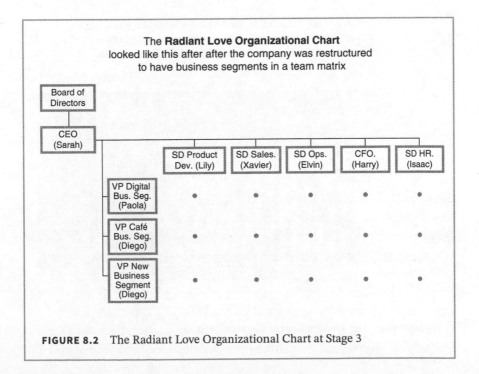

FIGURE 8.2 The Radiant Love Organizational Chart at Stage 3

segment. Her role was to oversee the development, sales, and delivery for the new app. Diego was hired to lead the café business segment.

Serving both were functional leaders and teams in Develop, Sell, Deliver, and Support. Lily, the IT team leader who oversaw the early development of the app, was promoted to lead the Develop function. Xavier continued to lead the Sell function. As you can see in the Enterprise Map shown in Figure 8.3, some functions were specific to the digital business segment, like those related to the development and optimization of the software. Others were specific to the cafés, like real estate identification or franchise marketing. But others served both, like brand awareness, quality assurance, or human resources (HR).

An **enterprise** is a portfolio of business triangles and functional capabilities designed and managed to create competitive advantage.

An **Enterprise Map** is a way to visualize an enterprise as a matrix of business triangles and functional capabilities.

Sarah's team created an **Enterprise Map** like this one to visualize key points of interdependency between **Business Segments** and **Functional Capabilities**

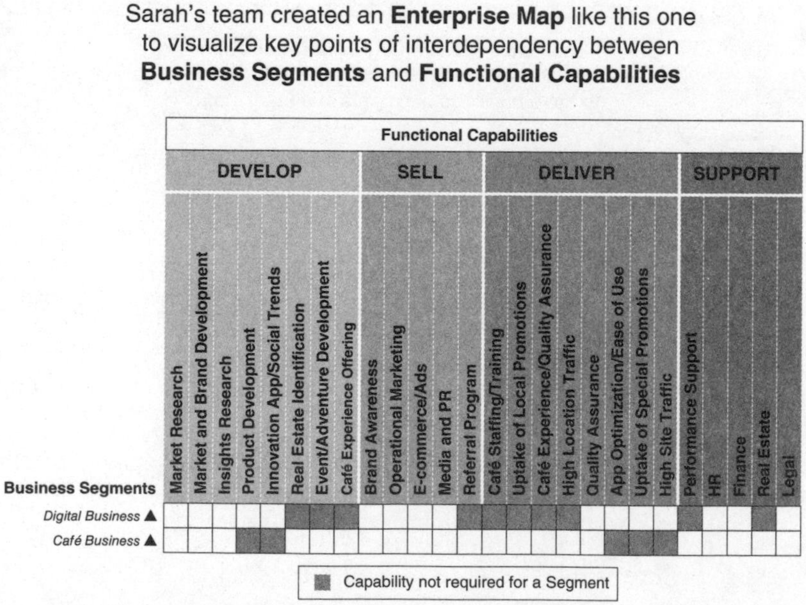

FIGURE 8.3   The Radiant Love Enterprise Map

The Changing Role of the CEO: From Executive Leader to Enterprise Architect

With all this talk of shifting power, distributing authority, and increasing organizational agility, leaders reading this may be wondering: What's my job now? Is there even a role for a CEO or leader in this newly empowered, evolved organization? Let me assure you, there is. When I say that change cannot be managed simply from the executive suite at stage 3, that doesn't mean leadership is not essential. It absolutely is.

Unlike some of the popular approaches to so-called flat or nonhierarchical organization, Growth River does not do away with leaders. Nor does our approach reflect any particular ideology about the role of management or the usefulness of corporate hierarchy. It's simply about what works and what doesn't work when it comes to leading change. At stage 3, there's still leadership, but what it means to be a leader changes, because the attitude at the top must be consonant with the changes we are seeking throughout the organization. In fact, a different type of CEO is required for a distributed leadership company.

Like most big changes in organizational life, this shift is largely about power. The move from stage 2 to stage 3 involves a massive shift of power in the organization. The power that was once invested in the CEO or a small, executive team can no longer reside at the top. In a directive leadership model, that CEO or team would have been responsible for all major strategic decisions, but at this new stage, the CEO or top leadership group recognizes that they can no longer "hoard" decision-making power if the organization is to remain agile as it grows.

Decisions need to be made at levels where the owners of those decisions have a clear line of sight to the impact they have on the client or customer. More specifically, decision-making needs to occur closest to where value is created—and closest to where the expertise and competent leadership resides to optimize that creation of value and manage the relationship with the client or customer. The goal is to push business acumen and competent decision-making closer to where decision makers truly understand the issues involved, appreciate all of the subtleties, and are better situated to respond. They own it or their team owns it. The top leadership team simply can no longer effectively function as direct decision makers for the business or in some cases multiple businesses. It's not a matter of competence—even a great detail-oriented CEO simply can't successfully provide that kind of leadership for an organization that has grown so complex. And if they try, they will likely fail.

So many leaders think that their job is to get the desired result to happen. To *do it*. Like a multitalented entrepreneur who has to be the jack of all trades, they attempt to drive results and just get things done. The "get 'er done" attitude is fine in many areas of life, but in a stage 3 organization, it's a recipe for failure. Leadership at stage three takes a level of nuance, sophistication, and leadership intelligence that often escapes the master-of-the-world, hard-charging, make-it-happen CEOs and entrepreneurs. Those people have many other wonderful qualities, but they're not effective enterprise architects. And that's fine—there will always be plenty of jobs for good directive leaders. But stage 3 organizations need the subtlety and skill of stage 3 leaders. The stage 3 leader's job is not to get it done themselves, but to create the conditions so that "it" emerges—"it" being whatever the organization needs to grow, thrive, and fulfill its mission. The leader's job is to build an organization and instantiate the system so that the rights things get done, by the right people, at the right time.

Sounds good, right? To which anyone who has been in a leadership role will probably say, "Yes, but . . ." What's the "but"? It's the hesitation about whether things will all fall apart if they take their hands off the wheel. Will people step up and respond to the right issues? Do they care enough and feel connected to the mission of the organization? Or will they just start pursuing their own agendas? Will they feel independently responsible? Will they see what needs to be done and do it? Or will they sit around and wait for someone to tell them what to do while things start to fall through the cracks?

It's important to note here that, although these fears are not unfounded, they are often misplaced. Failures in an organization are generally in the roles, not the people. So often I see leaders point fingers at the quality of their people and lament their lack of awareness or initiative. But, if you dig a little deeper, you'll find that it's not the person who is at fault, it's an issue with the role that person is playing vis-à-vis others in the business. It's too easy to blame people for something going wrong in their near proximity. But when things fall through the cracks, when issues go unresolved, when dysfunction gets entrenched, it's more often than not a result of a lack of clarity about the roles people are in, the responsibilities attached to those roles, and their relationship to other roles.

An individual naturally develops a sense of ownership when their role is clear, the scope of responsibility in that role is transparent, and the relationships with other roles in the business are well understood. Clarify the system of roles and a miracle occurs. Your people will look a lot more capable! Suddenly, everyone's visibility improves. And people start noticing and responding to issues that once were vague but are now obvious. Therefore, a big part of the answer to leaders' fears about relinquishing directive power lies in a complete overhaul of the organization's system of roles. In fact, this is a centerpiece of the shift from stage 2 to stage 3. And the new role for the leader is to be the architect of this system of roles. In this way, power gets carefully redistributed throughout the organization—not just vaguely conferred on people but embedded in a clear, complete, and effective system of roles.

This is captured in the stage 3 mission statement: *We, the executive enterprise team, are the architects of a complete system of roles in which our businesses are focused on the customer experience and our functions are focused on our businesses.*

The game of chess provides a useful analogy here. Everyone wants to know how to move the pieces around on the organizational chess board to get the best results. What's the best strategy? How do I deploy my best pieces? Which gambit will work in which situation? Unfortunately, that's not the secret to organizational chess when you reach stage 3. The question at this level becomes: How do you situate the pieces so that they start actually moving themselves? How do you organize the chess board so that each piece, or at least enough of them, becomes self-responsive and filled with enough responsibility and agency that the organization develops an independent strategic effectiveness that doesn't need to be directed from the top? It's no longer about the masterful strategy of the chess player; it's about the individual and collective intelligence of the chess pieces. But how effective and powerful a role they will play still depends partially upon the architectural talents of the chess player. It takes a different type of leadership intelligence to build that capacity into an organizational social system. Designing, cultivating, and being responsible for that "social-ware" is the leader's job. It's also one of the most difficult. Indeed, architecting roles is by far the most high stakes conversation for any leader to engage in—for it is where the aspirations of the individual team member encounter the needs of the organization.

Straightening the Spaghetti

So how does the leader or leadership team begin this monumental task? How does one start to architect an effective and functional system of roles? Don't think you can just do it by redesigning the org chart or releasing a memo. Before you can even begin the redesign, you need to deconstruct the system you already have. Organizations making stage 2 to stage 3 transitions aren't starting with blank slates. Wouldn't that be wonderful? Usually, their existing roles are a tangled mess—kind of like a heap of spaghetti that's been cooking away in a pot with no one tending it for a while and then dumped out on a plate. To architect an effective system of roles, you first have to undo that tangled mess—straighten out the spaghetti, so to speak. And in order to do that, you need to understand at least a little bit about how it ended up that way.

Imagine a new outpost town in the Wild West. (Forgive my abrupt shift in metaphor, but perhaps this is a spaghetti western?) In this pioneer settlement, there's a lot to do, so people just take on roles that seem necessary, natural, or appealing to them. One of the women offers to school the handful of kids. Everyone pitches in to build the church and the schoolhouse. There's no police department, so a few of the younger men form a militia. One of the wealthier settlers starts issuing loans to the townsfolk and effectively sets himself up as a bank. Unfortunately, no one has medical training, but the wife of one of the nearby homesteaders is used to doctoring cows, so people go to her when there's an accident or an illness. There's no top-down thought about who plays which role—it's a matter of necessity, and occasionally just chance. The upside is that things start to get done. The downside is that with few rules and even fewer law enforcers, all kinds of shadowy stuff gets tacitly sanctioned. Companies tend to develop in a similar way. The expanding business requires people to fill new roles—now! It desperately needs people to do X, Y, and Z, and the founders don't have too much time to think about how it all fits together. If you can do the job, no one is looking too closely at the "how."

As responsibility is doled out to accommodate the needs of a growing organization, the boundaries around roles start to get very confused. In fact, over time it often becomes completely tangled. There may be multiple businesses, with different types of support structures, some of which are shared with other businesses, and some of which are not. Some people have roles in multiple areas of the organization, sharing them with others. Perhaps there is a business with no clear business leader who can advocate for the business as a whole. Maybe there is a functional leader—head of accounting, perhaps—who has no clear way to divide up her time between two different business lines. She is simply pulled by whoever shouts the loudest or whoever seems to have more political power. Who is responsible for what function? Are there several people? What roles support which business?

The tangle is made stickier by the human tendencies to look for leverage, accumulate power, and avoid being held accountable. It's not always nefarious. It's part of how people try to get things done in dysfunctional organizations. I've seen situations in which one person might play two important roles in an organization, but because there is little clarity around those two roles and the differing needs of each, that person is able to always hide behind the "other" role to escape accountability. Sometimes people try to own different functions or roles in an effort to make it easier to do their jobs and to ensure that they get what they need. For example, someone might end up being both a business leader and the owner of another key capability. Naturally, they might tend to funnel resources to their own business line first, regardless of need or merit. There are endless ways that roles get tangled. Human social systems are complicated and even more so if they've evolved in an ad hoc manner.

These kinds of conflicts of interest get layered into the organizational structure and culture, explicitly and implicitly, and people grow resistant to any kind of change initiatives that might threaten their positions or take away their leverage. To return to our pioneer outpost, which has now become a small but thriving town, it's as if the assistant mayor is also the saloon owner. The saloon may get some special deals because of that connection! Maybe the town decides to spend money rebuilding the street in front of the saloon before fixing streets in other neighborhoods. The banker has legal training, so he's been acting as judge, but a lot of people are worried that he's harder on defendants who are behind on their loan repayments. In these kinds of situation, it becomes impossible to adequately prioritize, or even recognize, what's best for the entire town and its development because you have someone who has a natural vested interest in seeing things a certain way and is politically invulnerable.

When you decide the time has come to architect a new and more effective system of roles, you first need to clean up these outdated behaviors. There is a new sheriff in town, and all of the behind-the-scenes, that's-just-the-way-we-do-it political deals have to be transparently scrutinized to see what really makes sense. Otherwise, the town, or the organization, can't grow and really function in the way it needs to. If the leadership team is contemplating a shift away from directive leadership, and seriously intends to push power down through the organization, the last thing they want to do is empower something that's dysfunctional. If you push power down into a confused system, you'll just empower confusion. So the first task of the CEO as enterprise architect is sorting out and revealing the hidden power structures that prevent transparency and accountability. Illuminating dysfunctional structures may be uncomfortable in the short term, but ultimately, it a positive for everyone. Some may resist, but over time, they will hopefully see the power of the upgraded system, and how much more it makes possible. And remember, it's best if there is a temporary amnesty for lawbreakers in the old regime.

Why Roles Matter

I speak a lot about roles in my work at Growth River and it may seem like an odd idea to stake so much organizational mindshare on it.

However, I have learned that the remarkable power of roles to bring clarity, focus, and strategic coordination to human activity is generally underestimated.

A role is shorthand for a set of expectations. For example, think of a parent. We have a whole set of expectations, naturally, for what the parent role looks like. In some generalized sense, we all know what a good parent is and we know what a bad parent is, and those judgments are based on how well or how poorly the parents are living up to the expectations we have of the role. Obviously, there are a lot of gray zones here, but it's not entirely subjective. The role itself contains expectations beyond any specific person who may be embodying that role at any given moment.

A role is much more than a set of responsibilities or tasks. Fundamentally, it's a particular perspective—on the business, on the team, on the customer, on the organization, or on a certain stakeholder. Each role represents an organizational vantage point, an outlook from which I can see what is important, what is needed, and what is possible. Others do not have that perspective in the same way. Only I do, or my team. So when I adopt that role, it's about more than checking a few boxes; it's about embracing and being accountable to an entire perspective. When I inhabit a role, I'm now responsible to advocate for a particular set of priorities, needs, and outcomes—from that vantage point—that I now represent. I'm taking ownership of that perspective and its impact on the business and the enterprise. *Roles are the instantiation of a perspective.*

One of the remarkable qualities of being human is our ability to take on the perspective of a role and represent the values of that role without fully identifying with the role itself. We can even take on multiple roles, each with their own perspective. In fact, in any one day, a leader might take on the perspectives of two or more different roles. For example, I might put myself in the shoes of an accounting role in one conversation, and a marketing role in the next meeting. Each "hat" I wear will carry with it a certain set of priorities. Being able to effectively advocate for the perspective of a particular role, while still recognizing that other roles also have different, valid perspectives of their own, is critical to building an effective stage 3 distributed leadership.

A **role** refers to the function, responsibilities, and accountabilities assumed by a person in a particular situation, scenario, or system. Roles are the building blocks of organizational structures. Many times, roles are defined by their title; however, they are much more than the title itself. A role definition should include a variety of aspects of daily work, including:

Responsibilities: the duties to take action you are responsible for.

Accountabilities: your obligations to create outcomes or deliverables.

Interdependencies: any relationships you have with other team members or other individuals/teams where you are dependent on each other for mutual success. Interdependencies are points of intersection between roles that require aligned ways of working, processes, or information technologies to sustain collective higher performance.

Business capabilities: the strategic factors critical to creating value in a business or for a customer, such as people, processes, tools, or technologies. Capabilities answer the question, "What do we need to have in place to execute our strategy?" There are four types of capabilities around the Business Triangle.

A **system of roles** is a structure for dividing roles, responsibilities, accountabilities, and interdependencies in a group.

Architecting a Complete System of Capabilities and Roles

A well-designed system of roles is built on the foundation of a system of capabilities. As I discussed in Part I, capabilities represent the things the business needs in order to run smoothly—to develop, sell, and deliver its products or services and to support those activities. In order to achieve high performance, the team's organizational structure and division of roles need to be clearly specified to ensure every key capability and perspective has an owner. The optimal structure will leverage team members' specialties and expertise and allow them to manage and lead the domains where they are closest to the work being done. With time and iteration, a stage 3 company can reach a point where it has a complete system of capabilities and roles in place. That means:

- All key perspectives and capabilities are assigned owners, and none are missing.
- All key domains of work have assigned owners who lead and advocate for them.
- All roles and responsibilities are defined and assigned, delineations between roles are clear, and creative tensions are designed into the system.
- Points of interdependency among roles are identified and optimized.
- Decision mechanisms are clear, so that all key decisions are taken with quality and speed.

It's important to note that although the leader or leadership team is ideally the architect of this system, that doesn't mean they are sitting in the corner office designing it all by themselves and then presenting it to the team in a grand reveal as a finished object. The entire process is inclusive of the people who are playing the various roles—indeed, it's impossible to untangle the spaghetti without their honest and transparent participation. This is a journey that will take time and iteration, and early versions should deliberately stick to the broad strokes. As a new system begins to be envisioned, it's critical that it be tested against real-world scenarios, iterated, and adjusted in each team. This is where Crucial Conversation 4, Specifying Capabilities and Roles, comes in (see Chapter 16). Modern organizations and companies are like big spider webs, where each strand is connected to countless others. That's why we often hear them described as a matrix. Touching one strand will vibrate through the whole network. The challenge is to manage these interdependencies and ripples of change while each strand continues its work. When team members start to play their roles, they will figure out any gaps or conflicts that need to be resolved, allowing them to fill out the details and propose changes. The CEO may have ownership over the final decisions, but this process cannot be done by directive. And in some cases, a team might decide to pursue its own clarification of the system of capabilities and roles even if the larger company is not ready to do so.

Unleashing Strategic Intelligence

Clarifying each business segment, separating out the various capabilities that are intrinsic to each, and establishing clear accountability and ownership can be a godsend. It takes work and a lot of untangling of the entrenched system, but it can unleash tremendous performance gains. A well-architected system of roles, built on and aligned with a system of capabilities, forms the platform and is part of the "socialware," on which a stage 3 distributed leadership organization can run. This means that all the essential capabilities in the business ecosystem have been clarified and all of them are being owned by someone. When people get aligned and on the same page, everything starts flowing much more smoothly. The multiple businesses begin to function like powerful parallel processors; all fueling the company's further growth and development.

When this occurs, we see another system emerge: a system of strategies. In a directed-leadership context, the leader or leadership team is pushing strategies from the top down through the organization, so that the organization becomes largely an expression of the strategic will of the CEO or executive leadership team. In a distributed leadership context, strategies emerge organically from the bottom up. If people are given authority over their roles, ideally the right strategies become obvious. The right decisions will become clearer, accountability will emerge, and strategic priorities will reveal themselves. A complete system of roles, built upon a complete system of capabilities, is a social platform on which strategic business intelligence can be distributed more effectively through all of the layers of the organization. The leadership team will still provide overall vision and direction, but they are not pretending that they know all the strategic or tactical priorities to achieve those goals. Instead, those strategies emerge within teams through Crucial Conversation 6, Aligning Strategies (see Chapter 18). Leaders, meanwhile, focus on creating the conditions to unleash strategic intelligence throughout the organization, so that it becomes capable, adaptable, agile, and responsive.

Sounds good, right? I hope that after reading this chapter, leaders can say a wholehearted "yes" without the "but . . ." The shift to distributed leadership is a powerful and transformative breakthrough for everyone in the organization, from top to bottom. That doesn't mean it will be easy or comfortable. In fact, it takes a lot of courage to disrupt the ways things have always been done, to renegotiate the unspoken power-sharing agreements, to come out into the light and be accountable. No longer can people hide behind a muddled org chart and avoid the set of expectations that their particular role confers. No longer can people stake out their turf in order to protect their dysfunction. There is blessed clarity and transparency of expectations, and I say blessed because it's all too rare, and yet incredibly valuable. If your organization can achieve this shift, you've put in place critical architecture for the stage 2 to 3 transition. You've upgraded your "social-ware." You've created the context for distributed decision making and, importantly, ensured decision making occurs closer to where value is being created. In the chapters that follow, we'll look at how to optimize this "social-ware" through leveraging creative tension to build high-performing teams.

CHAPTER 9

Leveraging Creative Tension

Stage 3, Distributed Leadership, continued

I am not afraid of the word tension. *I have earnestly worked and preached against violent tension, but there is a type of constructive, nonviolent tension that is necessary for growth.*

—Martin Luther King, Jr., *Letter from a Birmingham Jail*

In the 1990s, the comic strip *Dilbert* became a comedic staple of American office life. Dilbert's creator, Scott Adams, was a master at both representing and lampooning dysfunctional corporate culture. One of the aspects of it that he captured so brilliantly was the tension between various parts of an organization. As an engineer, Dilbert, the protagonist of the strip, is always making jokes about the low IQ and poor ethics of marketing and sales, and is engaged in a constant turf war with other departments. The accuracy of Adams' scenarios made the strip both hilarious and close to home for those who have done their time in corporate America. Off the page, however, interdepartmental tension isn't so funny. Indeed, the politics and infighting that is common in most companies can be as nasty as it is counterproductive.

But does it have to be that way? Are power struggles inevitable? As we shift to a stage 3 distributed leadership model, how can we best work together to avoid these tensions? Or should we even try?

Many people imagine, or hope, that a more evolved organizational structure and culture would put an end to conflict. They envision a utopian workplace where everyone has a voice, decisions are made by consensus, and no one does anything they don't agree with. I would argue, however, that such a workplace would not be conducive to growth. There is nothing wrong with conflict. Conflict can be healthy and positive—in fact, it is necessary for organizational transformation and growth. Conflict is simply the outward expression of differing perspectives. And a complex social system is full of different perspectives, all of which potentially contain important information and intelligence for the organization. Perfect harmony or communal bliss is not the purpose of enterprise evolution—that would eliminate one of the most powerful elements of human social systems: their diversity of perspectives.

The challenge to organizational alignment is not conflict in and of itself, but conflicts that have no productive outlet for resolution. If conflict is allowed to simmer, the result is rarely beneficial for any individual or any department. Eventually, unresolved everyday tension will metastasize into debilitating personal grievance, departmental infighting, or large blow-ups that will torpedo an organization's ability to be effective, ultimately destroying trust.

To optimize the "social-ware" that a stage 3 organization runs on, we need avenues for turning conflict into what we call "creative tension" and resolving that tension productively. There is always going to be some tension between various roles in a business, because the nature of a role is that it represents a particular perspective that is different from the perspectives of other roles. It's rarely the case that one perspective is 100 percent right and the other 100 percent wrong. Rather, both contain important information that the other may not see, which needs to be taken into account. Creative tension naturally arises between roles as a result of specialization. It is a vital source of innovation in a stage 3 organization.

Stage 3 organizations leverage tension rather than attempting to suppress it. Believe me, you don't want a lack of tension. It might seem positive temporarily, but you'll eventually find that all you did was bury it. Sooner or later it will come back to bite. Important perspectives will not get a hearing. Critical roles will lack representation. Decisions will get made without key points of input. People will go underground to get what they need. Political maneuvering will encumber relationships and erode trust. Lack of creative tension is a common cause for stunted growth and failure to surface and resolve strategic trade-offs.

In a distributed leadership organization, we recognize that it's precisely in the tension that the opportunity for growth lies. Leaders at this level can't be conflict-averse. Quite the opposite. A well-architected system of capabilities and roles is actually designed to maximize continuous, open, well-intentioned, transparent tension and conflict. And at the same time, it minimizes the unhealthy ways in which conflicts disperse through a social system. We don't need blow-ups, resentments, and anger management therapy. No one benefits when long buried issues explode in dramatic disputes. We need forums to bring the key perspectives to the table, voice problems, identify constraints, and resolve the issues. We need people to feel liberated to bring all their passion, expertise, and experience to the conversation—to pound the proverbial table in defense of their perspectives; to be heard and acknowledged; and then constructively work through the issues together and navigate differences of opinion to create a holistic solution. In this way, we can actually resolve the inevitable tensions between various roles rather than engage in a winner-take-all death match for ultimate influence.

One of the concerns leaders often voice when it comes to distributing authority into a matrix structure and a system of roles is the challenge of trust. Inevitably, giving people more power increases risk. When do you give your teenager the keys to the car? And when you do so, what conditions can you create to mitigate the risks? Creative tension is one answer to this challenge. When decision-making authority is distributed in stage 3, it is not just *given to individuals* but *channeled through a complete system of roles* designed for creative tension. Risk is mitigated through transparent decision-making based on business logic that takes into account input from multiple perspectives.

Creative Tensions refers to differences of opinion or perspective that naturally arise between roles or between teams. They exist in the system of roles (in every team) and in the system of teams (in every company.) In teams, where team members are not intentional about how they work together, creative tensions can become sources of unhealthy conflict. However, in high-performing teams and organizations, creative tensions are intentionally "designed in" and leveraged as sources of insight and innovation. There are natural creative tensions between the functions and capabilities of Develop, Sell, Deliver, and Support around the business triangle. To leverage creative tensions, ask questions like: Is there a complete system of roles and perspectives? Are conflicts really just natural creative tensions that can be resolved in a healthy and forwarding way? See Figure 9.1.

The objective is to design in **Creative Tensions** as sources of innovation and people development.

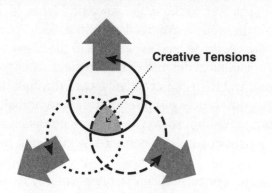

Creative Tensions

- Creative Tensions are the natural result of opposing values, roles, or perspectives.

- The objective is to design all the roles and perspectives needed for a successful outcome.

- Ongoing creativity and innovation is the result, because no single idea or solution will perfectly satisfy all roles and perspectives.

FIGURE 9.1 Creative Tensions

A Complete System of Roles Leverages Creative Tension

When an organization moves into stage 3, it constructs a complete system of roles, built on the strong foundation of a system of capabilities designed around the Business Triangle. This allocates clear ownership and accountability. It defines the relationships between the various parts of the business. It visually represents what it looks like when each capability has an accountable owner, who is advocating for that particular perspective. It brings about the potential for genuine alignment, because everyone's voice is at the table. Each role has a say in the outcome of important decisions. No single role dominates. This organizational structure allows for the ongoing, natural conflict between legitimate interests representing different roles and perspectives—indeed, it is designed to surface that creative tension and resolve it.

At Radiant Love, we saw how tensions arose between Xavier, VP of sales and the leader of coaching services, and Lily, the head of IT, over the design of the app. It wasn't personal, although it did get heated at times. Xavier's concern that IT shouldn't be in charge of the project arose out of his sense of responsibility for the knowledge passed down to him by Strega. Lily's frustration came from feeling like Xavier and the love coaches were withholding information about Strega's secret method from her team because he didn't like the fact that they were in charge. Plus, she knew Xavier was already overstretched and wasn't about to hand over the project to a team that had neither the time nor the technical know-how to drive it to completion. Their conflict revealed critical perspectives on both sides. The app did need to be infused with Strega's wisdom. It also needed to be technically sound. And it needed to be completed in a timely manner—something neither Xavier nor Lily could achieve, since both had other important responsibilities. The creative tension between the two roles allowed Sarah to see the critical importance of assigning a business leader to that business line who could give it their full attention, and work with both Xavier and Lily to ensure that their key perspectives were represented. Under the right conditions, these kinds of naturally occurring creative tensions can become a source of innovation and growth.

In a healthy system of roles, the surfacing and resolution of everyday tensions can act as releases of energy that move the system forward, almost like the small, controlled explosions that power an internal combustion engine. Creative tension is a powerful source of energy and momentum. It's good for people to feel strongly about the roles they represent, to advocate for the perspective of the customer that only they can see. In the end, even when a certain perspective temporarily fails to get its way, or obtain all the resource it desires, every side will actually win in the longer term, as constraints get resolved and the process of value creation flows with greater velocity around the Business Triangle.

The Natural Creative Tension in Business Triangles

The Business Triangle is designed to bring creative tensions to the surface. Each side of the triangle represents a necessary perspective to the success of the business. And the roles that hold each of those perspectives will be naturally in tension with each other. These are often expressed as stories people tell about other people—negative stories that reveal the areas of potential conflict. Strip out the particular personal and organizational details, and the underlying stories are the same. Take any *Dilbert* strip and you can probably boil it down to one of these archetypal narratives directed at either the Develop, Sell, or Deliver roles. See Figure 9.2. Here are the basic storylines:

- **Stories About Developing Roles:** "They are lost in models and focused on possibility, not practicality!"
- **Stories About Selling Roles:** "They will sell anything, regardless of whether we actually make it or if we want to!"
- **Stories About Delivering Roles:** "They are inflexible and rigidly focused on quality!"

I'm sure you recognize the truth in all these criticisms—at least the ones that don't pertain to your particular role! However, the other side of the story is that to grow, scale, and create competitive advantage, a

There are natural **Creative Tensions** around the **Business Triangle** that are necessary to drive innovation and growth—these show up as the same universal types of feedback between roles in all businesses

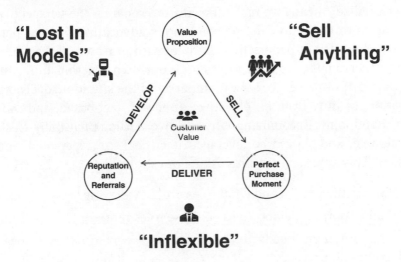

FIGURE 9.2 Creative Tensions Around the Business Triangle

business segment must have these three perspectives (and others) in creative tension with each other. It needs the unfettered imagination of Develop, the hustle of Sell, and the quality control of Deliver. Successful products and services require input from all these perspectives and more to achieve their goals and meet the customers' needs fully. The tension between them is what keeps their excesses in check, preventing any one side from dominating the others with its agenda.

Depersonalizing Conflict

One of the reasons people tend to avoid conflict or tension is that it can quickly get personal. Conflicts may originate in different perspectives about a business issue, but they often devolve into bad feelings and personal animosities, with people drawing negative conclusions about each other's motives and intentions. If we are to design systems that encourage and leverage the tension between roles, it's essential that we depersonalize the differences of perspective that arise. Often the blocker to resolving conflicts, leveraging creative tensions, and aligning roles is the unwillingness or inability of participants to ask these questions and discuss them in an objective, depersonalized way. To "depersonalize" means we make the effort to separate the perspective of a role from the individual person who is advocating for that perspective. And if that perspective conflicts with our own, rather than taking it personally, we seek to separate our own reaction from the perspective of our role. We seek to understand the situation, decision, obligation, or duty from an objective, unbiased, fact-based, and self-aware standpoint. Recognizing why creative tensions naturally exist, are valuable, and should be leveraged is critical for depersonalizing conflicts. This approach requires asking questions like:

- Who are the parties and what roles are they playing?
- What important perspectives do those roles represent?
- What are their needs and desires, and why do they appear incompatible?
- What can be done to resolve or leverage this creative tension?

Here's a great trick for proactively depersonalizing tensions: *Declare the hat you're wearing.* In other words, tell people which role you are advocating for when you share a perspective. This immediately signals that it's not just your personal opinion that you're stating, and it encourages others to respond from the perspective of their roles rather than from their personal reactions. All you need to do is to state your role or perspective before diving into the discussion itself. For example: "From my role as business leader, I think this isn't a good strategic direction for us"; "From my role as head of sales, I propose we discount that product to move inventory"; "From my role as VP of finance, I'm concerned that we don't have the budget for that project."

Declaring your hat(s) out loud will help clarify which perspective(s) you represent and will set up the discussion as depersonalized. This will allow team members to focus on the shared purpose and how each perspective contributes to it.

Another secret to depersonalizing and de-escalating conflict lies in the language we use. When you're trying to resolve creative tensions, pay attention to the tone of the conversation. Are people contributing in ways that are constructive and exploring possibilities, or are they guarded and limiting the discussion? Language that limits possibility either sustains the status quo or prevents resolution. The speaker's focus is on being right, why something is not possible, why something should be prevented, or maintaining power or status.

Conversely, language that opens possibility introduces and sustains access to potential resolutions. The speaker's focus is on being open, authentic, curious, and exploring what is possible. Language that opens possibility is the cornerstone of creating a high-trust environment in which creative tensions can be leveraged and resolved, and enabling two-way dialogue between all stakeholders in a business system. This is crucial for successfully leading and managing transformational change.

The Natural Creative Tension in Enterprises

Creative tensions play out around the business triangle between the different roles and teams. But there are also creative tensions that can be seen at the level of the enterprise as a whole. These, too, are powerful drivers of growth. When we look at the enterprise as a whole, the main creative tension that is apparent is between the horizontal perspective and the vertical perspective (see Figure 9.3).

The horizontal perspective is focused on optimizing existing solutions and processes in order to deliver more value, while the vertical perspective is focused on generating new solutions and significantly changing how existing processes work. As we discussed before, both are needed for companies to scale and grow in a sustainable way.

Some of the roles in an enterprise should naturally be more focused on vertical improvement and others on horizontal improvement. Enterprise leadership and business leaders usually lean more vertical, whereas functional leadership leans more horizontal. But which of these perspectives should come first? Which should take precedence? The answer is that the balance should be tilted slightly toward vertical improvement so that the system adapts and transforms fast enough to sustain industry competitive advantage. However, the tension should

The goal is healthy **Creative Tension** between horizonal and vertical perspectives—some roles will naturally be more horizontal and others more vertical.

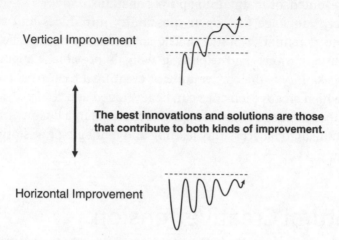

FIGURE 9.3 Creative Tensions in Enterprises

be embraced so that the horizontal perspectives can provide a healthy check on the pace of growth and change, ensuring that concerns like quality, brand integrity, cost control, efficiency, and culture are not trampled in the rush to transform.

Leading Through Creative Tensions

It takes a particular kind of leadership to skillfully navigate the creative tensions within a business and drive them to productive resolution without just taking sides. "Productive resolution" usually means a solution that works from the perspective of multiple roles, rather than just satisfying one. Such solutions can be harder to reach, because they require navigating trade-offs and grappling with multiple interests. But they're much more likely to actually solve the issue and create lasting value, because they're mutually beneficial for the many different perspectives that have a stake in the outcome. People tend to see the world from the perspective of the roles that they play. In any given situation, some perspectives may be more important than others, but if one perspective is allowed to dominate completely, it shuts down creative tension. At the same time, you can't just give all perspectives equal weight and attempt to reach consensus—that's a recipe for unproductive chaos. A wise leader is sensitive to the fact that some roles need to have greater authority and influence than others, but all perspectives need to be on the table in order for the right solution to emerge.

A few years ago, I was asked to consult on a business within Consumer Products Company. The current business leader had just been promoted. In her previous role, she had been head of sales, and as part of that role she had been responsible for a number of niche, specialized, one-off customers. In that role, she had grown frustrated with the inability of the Develop teams to meet the specialized needs of her customers and their hesitancy to develop niche products. Now that she was in charge of the whole business, overseeing all three sides of the triangle, she was happy she'd have more power to get Develop to create the products she knew customers wanted. For her, as for many successful salespeople, success had become equated to selling, and in her new role as business leader, she thought the key to growing the business was to sell more. Yet when I came in to consult with her, the business was struggling, margins were out of control, and performance was seriously degraded. She was thoroughly confused. What the heck had gone wrong?

What she hadn't fully internalized was that she was no longer head of sales! She was still seeing the business through the perspective of sales and empowering that part of the triangle at the expense of the others. She needed to realize that as a business leader rather than a functional leader, she was now responsible for managing a healthy creative tension between all sides of the triangle. She couldn't favor one over the others. They were all her children now, and she couldn't play favorites. She had to stop settling old scores, and using her power to push through all the bespoke and niche products that may have been wanted by sales but were not helping the overall business. Unbalances in the social system, especially unconscious ones, clog up the value stream.

Her mistake was thinking that promotion meant more power to promote her existing perspective on the business. But with a new role, increased power, and more responsibility comes the need to hold more perspectives, and often competing ones. That's how we build high-performing businesses. If the sales team starts deciding what kind of products get made, that's a problem. If the delivery group starts dictating how the sales team should operate, that's a problem too. There should be a healthy, creative tension between the sides of the triangle. The best solutions generally don't just satisfy one role. They work for multiple ones. Especially given that each side of the triangle has a critical role to play and a unique vantage point on the client or customer, and on the organization itself. They will each provide distinctive, valuable insights. If one gets de-emphasized or lost in the mix, the company will be harmed. All of them need to have a legitimate voice, so that conflicts can be understood, identified, and resolved in a timely fashion and the whole system moves faster and faster. In fact, this leads us to the formula for unleashing high performance in a business: *Every key capability has a single owner. And that single owner is advocating the strategy for that capability. And in that role, they are driving all key issues to resolution, and resolving all constraints.*

Banish the Scourge of Functionitis

There is a virus that often infects businesses, a debilitating condition can constrain and restrain their success. It can suck the life out of a company, frustrate and exasperate the best people, and tie an enterprise in knots. Simply put, it's what happens when any one of the functional perspectives—Develop, Sell, Deliver, or Support—oversteps its role and tries to exert power and control over other parts of the business. In other words, it stops contributing to or supporting the business and begins to imagine it actually *is* the business. It starts punching above its weight class. For example, when support functions overstep their roles, and try to act as if they are in control of some aspect of the business, things start to break down. It's all too common to see this happen with accounting, for example, so that controlling costs becomes the overriding priority rather than creating value. Another example, as demonstrated in the earlier Consumer Products Company story, would be when sales starts dictating what products should be developed. I call this *functionitis*. It's a highly curable but nasty disease. And it's all too common in corporate settings today.

The cure for functionitis is ensuring that the role of the business leader is being filled. It's the business leader's responsibility to hold a perspective on the whole triangle and the creative tensions between the different sides, while driving strategic alignment and clarity. If that vision is lacking, the functional leader's tendency to just "get it done" will step in to fill the void. At Radiant Love, a case of functionitis was partly to blame for the conflict over the development of the app. In the absence of the right kind of business leadership, Lily—a functional leader in the IT department—had stepped up. But she was driving the project from a limited perspective, with a focus on its technical attributes and timely completion. She was missing the key perspectives that were held by people like Xavier. When Sarah looked at the situation, she recognized that the perspective of a business leader was missing—someone who could integrate both Lily and Xavier's perspectives without losing sight of the larger business case for the project.

A North Star for Resolving Creative Tensions

Once again, when dealing with conflicts and tensions in a system of distributed leadership, the most important question we need to answer is, Are they productive? Are we able to resolve conflicts and tensions creatively in such a way that moves the whole system forward? But that brings up another, more fundamental question: How do we even know what constitutes "moving forward"? In broad strokes, the organization has a mission and vision, and the top leadership teams may have issued directives that provide general direction and orientation. But on the day-to-day level, these may not be enough to reveal the path forward. There are many important decisions that get made every day, and in order to make these decisions and take into account the sometimes conflicting perspectives of the various roles, we need a method for knowing what's most important. Where do we spend money? Who do we hire? For what job? Where do we put resources? What do we focus on?

Of course, business leaders and teams want and need their businesses to succeed, but again, what does *success* mean? People often answer this from the perspective of their function. Salespeople like my client at a global Consumer Products Company think "more sales." People in Develop roles think "more product lines." People in Deliver roles think "more quality and throughput." Each of these is obviously a very positive thing in a business. But for the organization as a whole, we need a brighter North Star that integrates all the functional perspectives and aligns everyone with the mission and vision. And we can't just resort to having all those decisions made at the highest levels, by leaders who are "above the fray" of competing perspectives. Part of coming to terms with organizational complexity is also coming to terms with the reality that the best decisions are often made by those for whom the results of those decisions, positive or negative, are most acutely experienced. You want your business teams to be highly invested in those decisions, to care about them, to be noticeably conscious of their impacts, and to carry them out with a high level of ownership and responsibility. That doesn't happen when they are passively executing some directives from on high. And yet, people will tend to see the world through the perspectives of their own roles. The North Star that can enable teams to resolve creative tensions for the higher good of the organization is competitive advantage—and in Crucial Conversation 6: Aligning Strategies (see Chapter 18), teams learn four metrics for weighing decisions in light of this North Star.

CHAPTER 10

High-Performing Teams

Stage 3, Distributed Leadership, continued

The strength of the team is each individual member.
The strength of each member is the team.

—Phil Jackson

As we've journeyed through the stages of enterprise evolution, you may have noticed one term appearing more and more frequently on these pages—namely, teams. At stage 1, the independent contributors who come together to form a business are barely a team—they're more of a loose confederation. At stage 2, you might see teams beginning to form around different functions or projects, but they're less important than the hierarchical reporting relationships that connect the business functions to the directive leader. At stage 3, however, teams become critical. The matrix structure of a stage 3 organization is not just a matrix of individuals; it's a matrix of teams—specifically, intact teams with clear leadership. So our discussion of stage 3 would not be complete without taking a closer look at teams—what they are, how they work, and how they can become high performing.

This last point—the creation of high-performing teams—is really the focus of this chapter and of the rest of the book. It's one thing to organize your structure around teams; it's quite another to have those teams be high performing. In a thriving stage 3 organization (and in stage 4, as we'll discuss in the next chapter) high-performing teams become the engine of growth, transformation, value creation, and innovation. The Seven Crucial Conversations in Part III of this book are the roadmap by which teams become high performing. But before we get there, let's take a closer look at what teams are and what makes them tick.

Teams at Work

What comes to mind when you think of the word *team*? Ask that question 50 years ago, and the answer would have been easy—sports. Today, however, the concept of the team is increasingly associated with the workplace as well. In their 2019 Human Capital Trends survey,[1] Deloitte found that 31 percent of respondents structure and operate their businesses wholly or largely on teams, while another 65 percent said that while their structure remains hierarchical, they do some cross-functional team-based work. And among those organizations that have not yet made the transition, many see the writing on the wall: 65 percent of respondents viewed the shift from "functional hierarchy to team-centric and network-based organizational models" as important or very important. And you only have to glance at some of the highest performing organizations today to see that the shift pays off, for those who execute it well. World class companies among my consulting clients that implement a structure built on high-performing teams include Chicos, Pfizer, Edward Jones, Johnson & Johnson, Lancôme, Mars, and Merck, just to name a few. As the report concludes, "The global trend toward team-based organizations is growing for a reason: It is a more effective model for operating in the dynamic, unpredictable business environment typically seen today. In the long term, we believe there will be no leading organization that does not work primarily on the basis of teams."

[1]Erica Volini, Jeff Schwartz, Indranil Roy, Maren Hauptmann, and Yves Van Durme, "Organizational Performance: It's a Team Sport," 2019 Global Human Capital Trends, Deloitte Insights, https://www2.deloitte.com/us/en/insights/focus/human-capital-trends/2019/team-based-organization.html.

I would wholeheartedly agree with this assessment. And yet teams by themselves don't a thriving organization make. A team at its best is far more than the sum of its parts—it's dynamic, intelligent, responsive, inspiring, and infectious in the best way. But it can also be nothing more than a grouping of people. To create a thriving, agile, intelligent team-based organization, we need *high-performing teams* at every level. This is a significant challenge for stage 3 companies—not just designing a team-based structure but unleashing high performance within those teams. And as the Deloitte survey noted, "deeper in the enterprise, many organizations are struggling to build programs and incentives that support teaming."[2]

Teams in an organization are like cells in the body. They may not stand out to the naked eye, but beneath the surface, they are determining the health of the entire system. If you want to transform your organization at a level that affects the functioning of the whole system, that means affecting the functioning of the cell itself—optimizing the power and capability of the team. A body, from one point of view, is a system of cells. Likewise, an organization can be considered a system of teams. I like to think of high-performing teams as the "secret agents" of transformation in a complex adaptive social system. Like transformation at a cellular level, transformation in a team is deep and sustained. And unless transformation happens at the level of teams, the organization will struggle to truly achieve high performance.

I have written quite a bit in these pages about the nature of an organization being a social system. Well, it doesn't get much more "social" than examining an organization and a business through the lens of teams. *After all, the fundamental currency of teams is relationships, and the currency of those relationships is the conversations we have with one another.* Therefore, transforming the social system of an organization ultimately means transforming the many conversations that collectively are defining that social system—its culture, its norms, its ways of working, its shared language, its perspective on the business and on the world. Those crucial conversations, as we'll see in Part III of this book, take place in teams.

If we're working to transform the social system, building new performance attributes into the system itself, that means affecting

---

[2]Ibid.

the ways in which individuals interact—how they come together and define their roles; how they solve problems; how they understand their work; how they organize around leaders; the quality of purpose and meaning they find in their work; and ultimately, the conversations they have about all of it. Indeed, if you want to get at the heart of the transformational journey in today's organizations, you have to directly impact the conversations that define and power its teams.

Understanding Teams

Let's begin at the beginning. Before there are high-performing teams with motivated members initiating crucial conversations, productively resolving creative tensions, building effective strategies, increasing competitive advantage, traveling together on a journey of transformation, and powering great organizations, there are just people. There are individuals with needs to be met, problems to impact, and issues to be resolved. Inevitably, they band together to do all those things, and as they do, again and again, teams are born—and in some cases, those teams form an organization. The story is as old as time. In fact, most teams evolve naturally. A *natural team* or *work group* is a group working together to achieve common interests in a way that is not structured by design. Families are probably the most common kind of natural team. In stage 1 and even early stage 2 organizations, work groups develop naturally, with little intentional structure. Shared ways of working are developed ad hoc, implicit agreements are formed about how things get done and who does what, power dynamics are navigated, culture develops, and so on. When a team gets a designated leader, it becomes an *intact team*.

The "performance" of a team—its effectiveness at achieving its aims—is, in the simplest sense, the sum total of the performance of its individual members and their ability to work in alignment with each other toward a common goal: to manage the complexity of their particular social system in order to optimize results. In a natural team, performance may not be something people are thinking too much about, let alone trying to improve. But for a leader who seeks to grow an organization or business, *high performance* becomes both an aspiration and an urgent necessity. Consider the difference between a group of kids who meet up at the local park to play a game of soccer, and a serious high school soccer team. The first group just happens to come together, and they play with whoever shows up that day. Some may be naturally gifted athletes, others less so. There's no coach or training program to help them improve. The second group is much more intentional in its creation. Kids have to try out for the team. They practice regularly, work with coaches to improve their skills, and create strategies for playing together in such a way that maximizes their talents. They are focused on becoming high performing in order to win more games.

It's the same in business, or any complex organization. But too many organizations take their teams for granted. They don't invest in them. They don't invest in coaches, training, or leaders. They don't develop a shared language for understanding and encouraging higher performance. They don't acquire the best technology to help support them. They don't pursue best practices. Perhaps most fundamentally, they don't consciously and actively commit to their success.

Mature stage 3 organizations are very conscious about how they build, structure, and run teams. Like the soccer team, they understand that high performance cannot be assumed. Certain conditions enable leaders, team members, and businesses to optimize their performance, individually and collectively. At Growth River, we've broken those down into a series of crucial conversations that will fundamentally alter the social system of your team and ultimately your organization.

Team structures refers to the different ways in which teams can be organized and led. Capabilities to build and sustain these different team structures roughly correspond to the four enterprise evolutionary stages.

1. **Workgroups or natural teams** refers to a group working together to achieve common interests in a way that is not structured by design.

2. **Intact teams** refers teams that have a single team leader who is responsible for team performance, dynamics, accountability, and continuous improvement. The team leader is fully in it with the team.

(continued)

(continued)

> 3. **High-performing teams (HPTs)** refers to an intact team that is designed and developed intentionally by the team leader and by implementing HPT ways of working.
>
> 4. **High-performing transformational leadership teams** refers to top leadership teams in companies that are HPTs and are responsible for leading transformational change across multiple audiences or stakeholder groups.
>
> 5. **High-performing self-managed teams** refers to high-performing teams that are trained and coached to be self-managing and not to require a single team leader. Self-managing teams will report into the leader, but they will not necessarily have all of the leadership strengths of intact teams. Self-managed teams enable companies to scale leadership and to build flat agile organizations by having multiple self-managed teams report to a single leader.

The Building Blocks of High-Performing Teams

The amount of ink that has been spilled in an effort to improve the performance of teams is daunting. And yet, we forge ahead. Why? Because any little advantage in the quality and performance of teams is like discovering a vein of gold in the walls of a business. It yields extraordinary dividends. Here are a few important lessons I've learned from observing and creating HPTs over several decades.

HPTS are built by design. They are intentional. They are purposeful. They don't happen by accident. They are built consciously.

HPTs are not too big, not too small. Teams should ideally be about 6–10 people but not more than 12. Too many people on a team will inhibit performance and reduce its effectiveness.

HPTs are led. In natural teams, leadership might organically form. But in an HPT, there is a leader who is explicitly responsible and accountable. That doesn't mean leadership has to be "command and control," but neither is it vague, spontaneous, or organic.

HPTs are authentically a team. This may seem obvious or repetitive, but it's crucial. Members authentically feel like they're "in it together." The journey of an HPT is deeply shared. There is a sense of collective purpose, not just an individual one. Team members are accountable to each other, develop camaraderie and trust, and feel a sense that each person has the other's back.

HPTs are on a mission. Perhaps most important, high-performing teams don't just exist in a vacuum. They are on a mission—a continuous improvement journey, fulfilling their own purposes and the purposes of the organization.

Now that we have those basics in mind, we need to turn to another key element of HPTs that is easy to take for granted. It involves the shared information ecosystem that will inevitably develop among team members. This needs to be explicit and transparent. How are we going to work together? What role is each person representing? What skill-sets do we need to achieve our team goals? Don't assume the answers to these questions are naturally understood. Make sure that everyone is singing from the same hymnbook, and understands the words to the songs! Such clarity begins with the most simple but underappreciated cultural achievement that all high-performing teams exhibit—a shared language.

Shared Language

George Bernard Shaw is said to have once described England and the United States as "two nations divided by a common tongue." The same could be said of many individuals working together in teams and organizations today. They might use the same words and utter the same sentences, but their meaning is continents apart. You might be sitting in a meeting discussing a business problem when someone exclaims, "We need marketing!" Everyone agrees. And then you leave the meeting and the sales guy walks out thinking he's going to create a brochure, while the product guy thinks he's going to do a study to design a new value proposition. Both of those are meanings assigned to the word "marketing." This happens all the time in business. Trains crash and lots of damage is done only because people use the same words to mean different things. It's little wonder they often find it hard to align and coordinate, let alone to grow and thrive.

All tribes, big and small, develop their own language. It's a natural part of being human. It's part of how we define in-groups and out-groups. Indeed, we've all had the experience of being in a group of people who share a lexicon—perhaps the jargon of a particular industry, the fan-speak associated with a sport, the lingo of a subculture. It can be frustrating to feel like you're on the outside of such a group. Certain words or phrases are sacred, but you don't appreciate why. Everyone else is laughing but you don't get the jokes. They finish each other's sentences, while you don't understand the references. For those on the inside, the common meaning they associate with certain words or phrases creates not only mutual understanding but also a sense of camaraderie. The laughter they share is bonding, creating a tribal sense of connection. They're "in it together" because they speak the same language. From a cultural standpoint, we want our teams to feel camaraderie and mutual understanding and avoid the common misunderstandings that can lead to mistrust and breakdowns in relationships. Teams, as social systems, are fragile constructs. Small misunderstandings, miscommunications, and assumptions can derail even successful teams and cause doubt, mistrust, and insecurities. The surest way to avoid miscommunications is simple—communicate! If you want to ensure understanding and alignment all around, you must discuss the issues out loud so that everyone in the room can respond. You must resolutely insist on achieving something all too rare in the business community—a commonly understood language for working together.

High-performing teams are conscious and deliberate about the language they are using. It's important to know that everyone is on the same page. It will help bind the group together. In a very real sense, the shared language of a team creates a kind of cell membrane around the team that defines what is inside and what is outside. Don't ever take for granted the importance of developing and cultivating a shared language that everyone understands. And this is not something that is done once and put aside; it's an ongoing process, a shared experience that must be continually cultivated.

Creating a shared language, clear roles, explicit ways of working, and a clear structure for team interactions doesn't have to result in a team dynamic of conformity. We're trying to inspire autonomous team members, not create drones! Diversity of opinion is fine. Disagreement is fine. Creative tension is essential to HPTs. But tension is much more likely to be creative if that diversity of opinion and disagreement is happening in the context of a shared language, and the basic structure of team interactions is understood. If the roles that team members play are clear, and if the overall direction and goals of the team are transparent, it's much easier to have productive discussions and even disagreements. In that context, the energy of creative tension has the power to move the team forward, not waste energy in unproductive conflict, often driven by miscommunication.

Shared language needs to be developed intrateam, but that also highlights the importance of interteam communication. Do different teams in different parts of the organization communicate effectively? Does the organization as a whole have a shared language for common business activities and protocols? When language gets codified across the organization, we begin to develop more effective cross-functional business processes. All the little confusions and disharmonies that come from singing in different keys begin to work themselves out. Suddenly, and often surprisingly, disparate teams and functional silos start to sync up.

At Growth River, we have developed a language that has very specific meaning, and in our methodology, we strive to be clear and precise about language and attentive to the relevant audience lives inside our shared language membrane. I have shared some of that language in these pages, calling out key definitions. Honestly, if you revisit our methodology in five years, I expect the language to have changed and evolved. That's simply due to the fact that we are always working on our language, striving to be clearer, endeavoring to express our meaning with greater precision. I encourage you to do the same, whether you are working with a Growth River methodology or on a system of your own creation. A huge degree of complexity in organizational social systems can be ascribed to a failure of shared language, to the dangers of assuming others know what you're talking about. A glossary and a snapshot of the current key terms in the Growth River Operating System is included at the end of this book.

Developing a more conscious, explicit method of communication, and knowing—not hoping or assuming—that team members understand exactly what you are saying, is an indispensable step in the process of forming and sustaining an HPT.

Beware of Toxic Rock Stars! They exist in most organizations. And they are oh, so hard to let go. But it's essential. Toxic rock stars are highly productive jerks, excuse my French. They seem vital to a team from a performance perspective. They're often independent, and they get things done. There is just one problem—they're toxic. They don't up-lift those around them. They can't work with others. They can't function in teams. They lower the performance of the team, even as they seem to hold everyone hostage with their impressive individual productivity.

In a stage 2 organization, toxic rock stars seem like a necessary evil. I've had people tell me "Yes, this person doesn't work well with others, I know they're not creating a healthy environment around them, but they're responsible for half my business! How can I possibly let them go?!" Maybe they are. But if you want to rise to stage 3 performance, that toxicity has no place. Otherwise, it will undermine any attempts to create the type of high-performing teams that will ultimately be a much better foundation for the company's growth and success.

Toxic rock stars thrive in otherwise low-performing organizations. But when those around them start to transform and rise up, the environment that excused and allowed that toxicity will have to change as well. It's a hard truth, but if you want the power and benefits of distributed leadership, and your toxic rock stars won't change, then they have to take a hike.

Secret Agents of Transformation

For some teams, major renovations will be required to attain high performance. The entire social structure will need to be rebuilt from the ground up. A new lexicon of shared language and perspectives will need to be established. Multiple ways of working will need to be redesigned and implemented. Key skillsets will need to be developed. In other cases, there may be simpler changes needed—a new coat of paint, a reinforcing beam, a few key realignments. Whatever it takes, the team shares an intention to become the most effective version of itself, and all team members recognize that this process is a developmental journey to be navigated, not an initiative to be checked off.

When a team attains high performance, it will be obvious. High-performing teams get noticed. They may be a functional team, a business team, or an enterprise team, but wherever they sit on the org chart, the quality of the group dynamics and the power of their shared work will be felt in the organization. They have impact. They grow, learn, and improve. They become more and more effective. They inevitably put positive pressure on the rest of the organization. They are hard to ignore. And over time, they will naturally break out of their own internal workstreams and connect with other teams (or HPTs) in the organization. In fact, one way to think of a company is simply as a system of teams that interact with each other in similar ways to the way members within the team interact. If intrateam dynamics are powerful and positive, it's more than likely interteam dynamics will be as well. An HPT will only fly under the radar for so long. Its influence, power, and obvious effectiveness will tend to infect those around it. It will stand out. It may even be disruptive. It may challenge conventional organizational wisdom, and in so doing, even step on a few less-than-high-performing-toes. Sooner or later, it will be noticed.

HPTs are, for lack of a better word, *awake*. They are intelligent, adaptive, and continuously learning. In their emergence, the promise of distributed leadership becomes realized. The business, the organization, the social system is no longer sleepwalking, semiconscious, and responsive to only the biggest shocks from the market or from management. It's alive and attuned, capable of adapting, adept at learning—driven forward by the types of conscious conversations that inspire teams, and ultimately individuals, to realize their potential.

High-performing teams are the essential driver of high-performing organizations. They commit to the journey, they do the work, they don't skip steps, they're in it for the duration, and they reap the rewards. In fact, the journey of a high-performing team could provide the material for an entire book of its own. It's that important. But it's also a fitting amalgamation of the Growth River journey, as we've described it throughout. So much of the work to create high performing stage 3 and 4 organizations will stand or fall, succeed, or fail, based on the development of high-performing teams.

Another important reason for developing teams is that most individuals in organizations, even most leaders, simply do not have the authority to implement change initiatives at the scale of the entire organization. Their transformational ambitions must inevitably start on a more limited canvas. But most people in organizations are part of teams. And teams can be powerful agents. They can surprise. That's why I call them the secret agents of transformation.

Besides, top-down initiatives so often flounder. Even the most well-intended initiatives rarely reach all the way to the ground, and therefore fail to have the desired impact. Leaders fall in love with the adrenaline rush of designed change, and as a result they keep looking to the next big re-org. In fact, the most transformative changes are often small, even mundane. Transformation happens because of a million little choices plus a few big collective ones. The question is, how do you create energy and commitment to the million, not just the few? I think you create that through building them into teams at every level. Establishing HPTs is something more resembling an "inside-out" transformation. A true HPT—confident, empowered, and intelligent—knows how to digest a transformational journey. It can understand its components, appreciate how it intersects with the team, identify the capabilities involved, connect it to the team's purview, and implement and adjust where necessary. And it can even start to engage other teams around those issues and help facilitate its smart adoption throughout the organization.

Indeed, HPTs are infectious. Eventually, if enough teams in the social system begin to exhibit these characteristics, they will influence those around them. That will drive curiosity and interest in this methodology, and possibly some resistance as well. That is natural. When one team achieves higher performance and begins to advocate for its perspective with a single voice, others will start to listen. Initially, it may challenge the status quo. But it will also inspire and uplift. And as other teams rise up, they will emerge with their own distinct voices. That generates creative tension across the organization—a sort of race to the top. After all, once you've been part of the journey of a truly HPT, you won't ever want to go back to the status quo. It's hard to put the genie back in the bottle. When HPTs align with other HPTs through applying the Seven Crucial Conversations, the organization as a whole is profoundly impacted. Build enough HPTs and eventually the result will be as inevitable as it is desirable—a high-performing organization.

To actualize stage 3 potentials, it doesn't matter whether the team is a functional team working deep down in the organization on one side of the Business Triangle or a high-profile executive team overseeing multiple businesses, the same principles apply. If you want to initiate a transformative journey in your organization, I invite you to begin a series of crucial conversations with the people on your own team.

CHAPTER 11

Toward a Flat, Agile Organization

Stage 4: Leaders Leading Leaders

A world of flat organizations and tumultuous business conditions—and that's our world—punishes fixed skills and prizes elastic ones.

—Daniel H. Pink, *To Sell Is Human*

In following the journey of organizational evolution through the first three stages, we have devoted particular attention to the momentous shift from stage 2, Directive Leadership, to stage 3, Distributed Leadership, and to unpacking stage 3 in detail over several chapters. In contrast, this chapter on stage 4, Leaders Leading Leaders, will be brief. There's a simple reason for that: the transition from stage 3 to stage 4 is not as definitive as between the other three stages. Stage 4 is more like a maturation of stage 3, and therefore many of the principles we've already discussed in stage 3 apply in stage 4 as well, with a few key points of difference.

Stage 4: Leaders Leading Leaders. *A flat organizational structure with a system of intact teams at the top and self-managing teams reporting into those teams. Aligned leadership is driven by high-performance-team (HPT) ways of working. The top leadership team is a sensing team, operating from a strategic purpose-driven perspective.*

There is, however, a distinctive tipping point from stage 3 to 4. Before this point, when an organization's top leadership recognizes a critical issue, concern, or gap, in order to ensure clear accountabilities, they will need to assign it to one person, who then leads it to resolution (developing an intact team as necessary). This is part of what makes the CEO role scalable in stage 3, with the CEO as enterprise leader being freed up to distribute authority and decision-making power throughout the organization's matrix of intact teams. But in the developmental logic of a transformational journey, every good thing eventually becomes an obstacle. The progress of one stage becomes the pathology of the next. One stage's solutions become the problems that spur the development of the next stage. In late stage 3, the need to have a single accountable leader for every issue becomes a bottleneck, just as the single directive leader became a bottleneck in late stage 2. You end up with a limited pool of trusted middle managers, a layer of leadership that operates between top management and the rest of the organization. A mature stage 3 organization starts to chafe against the need for everything to go through this layer. In the transition to stage 4, the company resolves this bottleneck, reaching a level of high performance at the team level that transcends the need for those team leaders. In other words, teams become truly self-managed. This occurs when the organization has developed the critical level of HPT ways of working and support capabilities that is required to charter and sustain high-performing self-managed teams. In stage 4, top leadership will have the confidence that self-managing teams are a trustworthy mechanism for addressing significant strategic and operational challenges. And that opens the door to building flat agile organizations.

> **High-performing self-managed teams** are high-performing teams that are designed, built, led, and supported to be self-managing. The team reports to a single leader, so that there is a clear leadership mechanism, however that leader is not responsible for managing the team's HPT journey, so it is not strictly an intact team. Instead, the process of chartering the team and managing its developmental journey and tracking its performance as a team is supported by formalized cross-functional capabilities and processes. As a result, the company is able to develop and leverage self-managed teams to build *flat agile organizations,* which require very few middle managers.

In stage 4 companies, as in stage 3, the structure is a matrix of teams designed to provide Develop, Sell, Deliver, and Support capabilities across multiple Business Triangles. At the top level, the senior teams, in charge of Business Triangles and various capabilities will be intact teams—with single accountable leaders. These include the following:

1. Enterprise leader and team
2. Business leaders and teams
3. Develop capability leaders and teams
4. Sell capability leaders and teams
5. Channel leaders and teams (in some companies)
6. Deliver capability leaders and teams
7. Support capability leaders and teams

Among these team will be team connectors, leaders of teams that are members of other teams and are responsible for aligning across teams. So, the members of the enterprise team, and the business teams, will include the leaders of various capability teams, as is required to ensure all key roles, perspectives, and creative tensions are represented.

The enterprise team will be the one place in the company where all the roles and perspectives across the company come together. In stage 4 companies, the goal is to enable that enterprise team, to operate more as a "sensing team" than a "doing team"—to be "in it together" at a strategic level, viewing from the balcony not the dance floor. This does not, in any way, imply that top leadership is disconnected from the salient business details or operational results. Indeed, they will be leading teams where those details are managed and executed.

Sensing is a way of working in which leaders intentionally create and apply dynamic learning relationships with other leaders to clarify shared intentions, surface intuitions, and follow a gut sense to creatively anticipate risks and create opportunities. What is the ideal future state for the company? What are the gaps in the current state? What are the target milestone breakthroughs for the company, as a business social system?

In stage 3, it is often the case that the top leaders who are members of a company's enterprise team will think of their role on that team as being to represent the needs and perspective of the separate business or capability teams that they lead. Therefore, they will come to enterprise team meetings with the intention to protect the interests of these subteams. However, in stage 4, an important shift occurs in which they choose to think of the enterprise team as their "home team."

Home team refers to a high-performing senior leadership team in which team members are held accountable as leaders for developing and leveraging strong dynamic peer-to-peer relationships, that enable them to collectively rise above operational concerns and to engage in sensing conversations toward shared purpose. A common misinterpretation of this idea is that your home team is one that you lead or a place where you spend most of your time; this may or may not be the case.

Another characteristic of stage 4 companies, particularly larger ones, is the emergence of a kind of "internal consultancy" function that can support and guide teams across the company in their HPT journeys. You see this, for example, in a large stage 4 company like Google. For companies to progress from stage 3 to stage 4, they need to formally develop the process capabilities for establishing or chartering intact high-performing teams, and high-performing self-managing teams and then tracking, managing, and supporting the developmental journeys of those teams—all of which occurs through the template of the Seven Crucial Conversations. Growth River's reason for being is to enable organizations to develop their own capabilities to develop and accelerate high-performing teams, businesses, and companies.

Enterprise Evolution Shouldn't Be Rushed

When we last checked in on our friends at Radiant Love LLC, they were still early in stage 3. Sarah, as enterprise leader, has led the organization through the process of redesigning its system of capabilities and roles around two distinct Business Triangles. The introduction of the two business leaders, Paula and Diego, was key, allowing the functional leaders to focus on developing and aligning their capabilities. The newly aligned team was able to move forward with acquiring and building the necessary technologies, skills, and processes to successfully create and run a digital app business. About a year after Sarah took over the helm, the Radiant Love app was launched. With its proprietary algorithm inspired by Strega's unique approach to matchmaking, the app allowed the company to successfully compete with much more established players in the dating app field. It also provided an unexpected boost to their other business line, promoting the cafés and love coaches. Special events at the cafés sell out almost immediately thanks to the reach of the app.

The organization itself continues to evolve as the enterprise team and all the other teams develop their HPT ways of working. Radiant Love may continue to thrive and grow in stage 3 for many years to come. However, it is easy to imagine Sarah and her team beginning to anticipate the need to invest in the capabilities required to create and sustain self-managing teams to tip the organization into stage 4. My advice to her? There's no hurry. Don't get ahead of yourself and try to jump to stage 4 before the organization has truly integrated stage 3 learnings and attained high performance in every team. It's not always true that "higher stage = better." What's best for any company depends on where they're at in their journey, and the beauty of development is that when the time comes for a shift to a new stage, you'll know it. It will become a matter of pressing urgency—a wake-up call that cannot be avoided. But you won't even encounter the problems that necessitate that shift until you've deeply inhabited the previous stage.

This advice isn't limited to Sarah and her team. Very few companies today have matured in stage 3 to the point where stage 4 becomes a compelling possibility and even a necessity. We're all still learning the limits of distributed leadership, and as we begin to bump up against them, stage 4 will come into focus, with its own unique solutions, challenges, and opportunities. Until then, the task at hand for teams at every level of the organization is to accelerate their journey to high performance. To do so, let's turn to the Seven Crucial Conversations . . .

PART 3

The Seven Crucial Conversations

U p to this point in the book, we have examined organizations from the outside in. We began studying them as a whole and then proceeded to look more closely at the various parts as they evolve through the four stages of enterprise evolution. For this final part of the book, the Seven Crucial Conversations, I want to reverse that lens. Instead of starting with the whole, we will work from the inside-out, starting with the essential units or parts of the social system and examining how they impact the whole. Stage 3 and 4 organizations are designed as a matrix rather than a traditional hierarchy. And as discussed in the last few chapters, the key units in this matrix are not individuals, but teams. When it comes to implementing the methodology of Growth River, and enacting the transformational journey of stage 3 and 4 organizations, we do it in teams. And we structure that process around the Seven Crucial Conversations.

If you want to escape the Swirl, and move into higher performance, the transformational journey ultimately has to reach all the way down to the ground—to the level of individuals and the teams in which they work. The urgency of change must take root in team members' hearts and minds. People need to authentically care about it. And here is the truth that all leaders must understand: With some exceptions, individuals don't outperform for a beautiful idea or a lofty goal. They don't transform themselves and reach new creative heights simply because they care about the mission statement. Such things may certainly inspire, but on-the-ground results often require another key catalyst, one much closer to home. It's the person next to them, the colleague across the table, the friendships they've developed with the people in their group, the joy of competition and collaboration with those with whom they are sharing the proverbial foxhole. Individuals go the extra mile, in other words, for the team—for the people they've come to trust and care about. So how do we release human potential? We must find ways to upgrade, enhance, and empower the quality of relationships and the sense of possibility that is shared among members of our teams. That's what the Seven Crucial Conversations are designed to do.

CHAPTER 12

Organizations Evolve at the Speed of Conversation

No matter how brilliant your mind or strategy, if you're playing a solo game, you'll always lose out to a team.

—Reid Hoffman, LinkedIn co-founder

Brilliant strategy; no results.

That issue, I have discovered, is more common than many realize. Of course, not all strategies deserve the label "brilliant" or even "good," but sometimes organizations do develop business strategies that by all accounts are clear and compelling, even urgent, only to find that implementing them is like having a conversation with a wall—it's one-sided, frustrating, and in the end, very little ultimately happens. Somewhere in the conversational space between business strategy and execution, the strategy seems to almost dissolve—forever dispersed in the confusing maelstrom of the Swirl.

I once worked with a diagnostics company in the life-sciences industry that had a very specific problem. They hired a large, well-known consulting company to work on a business strategy for them. This firm created a strategy, and by most accounts it was a good one. And this strategic document sat on a shelf—literally. Finally, the board began to put pressure on the CEO to implement the details of the strategy, but he was struggling. It was hard to get the leaders of his teams to take it seriously, to read it, to consider it, much less to implement it. He encountered resistance all the way down.

I was called in to work with his teams to try to build a bridge between the strategy, which seemed as if was written in a foreign language to many of the principals in the company, and the actual on-the-ground realities of the organization. I certainly didn't do it by trying to sell the brilliance of the strategy. How would I even judge its merit? What I did know was that, if it was going to work in the company, there had to be an entirely different level of authentic, internal buy-in. So, I approached the challenge from the ground up. I worked with the critical teams to develop a language and a culture among themselves that was empowered to take a document like that and really break it down in ways that worked for them and for the company. High-performing teams are perfectly capable of knowing how to engage with such strategies and implement them in a workable way. But to create that breakthrough, we had to build that internal muscle; to develop the type of confident, capable, internal culture that would know how to digest the strategy and metabolize it throughout the various roles and responsibilities in the organization's social system that were critical to its implementation.

Organizations evolve at the speed of conversation. That claim is at the heart of Growth River's approach. In fact, it describes a foundational truth of any complex adaptive social system. How effective that system will be, how creative and innovative, how capable of change and adaption, is largely dependent on the quality of the conversations within the social system. And notably, these conversations don't start with strategy or implementation. If you always start with strategy and ignore what I would consider more foundational conversations about leadership, culture, roles, and so on, you will not be creating the beneficial conditions necessary for great strategy and execution to succeed. The shared language necessary for making effective and efficient decisions will prove elusive. And you will struggle to achieve high performance at the team level and at the organizational level. As discussed earlier in these pages, change unfolds through a natural pathway or sequence through the *three domains of change*

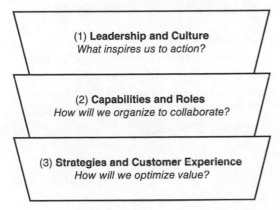

Organizations evolve at the speed of **Crucial Conversations** and in the direction of the **Three Domains of Change.**

(1) **Leadership and Culture**
What inspires us to action?

(2) **Capabilities and Roles**
How will we organize to collaborate?

(3) **Strategies and Customer Experience**
How will we optimize value?

FIGURE 12.1   Transformational Change and the Three Domains of Change

(see Figure 12.1). If you try to bypass this sequence, it's unlikely to go well. The gap, as in the earlier example, between high-level strategy and actual organization-wide or business-wide implementation will be more like a chasm. And your efforts to close that gap will remain a frustrating monument to missed opportunities.

For teams that want to truly engage in a transformational journey through those three domains, the Seven Crucial Conversations provide a roadmap. They are a series of structured dialogues or multilogues that generate breakthrough insights, encourage continuous improvement, and lead to higher and higher levels of productivity and performance. When we are part of an high-performing team, we aren't just getting together and hoping for positive results. We're focused and intentional. We're building something together, and the quality of our shared engagement reflects that intention. Being a part of an HPT should be powerful, engaging, even memorable. It should challenge us and incentivize us. An HPT establishes a culture of ongoing development. We're not just getting stuff done, or meeting for meeting's sake. We're going somewhere together, connecting, refining, and improving as we move further down the road. We're fellow travelers in this organizational journey, focused and incentivized at each step along the way.

> **Crucial conversations** are structured dialogues or multilogues that are able to generate breakthrough insights, encourage continuous improvement, and lead to higher and higher levels of productivity and performance in a team.
>
> **The Seven Crucial Conversations (the 7CCs®)** is a system of thought for building teams and growing and scaling companies toward competitive advantage through an optimal sequence of crucial conversations. This sequence aligns with the natural path of the three domains of change. As such, the 7 Crucial Conversations are a roadmap for transforming teams and companies. They include:
>
> *Leadership and Culture*
>
> 1. Activating Purpose
> 2. Driving Focus
> 3. Shifting Mindset
>
> *Capabilities and Roles*
>
> 4. Specifying Capabilities and Roles
> 5. Streamlining Interdependencies
>
> *Strategies and Implementation*
>
> 6. Aligning Strategies
> 7. Implementing Initiatives

These Seven Crucial Conversations play several roles in the journey of a team and organization. They establish the key conditions that a transformational template is based on. Each conversation includes specific **ways of working** that outline the basic ways in which the team is going to interact and work together, becoming a shared language for a team's performance and growth.

> **HPT ways of working** are impactful agreements, deliverables, and processes that enable teams to reach and sustain higher performance.

These conversations are an effective dashboard for tracking progress. They are essential to planning. And most of all, they are a roadmap of milestones by which a team can measure its progress. Following is a taste of the kinds of questions you can expect to engage with in each conversation. In the chapters that follow, we'll unpack each conversation, including some of its key ways of working, in more detail.

1. **Activating Purpose:** Does this team have a leader willing and able to activate a shared team purpose? How will decisions be made in this team? What is the shared purpose of the team? Are the needs of the customers and stakeholders whom we serve clear?

2. **Driving Focus:** Are team members focused on a shared journey? Is the destination clear? Have blockers been identified? Are next steps and priorities clear?

3. **Shifting Mindset:** Are team members able to bring their best efforts to the team's success? Are they accountable and coachable?

4. **Specifying Capabilities and Roles:** Does every key capability and concern in the team's purview have an owner advocate? Are the roles and responsibilities clear? Are creative tensions leveraged?

5. **Streamlining Interdependencies:** Are the points of interdependence within and across teams explicit? Are shared processes and handoffs efficient? Do rewards and incentives support working as a team?

6. **Aligning Strategies:** Is there a strategy and a strategic planning process in place? What is the role of the team in this process? Is the path toward competitive advantage clear?

7. **Implementing Initiatives:** Do team members plan and manage programs and projects effectively? Can the team forecast and budget their projects? Are there sufficient dashboards for measuring and tracking performance?

The seven conversations that will transform your team do not comprise a perfectly linear system—once through and presto!—but order does matter. You can't ignore Conversations 1–3 and hope for the best with 4–7. Don't tempt fate and ignore the dustbin of business history filled with underperforming companies that ignored this reality. The 7 Crucial Conversations help you develop an organic team-based intelligence that can perform at an unusually high level. And each conversation adds something critical to that emergent, collective intelligence.

These seven conversations are also not a one-way street. As the team develops, it will return to the conversations again and again. They must all be engaged, and to some degree, continuously so. And when initiatives struggle or fail, these conversations can act as a diagnostic to pinpoint the underlying issue. The problem and ultimate solution is not always to be found in a postmortem of the initiative itself. All Seven Crucial Conversations are implicated and need to be examined. To illustrate this basic idea, I'll use a sports analogy. The goal in a football game is for the defense to perform at a high level, but if a linebacker misses tackles consistency, the corrective to that failure might not just be found in the game film. It may be that he doesn't understand his role clearly, or how his role interacts with others around him. It may be that his practice habits have not been well established. There may be problems in other areas of the defense. It may be that the defensive strategy was ill-conceived. In other words, there may be all kinds of important issues that are not directly traceable to decisions made on specific plays.

It's the same in organizational teams. The legwork matters. If you're struggling with issues related to later conversations, perhaps the earlier ones need more attention. If you're unable to develop effective strategies, perhaps more work needs to be done on roles, or purpose. It's not all about implementation. It's not all about what happens on gameday.

My Growth River team and I have recently been working with the executive team at a hundred-year-old late stage 2 Directive Leadership company. Over the past three years, we have restarted at the top of the 7 Crucial Conversations with newly configured top teams three separate times. From the outside, this could look like slow progress, when in fact it has really been a very accelerated transformational learning curve. At each step, the senior team has versioned its way forward, testing and learning what is required to lead transformation in a large and complex social system. And with each step, it has released greater levels of human potential.

The first iteration was with a small executive leadership team, leading a single Business Triangle. We applied the 7 Crucial Conversations to assess the state of the team and the company. At the time they had a high-level five-year business plan, but they didn't have a complete business strategy with the level of sophistication required. They wanted to create one, but they didn't have the right system of roles on the senior team that would have been required. They also didn't have the buy-in from the organization that they would require to broadly restructure the system of roles at the top. So, we decided to implement a next small step, a transitionary leadership structure, to move the organization in the intended direction.

In the second iteration, we applied the 7 Crucial Conversations in parallel with two interdependent teams at the top of the organization, an enterprise strategy team and an operations management team. As a result of this iteration, the organization began to establish a robust change leadership infrastructure. At that point, we were able to make the move, with sufficient buy-in, to implement a matrix organizational structure, with multiple business triangles. At that point in the journey, the company was moving from stage 2 Directive Leadership to stage 3 Distributed Leadership.

We are now in the third iteration, applying the 7 Crucial Conversations with a newly combined enterprise team. I expect this basic configuration to be stable for a long while, although the team's system of meetings and roles will evolve. The point is that the 7 Crucial Conversations are neither a step-by-step plan nor a random set of conversations. Instead, what they are is a "cascade of key conditions" that enable leaders and teams to identify and align the fastest path to team and company transformation, including what moves are or are not feasible given the current state of the team and organization's culture.

Cascades of key conditions is a method for identifying primary constraints using lists of key conditions. The set of key conditions that follows is an example.

By a cascade, we mean that the most interdependent conditions are at the top of the list and the most independent ones are at the bottom. Changes to conditions at the top of the list are more likely to cascade down and impact conditions later, whereas changes to conditions at the bottom of the list are less likely to impact up. Primary constraints are revealed when this pattern is applied using data as part of a gap analysis.

(continued)

(continued)

In this example, a team applied a **Seven Crucial Conversations** checklist to identify its current **Primary Constraint** and to plan the optimal intervention needed for a **Breakthrough**.

Crucial Conversations	Gaps in the Current State Based on Data	Ideal State Checklist	
Domain 1, Leadership and Culture			
1, **Activating Purpose**	• Team leader is not willing or able to make key decisions • Team gets stuck in consensus decision-making • Team purpose is not aligned	✓ Responsible Team Leader ✓ Effective Decision-Making ✓ Clear Team Purpose ✓ Customer Focus	⬅ **The Primary Constraint**
2, **Driving Focus**	• Focus and priorities are mostly tactical and not strategic	✓ Clear Destination ✓ Shared Work Is Clear ✓ Clear Roadmap ✓ Clear Priorities	
3, **Shifting Mindset**	• A culture of infighting and blame	✓ Leadership ✓ Authenticity ✓ Authenticity ✓ Transparency	
Domain 2, Capabilities and Roles			
4, **Specifying Capabilities and Roles**	• No missing roles • Unresolved conflicts	✓ Complete Capabilities ✓ Complete Roles ✓ Effective Creative Tensions	
5, **Streamlining Interdependencies**	• Team members mostly work in silos, not together	✓ Effective Interdependencies ✓ Aligned Roles within Team ✓ Aligned Teams across Company	
Domain 3, Strategies and Customer Experience			
6, **Aligning Strategies**	• No clear team strategy	✓ Complete System of Strategies ✓ Decision-Making Aligned toward Competitive Advantage	
7, **Implementing Initiatives**	• Some plans • No budget • Suboptimal execution	✓ Clear Plans ✓ Effective Budgets ✓ Effective Execution	

FIGURE 12.2   Example Gap Analysis Against the Seven Crucial Conversations

Cascades of key conditions, like the 7 Crucial Conversations work like a GPS, revealing the most impactful path to higher performance. Constraints theory applies here as well, as illustrated in the HPT Assessment Report above. In an ideal world, a high-performing team would be firing on all cylinders—understanding their purpose; focused and aligned; fully inhabiting their various roles; resolving creative tensions with a clear eye toward competitive advantage; unleashing powerful strategic intelligence. If this were true, the only actual constraint would be found in Conversation Seven. The only limit to that team's performance and productivity would be its capacity for implementation. Everything else is lined up for success. But that's an ideal scenario that rarely exists in the real world.

Even in genuinely high-performing teams, it's perfectly natural to have constraints show up. The problem in an HPT or high-performing stage 3 organization is not, well, having problems. Constraints are inevitable, in some form, and new ones will arise as the team or organization moves forward on its journey, which necessitate revisiting earlier conversations. We may realize that the company's ability to implement its strategy is being stymied because key roles are not being filled. By going back to Conversation 4 and applying the Business Triangle to map capabilities and roles, we can resolve that issue. Such constraints are normal in both social and business systems. It's how we respond to them that makes the difference. Are we consistently asking the right questions? Is our forensic analysis effective and accurate? That's what makes all the difference. The power of a high-performing team does not come from negotiating calm, flowing waters. It comes from our skill in navigating rapids and rocks, from knowing when to catch a current, and when to pause and do some reconnaissance on the next section of river. Indeed, the true measure of a high-performing team is not a brief period of remarkable outperformance; it's the speed at which a team can respond to constraints, move through obstacles, and return the team, business, and enterprise to high performance. In that sense, the 7 Crucial Conversations are a toolkit for troubleshooting and a dashboard for tracking the journey of a team toward being able to have the maximum impact on a business and company.

Setting the Stage for the Seven Crucial Conversations

My purpose in the following chapters is to capture the spirit of each conversation and a few of its key elements. I won't pretend this roadmap includes all the milestones, signs, traffic lights, speed limits, detours, and other information that would be naturally featured in a workbook or practice manual on the 7 Crucial Conversations or worked through in a consulting engagement. I want the reader to understand the core components of each conversation, to appreciate the overall integral system that these conversations enact, and to get a sense of how each conversation serves to take its place in a cascade of key conditions that sets the foundation for growth and ultimately helps teams achieve extraordinary results. I hope to also give readers a taste of what those results might feel like. In an HPT that is deeply engaged with all these conversations, here's what you might find:

- People are inspired, energized, and aligned around a shared *purpose*.
- People are *focused* on a shared journey toward a goal state.
- People have transformational leadership *mindsets*.
- Individual roles are clear, within a complete system of *capabilities and roles*.
- The matrix of roles is in which people collaborate is supported by effective processes and systems at key points of *interdependency*.
- People align local decisions in the context of clear overall *strategies* for creating value and competitive advantage.
- People have access to sufficient *implementation* resources and know-how.

With all these conditions in place, growth becomes not only attainable but inevitable. So, let's begin the conversation!

CHAPTER 13

Conversation 1: Activating Purpose

Does this team have a leader willing and able to activate a shared team purpose?

How will decisions be made in this team?

What is the shared purpose of the team?

Are the needs of the customers and stakeholders whom we serve clear?

How many meetings have you been in that caused you to ask yourself: Why am I here? What am I doing? What's the purpose of this meeting? Are we accomplishing anything? Such is the character of the Swirl—high activity, low focus; intensive motion, little direction. And it's exactly what the experience of a high-performing team should *never* be. Activating Purpose is an antidote to precisely that kind of organizational drift. In an HPT, we know why we're meeting, why we exist, what we're seeking to accomplish, and how we are doing it. All of that begins with clarity around purpose and leadership.

Activating Purpose can also apply to the larger organization. Indeed, given today's proliferation of books and content on business leadership and organizational development, it is perhaps a cliché to say that great companies are alive with a higher purpose. But it's true. Every company or organization that aspires to do important activities in the world has a purpose, a telos, that animates the energy and productivity of the social system. They are moving; they have a direction; they are going somewhere. That sense of purpose provides an emotional connectivity across an enterprise, bonding together the larger tribe and its shared project. It's not about words on the wall or some pithy, inspirational statement. That's not where purpose lives. Real purpose is something you can feel in the air of an organization—a sense of commitment; an atmosphere of shared, focused energy. It's an arrow that resides deep in the soul of the company that communicates a consistent message: "This way." Consciously or unconsciously, every key decision is inevitably evaluated in the light of that directional arrow.

While organizational purpose and its importance is a well-traveled path, few appreciate that great teams are also animated by purpose. It doesn't have to be a world-changing purpose—some high-minded or altruistic ideal. It can be straightforward, simple, even functional. But high-performing teams have a clear raison d'être, and it's important that the purpose is explicit and understood by everyone on the team. And perhaps it goes without saying, but that purpose is not freestanding; it should have a clear relationship to the larger organization. And if you're a senior executive team, it may be that part of the work of the team is to enact or be responsible for that organizational purpose. But that's certainly not the work of every team (though I've seen less-senior HPTs in a company recognize that an organizational purpose was inadequate or missing, and advocate for that to be addressed).

In the list that follows, we can see the many types of teams that exist in a large organization. Each has its own purpose and orientation in the "system of teams" of an enterprise. Each one has its own customers and/or external stakeholders that it needs to be focused on. Each one has a different orientation to the overall social system of the enterprise.

What type of team is your team and what is its purpose?

> **System of teams** refers to the matrix of different types of teams and the division of responsibilities that ideally develops in an enterprise to optimally grow and scale. The logic of this system corresponds with Business Triangles and Enterprise Maps.
>
> 1. **Enterprise Leadership Team:** The purpose of this type of team is to lead, manage, and continuously improve a company's portfolio

of businesses and functional capabilities toward overall competitive advantage.

2. **Business Segment Leadership Team(s):** The purpose of this type of team is to lead and align Develop, Sell, Deliver, and Support capabilities to provide products and services to target customers in a way that creates targeted competitive advantage.

3. **Develop Capability Leadership Team(s):** The purpose of this type of team is to develop winning value propositions (including technologies, products, and services) for target end-users, channels, and buyers.

4. **Channel Capability Leadership Teams(s):** The purpose of this type of team is to lead and align Sell and Deliver capabilities to create perfect purchase moments with target channel partners in target markets for target buyers and target end-users and to provide a winning experience for all key stakeholders.

5. **Sell Capability Leadership Team(s):** The purpose of this type of team is to gain access to target markets and to create perfect purchase moments in target channels for target buyers.

6. **Deliver Capability Leadership Team(s):** The purpose of this type of team is to deliver products and services through target channels to target end-users as promised and as a result to generate positive referrals.

7. **Support Capability Leadership Team(s):** The purpose of this type of team is to provide support services and capabilities that create economies of scale or mitigate business risks for internal customers and stakeholders.

In Conversation 1, the team will identify its purpose and create what we call a **team charter**. This document, and it's helpful to put this in writing, clarifies the team's purpose, leadership, outcomes, and in-team commitments—the everyday agreements that define how the team comes together to fulfill its purpose. For example, is the team being clear and explicit about how they will meet together—timing, style, method, and so forth? Also, are the skillsets needed to fulfill the team's purpose present on the team? Are the team's members clear about the language being used around purpose, leadership, and alignment? These building blocks are part of a strong foundation. As shown earlier, different types of teams in a company's system of teams will have different purposes, as well as different customers, stakeholders, and end-users. Understanding exactly where the team sits in the larger organizational matrix and identifying these elements is part of the process of clarifying the team purpose.

Effective Decision-Making

An HPT not only has a purpose; it has clear leadership. The leader, or leaders, on the team are responsible for making sure that there is general "buy-in" to the team's purpose. In other words, people are committed to being a part of the team's journey. Again, purpose is a declaration that "we're going this way" that comes with an explicit request to get on board. This is not about forcing anyone to be part of anything. This is not about ensuring sullen compliance; it is about requesting the free choice of authentic alignment. If people can't align, they shouldn't be on the team.

For team members, Activating Purpose is about understanding the mission of the team and making a choice to align, and in so doing, accept the team's leadership mechanism. Whether or not they perfectly agree, they are fundamentally aligned with the team's purpose, and are ready to move forward together. This may require the temporary subjugation of their personal opinions, preferences, or desires. Of course, HPTs are not little dictatorships; there will be opportunities for each team member to contribute with all of their energy and ideas. But that needs to happen in the context of healthy leadership and a "buy-in" to the decision-making mechanism of the team.

Decision-making is an activity every team must engage in. A significant part of Activating Purpose is about the team's capacity for making healthy decisions on their journey. In some types of teams, there is a naturally strong leader who takes over the decision-making functions independent of any clear, collective decision. This autocratic approach may get certain things done, but it also lacks important input from the team and can alienate other team members. Ultimately, it will prevent high performance and the type of buy-in and distributed accountability that makes an HPT stand out.

Higher performance, in teams and organizations, occurs only when individuals are expected and encouraged to exercise agency and choice. When people are allowed to simply comply, without explicitly making the choice to align, sustaining higher performance is unlikely. If you don't choose, you lose. And most importantly, the whole team loses. Authentic alignment always trumps rote compliance. As I mentioned in the discussion of creative tension (see Chapter 9), alignment doesn't mean enforced agreement. It can even include disagreement. But it does mean there is a shared commitment to moving forward on the same pathway as the team and the leadership of the team. A "command-and-control" leadership is ineffective for creating high performance because it fails to consider most people's deep need to exercise their own agency and choice, and it fails to respect people's need to pursue their own developmental journey. In contrast, HPT members expect one another to actively engage in a journey of growth; explicitly "choose in" to the shared perspectives and ways of working that the team identifies as contributing to its forward momentum, and demonstrably align their actions and behaviors with the team's trajectory of transformation.

For team leaders, respecting and expecting agency from team members is critical. Effective change leaders communicate authentically, engage meaningfully, and create compelling choices for people. People may buy-in to their leadership, but not out of coercion or fear. Those leaders demonstrate empathy and trust, and as a result they evoke the same in others. This leadership style creates the conditions that enable people to "choose in," align, and bring their creativity. Authentic buy-in by team members allows agency and independent thinking to thrive in the context of team alignment, and that is a sweet spot for an HPT.

In contrast, ineffective leaders depend on positional power and coercion, treating people like parts in a machine to be swapped out or fixed. This leadership style may create the conditions for people to understand and comply, but it does not create the conditions for them to choose-in and align. The inevitable result is resistance, in many forms, both subtle and overt. And believe me, if people want to resist your leadership, they will find effective ways to do it, even if you never hear about them.

It's also possible that no strong, decisive leader emerges in the formation of a team. The danger here is that the team defaults to a consensus style of decision-making. That can paralyze the team and make it hard to move forward. An HPT needs to agree on a form of decision-making that avoids both the trap of the autocratic style and the trap of the consensus approach. We call this *consultative decision-making*. It means that there is clear and explicit leadership on the team, that every decision has an "owner" who is responsible to drive it to resolution, and in the process, that owner must seek input from key stakeholders and the smallest number of people required to make a final call. This combines some of the positives of both autocratic and consensus-driven approaches while avoiding their downsides.

Three Forms of Decision-Making

There are three main styles of decision-making:

1. **Autocratic:** One person, usually the leader, decides with minimal input from team members, who are then expected to comply with the decision.

2. **Consultative**: With input from the team, and process support from a Single Journey owner, a call is made by a designated decision-maker and communicated with clear rationale. Although agreement may be desired, alignment will be expected. A decision analysis process may be used to structure this alignment conversation. To achieve alignment, it may be necessary to clarify a date or other conditions for when it will be okay for team members to revisit the decision.

3. **Consensus:** All team members are involved in agreeing on a course of action (majority rule). Individual team members may have veto power. Once the decision is reached, all team members are expected to comply.

Effective decision-making is one of the critical *ways of working* that teams learn through Conversation 1. It's easy for a team to default to either autocratic decision-making or consensus decision-making, but either of those will undermine the team's performance. Consultative decision-making means that the team is not endlessly dwelling on decisions, having unproductive discussions, or pointlessly speculating. Rather, they are designating specific individuals to own each issue, gather input from the smallest number of people required, and drive it to resolution. When HPTs develop the instinct to consistently practice this powerful form of leadership, it will not only save time, but it will literally help the entire team focus on what's most important.

The Law of the Lid

Purpose is inextricable from leadership, so Conversation 1 includes essential insights around leadership. One of these is "The Law of the Lid"—a phrase coined by author John Maxwell, stating that the potential of the team will be constrained or even determined by the capacities of the leader. The ability of the leader creates a "lid" or ceiling on the overall potential of their team. If the leader's ceiling is high and moving higher, so too will be the potential or ceiling of the team's performance. If the leader's abilities are unremarkable, and if their willingness to change and evolve is also limited, the Law of the Lid states that this will inevitably constrain the overall performance of the entire team.

> The **Law of the Lid** refers to the principle that a team or company can never sustain performance at a level higher than that of its top leader(s).[1]

The Law of the Lid should always be a sobering reference point for leaders, a reminder that leadership cannot be haphazard or accidental or half-hearted. Nor can it be overbearing or an excuse for the random exercise of power. It should incentivize them to look in the mirror and to do everything they can to develop and evolve so as not to hold back the potential of the teams they lead. How many leaders have I worked with who struggled to understand how critical their role is in setting a positive, healthy work context, with clear communication and expectations, in which team members can thrive? And honestly, that's just the table stakes. In a true HPT, leaders also need to be able to be fellow travelers with team members on a journey of development and transformation. *That takes a lot more than effective execution; it*

---

[1]The Law of the Lid comes from *The 21 Irrefutable Laws of Leadership* by John Maxwell, a thought leader and motivational speaker in the realm of leadership. Maxwell uses the Law of the Lid to explain how leadership impacts every aspect of your daily life.

takes good relationships. It takes being in it together. It takes activating shared purpose. And most leaders need some help on that journey. In fact, that's part of the journey of an HPT. There is no shame in not having that skillset already tucked away in your bag of tricks. Most do not. That's acceptable; pretending otherwise is not. In that sense, most leaders need the support and feedback of their team members, which we'll talk more about in Conversation 3.

These are just a few of the key elements of Conversation 1. By engaging seriously with this conversation as a team, you do some of the most important work up front, to avoid breakdowns later. Of course, not everything can be dealt with up front. But you don't want people complaining about the team's leadership mechanism three months later. Or questioning the team's purpose after the team is already knee-deep in implementing major initiatives. The time spent up front on clarity around purpose and alignment can prevent multiples of that time being wasted over the long term.

CHAPTER 14

Conversation 2: Driving Focus

Are team members focused on a shared transformational journey?
Is the destination clear?
Have gaps and primary constraints been identified?
Are next steps, and priorities clear?

Whereas Activating Purpose is all about the structure, format, and shared vision of the team, Driving Focus is about getting clarity around priorities, visualizing the team's work together, and energizing around the goals of the team. In this crucial conversation, we are still in the first domain of change—Leadership and Culture. And developing a shared sense of being "in it together" should be one of the outcomes of this crucial conversation, especially as the team priorities come more into focus. This is also a conversation in which it can be helpful to work with constraints as the team tackles its shared work. But perhaps the most significant element of the culture we are building when it comes to the Driving Focus conversation is the willingness to engage in a shared transformational journey.

A Shared Transformational Journey

The Driving Focus conversation is about the team's overall commitment to a journey of continuous improvement. We have spoken a lot about transformational journeys in this book, but this is where that set of ideas takes root at the team level. Are team members up for that? This is not something to simply give lip service to. Is the team ready to step together into the unknown?

There is a delicate dance of leadership that is required at this juncture. A leader on this transformational journey needs to plant a stake in the potential future—what we at Growth River call the "ideal future state"—a shared vision for the upper reaches of the team's potential. This is not a static point in time; the future is open, flexible, and fluid. This may sound paradoxical. But the open-ended, unformed nature of that ideal future state doesn't in any way prevent us from bearing witness to its potential, and actively calling it into being through everything we're doing in the present. The leader's job, therefore, is not to "know" that future in a literal sense. Rather, it is to help it evolve and emerge, and to help others on the team to see its potential even as they work to bring it into being. This is true both of a leader of the organization and of the high-performing team. A leader, in a sense, needs to co-create this vision with those around them. This is very different from providing the answers or even simply giving direction. It is more about making sure that the team is collectively committed to an authentic journey of growth, to reaching for higher potentials. A leader who can engage the group in that conversation has the raw materials for a truly high-performing team.

I'm reminded of the work of Otto Scharmer at MIT, whose work calls on leaders to put aside the structures of the past and to "sense" and "presence" what the emerging future holds. This inevitably involves passing through a period of not knowing, or emptying one's mind (and the collective mind of the team culture) of its preconceptions, and/or hidden assumptions. Only then can we truly embark on a journey of authentic transformation whose future is not largely determined by its past. We can certainly do that individually, but leaders also need to help facilitate this possibility in the teams around them.

This may be anathema to some leaders who feel responsible for *having* most of the answers, but there is a great power in not knowing, in *not* having all of the answers, which is quite different than the usual authority we reserve for those who seem to know exactly what to do all of the time! It's only when a leader is to some degree able to embrace this vulnerability, this uncomfortable absence of certainty, that they will paradoxically discover the ability to understand the meaning of a transformational journey. It starts with clearing some of the accumulated debris of the past. Indeed, the first rule of any transformational journey is not to tether the future to the ballast of the past. Or, to put it in the context of the stage 2 to stage 3 transition, we don't want the constraints of the Swirl to define the possibilities of the flow.

When we authentically recognize that we don't know how things will unfold, and short-circuit the pretense that we do, we can begin to envision a future that is genuinely new. And not only that, we can actually co-create it with others! It's the space from which to envision the conditions of an "ideal future state" in which the team (or organization) is fulfilling a new, higher potential. That vision doesn't have to be perfect or exact or detailed. It will never be. Reality will always surprise, hopefully on the upside. But the point is that a leader's job is to plant a stake in that possibility, to inspire the team to continually co-create, discover, and enact it.

A Transformational Journey Plan

Envisioning that "ideal future state" is the first step in being on a transformational journey together. Here's a four-step process for mapping out a shared transformational journey for a team.

1. **A Vision for a Better Future:** What is the ideal future state you're working toward?

2. **The Urgent Need for Change:** What is the current state, including the gaps and constraints? What is the primary constraint?

3. **Priorities for Tomorrow:** Given those gaps and that ideal, what are your priorities from today to tomorrow? How can you get your immediate needs met? What initiatives will drive horizontal optimization of your current state?

4. **Breakthroughs to the Future:** What are the breakthroughs you're targeting to move from tomorrow to the future? What do we need to learn? What skills do we need to master? What initiatives or ahead-of-the-curve investments will drive vertical transformation?

If you're not aligned around these four elements, you're not on a transformational journey together. Once you are aligned around these, the team truly comes into focus. And it removes the anxiety that change often creates.

One final note on this transformational journey: Driving Focus is not just about far-flung potentials. It is also about getting on the same page about individual and team priorities in the near term. Indeed, if you're clear about the difference between today-to-tomorrow priorities and tomorrow-to-the-future breakthroughs, you can begin to distinguish *event horizons*—points in time beyond which you cannot yet know what's coming. See Figure 14.1. The beauty of that is there's no point getting hung up on them. Trying to control what you can't influence just creates worry and unproductive stress. Instead, you can focus on working though the priorities that are clear and present, as well as creating the conditions for the next breakthroughs. Those steps that lie beyond the event horizons are by definition beyond the team's control.

A good example of an event horizon in many people's lives is becoming a parent for the first time. The transformation can't be understood until it is experienced, nor can it ever truly be reversed. In the context of an organization or a team, vertical improvement, transformation, and breakthrough experiences can often create feelings of uncertainty. That is because the team or company is facing an event horizon, and they can't see what lies beyond. In the life of an organization, an event horizon might be a major organizational restructuring, an introduction of a new service or product, the launch of a new outside competitor. It might even be a seemingly small event such as a personnel change in the leadership team, or the introduction of new software for managing files.

Transformational change refers to irreversible changes in living systems, including people, teams, and companies, in order to adapt to different challenges in the environment.

Event horizons refer to any significant transformation point in time where you cannot envision how the system will react and adapt in the future. Managing the uncertainty before and after event horizons is the core challenge of leading transformational change. Event horizons are often the result of breakthroughs caused by the resolution of primary constraints.

Disruption refers to radical changes in an environment that make new ways of working necessary.

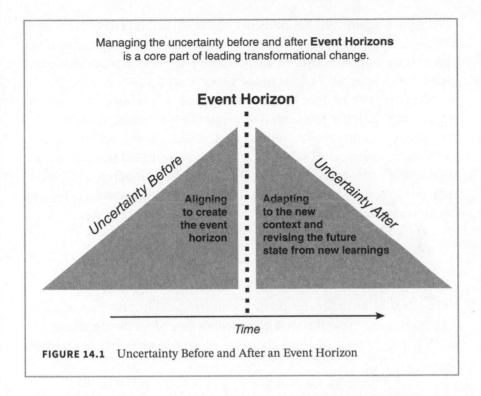

Managing the uncertainty before and after **Event Horizons** is a core part of leading transformational change.

Event Horizon

Uncertainty Before

Uncertainty After

Aligning to create the event horizon

Adapting to the new context and revising the future state from new learnings

Time

FIGURE 14.1   Uncertainty Before and After an Event Horizon

So, how do you plan and manage event horizons? The key is to understand the nature of the uncertainty. The cause of uncertainty is different when preparing for an event horizon than it is in the period right after the change (see the definition of event horizon earlier). *Before* the event horizon, the uncertainty stems from the team's inability to predict how the event horizon will change their ways of working. At this time, it is easy for people to get distracted by speculating what the new context is going to be like, or how they will respond. However, these speculations are helpful only to a point, and can become time-consuming, worrying, and a source of needless preoccupation. When team members are working toward an event horizon, a transformational journey mindset is critically important. You and your team will have to be ready to walk the path and stay engaged even when the full implications of the next steps are unknown. Once the event horizon has taken place, the nature of the uncertainty changes. *After* the event, it revolves around learning new ways of working needed to adapt to the new context. Sometimes those changes will be minor, but often they will require significant adjustments and learning. It is easy for people to cling to the old ways of working and to resent having to change. That can also be unproductive, as the only way forward is to embrace the change, and learn and adjust in the new context.

There is nothing that bonds a team quite like being on an authentic transformational journey. It's invigorating to share a continuous improvement journey with others on the same team, and to feel the joy of camaraderie and shared aspiration. And it also leads us to our final crucial conversation in the domain of Leadership and Culture, which involves a shift in how we relate to our fellow travelers on this collective journey of growth.

CHAPTER 15

Conversation 3: Shifting Mindset

Are team members sober and honest about where they are on the journey and where the gaps are?

Are team members able to bring their best efforts to the team's success?

Are they accountable and coachable, giving and receiving feedback?

Do they resolve conflicts directly at the source?

Do they build dynamic interpersonal relationships?

How do individuals build trust in each other? How do we inspire ourselves and each other to keep our commitments? How do we move forward together when each of us has such a unique and different perspective? These questions become incredibly real when it comes to ambitious teams that aspire to do great work together. How do we negotiate a profound diversity of perspectives? Is negotiate even the right word? How do we go from a cacophony of individual opinions to the harmony of a team? Believe me, the more high-performing independent-minded individuals that are part of any team, the more urgent these issues become.

Shifting Mindset is about embracing a team's diversity of perspectives and transforming it from a debilitating liability into a tremendous asset. But this means developing new agreements to support each other, be accountable, and coachable. In a sense, Shifting Mindset is less about what the team does, or will do, and more about who they are. Is everyone ready to be on a high-performing team? Are they ready to be honest and authentic? Can each individual put their ego aside long enough to be frank and real and address the challenges the group faces?

To create a team culture in which we authentically care about the growth, health, and development of the person sitting next to us, and moreover, the performance of the entire group, we need to be well grounded in two wonderful and terrible truths—how things actually are, and how much could potentially change. Neither can be assumed. These two truths go together. The latter without the former will never work, and the former without the latter will never be enough. Many teams I work with are far removed from the reality of each. They struggle to admit and authentically engage with the actual problems and challenges they face. And they rarely feel collectively engaged in an authentic journey of development, one in which they can feel the energy and enthusiasm that comes from setting their sights on higher and higher levels of individual and collective performance. The point is not to create an encounter group. This isn't therapy. Rather, it's simply to ensure that we can have truly frank discussions. Honest—but not punitive or harsh—conversations are all too rare in the world of business, but they're crucial.

This also means getting beyond the superficial niceties and starting to develop a deeper layer of trust. This is the kind of trust that must be earned, through how we show up every day, how we keep our commitments, how we hold ourselves and others accountable. *I define trust as the residue of kept commitments*. It's not a sudden leap we take; it's something that develops among team members over time. It's a byproduct. It can't be manufactured out of thin air.

Some degree of tension and even conflict is inevitable in a group of individuals who care about doing great work and delivering on ambitious goals. Resolving those conflicts by understanding the value of creative tension is a critical skill for a high-performing team, as we discussed in depth in Chapter 10. The more that a team can productively resolve tension and conflict, not just sweep it under the rug, the more trust will grow among members.

Trust is also the result of deeper understanding, and that means attending carefully to our shared language and speech. Words have power. If someone has ever told you "You're fired," or "I'm sorry," or "I will love you forever," you know that such utterances make an impact that is far more than the simple conveying of information.

In linguistics, these are called "speech acts"—utterances that are made with a particular intention and have a particular effect on the listener. Speech acts are words that get things done, or shift how we see and engage with the world. As you pay attention to team dynamics, you will become more aware of your own choice of words and the language others use to express themselves. It is important to consider how the language you choose will impact the listener.

Speech acts can be pivotal to the conversation. They change and align shared understanding around situations, relationships, and probable outcomes. Speech acts lead to some important changes in how people view a situation—for the speaker, the listeners, or their shared understanding. Oftentimes, conversations cannot be considered complete until the relevant speech acts have occurred. Without a speech act, how can you know whether team members are on the same page? A clear, out-loud declaration of alignment and/or agreement is necessary to make decisions, assign responsibilities, or mark other significant moments. A spoken act of commitment is a bond that creates clarity, momentum, and certainty on the path forward. This is essential in transformational contexts where learning is critical. As an HPT, the goal is for all leaders and team members to be aware and intentional in their speech acts.

Building Trust

Trust, transparency, and accountability stand out as being key features of Conversation 3. But it's easy to mouth the words and declare the quality of these worthy virtues. In the everyday real-world context of a business, difficult issues are going to come up that pit team members against each other, trigger people, and easily lead to mistrust. This is where coachability and giving and receiving feedback become essential.

I know I'm a broken record, but I'll say it anyway: Accountability starts with leaders. It's so important for leaders to model the behavior that they want the team to encourage. Leaders need to recognize that in some unavoidable way, the culture of the group begins and ends with them. A transactional leader creates a transactional team. A victimized leader quickly trains team members to express victimization. A directive leader creates a team that is obedient and follows orders.

I'm not saying that every team behavior can be traced back to the leader. It's not always that simple. But without question, the leader can and often does define the basic culture of the team and unconsciously reinforces what the limits and boundaries of that culture are. That's why one of the most important skillsets for a leader is to authentically seek out diverse perspectives, to utilize the insights and abilities of team members.

Team members also need to be coachable. They need to be able and willing to learn, as well as to accept constructive feedback. Coachability can often be much more important than innate talent. The ability to learn and grow and accept good coaching is one of the most underrated skillsets. The way you raise its value in an organizational context is to make it a key criterion for promotion, and a decisive factor in choosing leadership opportunities. Too often, subject matter expertise or previous experience overrides coachability, but the latter is often more indicative of future success.

Beware of Efforts to Sweep the Leg

In the iconic movie *The Karate Kid*, the rival of the main character is losing the pivotal bout, and so his coach, or sensei, leans over and instructs his fighter to "sweep the leg." In other words, he should short-circuit the legitimate unfolding of the fight and try to end it quickly by playing dirty. Organizational politics are not hand-to-hand combat, but they have their own version of "sweep the leg" and HPTs need to be aware of it. Too often, I've seen this tactic play out. At some point in the development of a new HPT, somebody will lose patience, for whatever reason, and it's often to do with a well-intentioned but misguided sense of urgency. They want to put an end to it—get rid of the team, remove a leader, replace one or more members, or in some other way make a dramatic change. But the development of legitimate HPTs doesn't happen overnight, and it doesn't satisfy everyone's timeline. The process needs time to play out. Beware of the wrong type of impatience. Is the team moving in the right direction? Is it developing? It takes time for an HPT to find its feet and prove its merit. Don't let internal politics or even the simple insecurity of an unfamiliar process lead you to pull the plug too early. Beware of efforts to "sweep the leg."

Right up there with coachability is another critical way of working: the ability to give and receive feedback. Most team members need practice with this one. The ability—which often comes down to humility—to authentically take in someone else's constructive feedback and even to actively seek out that feedback when needed, is a skill that will serve any team member extraordinarily well. For the team to develop we need good, constructive feedback, the kind that won't create its own reactions and antibodies.

Feedback is not just advice. We're all experts at giving advice! Good feedback is developmental; it's not about changing people or simply expressing opinions. It's about the other person and what's going to truly help them to be more effective at their job. Remember that the most effective feedback is never a reflection on the quality of the person, good or bad. It's a helpful spur to development in a particular area of work. Also, good data is always a nice companion to feedback. It helps ground it and takes it further outside the realm of personal opinion.

Feedback should never simply be negative. Keep in mind organizational development expert Ken Blanchard's wonderful notion of "catching people doing something right." Leaders and team members should avoid getting in the mode of just looking for what's not working. An HPT needs to have a strong sense of overall forward-looking positivity. Although we have to be honest about things that aren't working, that should never be where our focus is. Positive energy may sound like a cliché, but we all feed off each other's energy, and dwelling too long on problems is rarely much of a solution for anything, much less for a culture of continuous improvement and transformation. Authentic appreciation for a job well done is often, well, underappreciated! Don't withhold your gratitude for the contributions of fellow team members.

The goal of Shifting Mindset is a healthy, positive, culture of growth. It's not about perfecting the personal dynamics or overcoming every development challenge among team members. There is a reason it comes after Driving Focus. Shifting Mindset is in the service of the goals and purpose of the team, not the other way around. Team spirit is great but not as an end unto itself. This conversation is about recognizing and engaging with personal, interpersonal, and team issues in such a way that makes abundant space for the larger project and goals of the team to take center stage.

CHAPTER 16

Conversation 4: Specifying Capabilities and Roles

Does every key capability and concern in the team's purview have an owner advocate?

Are the roles and responsibilities clear?

Are creative tensions leveraged?

In an organization moving from stage 2 to stage 3, the conversation about capabilities and roles will be company-wide, as I emphasized in Part II. But even if that larger conversation is not yet active in the whole company, a team can still enact many of the elements that define a healthy system of capabilities and roles. Where does the team sit on the Business Triangle? Is it a support team? A sales team? An enterprise team? It's critical that the team understands the scope of its own purpose relative to the four enterprise capabilities. Mapping the specific capabilities that each team owns on the Business Triangle and on the overall Enterprise Map illuminates its purpose in the context of the larger organization and it leads on to the next questions: Which roles on the team are accountable for which capabilities? What perspectives do they represent? What value are they accountable for creating? As each team member understands the answer to those questions, the relationships between team members and their roles become clear. And healthy creative tension between roles is born.

A word of caution is appropriate here. When we specify roles, we are also, inevitably, distributing power—to some degree or other. You may have noticed that people tend to be highly reactive when it comes to gaining or losing power, or even the perception of doing so! Such dynamics can impede the development of a team. Many efforts at transformation fail at this point. That's why, when it comes time to specify roles in your emerging HPT, you will be very glad that you have spent productive time on purpose, focus, and mindset, building a healthy culture of trust that can support transparent, real, and honest conversations that aren't derailed by concerns over the allocation of power. The culture of the team (and the organization) needs a high level of maturity to handle the inevitable tension and conflict that comes in Conversation 4, as power is redistributed. Without that maturity, Specifying Capabilities and Roles can easily morph into a large pothole that will derail your efforts to move into a more beneficial system of roles.

Of course, any high-performing team sits in a larger organization that may itself have a tangled system of roles. Even so, engaging these issues at the level of the team will help in those external facing conversations. It may even begin to exert a subtle pressure on other parts of the organization to get their act together regarding roles. To be in an HPT that is very clear around capabilities and roles is to experience a refreshing oasis in an otherwise bleak landscape. People will notice.

In order to architect a new, more effective system of roles for the company, it's important to start at the level of capabilities. Don't reverse that order. The conversation around roles can be challenging regardless, for reasons I specify later, but even more so if you try to dive into it without mapping capabilities first. Here again, the business triangle is your friend. By modeling your Business Triangles for both current and future businesses (see Chapter 2, you can lay out a system of capabilities that becomes an essential blueprint for building out a successful and effective system of roles for any particular business. The capabilities you identify will represent the building blocks of how you create value for your customers in the present, or how you intend to create value in the future.

There's no perfect set of rules to explain what constitutes a capability in any given business, but it's helpful to keep asking yourself,

Does this activity create value for a particular customer and in what way? This will help you break down broad or vague terms into more specific and useful ones. For example, marketing is a broad term that can mean many things. If you try to put "marketing" on the Business Triangle, you'll quickly find that it's hard to know where to put it. In one situation, it might mean doing market research, which is an important function and a key capability in Develop. It can also mean creating marketing and messaging material for the sales team, which is part of Sell. So breaking the term *marketing* down into capabilities like "market research" and "marketing communications" allows you to place those capabilities accurately on the triangle. This may sound obvious, but without the clarity of something like the Business Triangle, the blurring of these terms can create a lot of confusion and impede value creation. Never underestimate the power of clarity when it comes to capabilities and roles.

As the system of roles gets more transparent, a subtle but important breakthrough often happens. Team members become aware that in their roles, they own a set of capabilities rather than simply being responsible for a selection of activities. That ownership becomes crucial. For example, if you own a set of sales capabilities, that may demand a high degree of creativity in figuring how to upgrade them and expand them. It may require hiring new people, expanding skillsets, and advocating for all of it. That's a very different perspective than simply fulfilling a set of tasks. It's not "you do these things"; it's "you own these areas." And as the strategic landscape in the team and organization shifts and changes, the owner of those capabilities will be able to advocate appropriately for them and translate those strategies into on-the-ground execution. I often say that *strategy is spoken in the language of capabilities*, and unless there is clarity around ownership of those capabilities, the words of strategy, no matter how elegant, will fall on deaf ears.

The conversation about roles isn't just limited to individuals. The team itself has a role as well. Depending on where your team sits in the overall organizational chart, you may be more responsible for what I would call a horizontal perspective or a vertical perspective (see Figure 16.1). A vertical perspective naturally has more of an oversight role in the larger organization—for example, an enterprise executive team. They aren't deeply involved in one particular side of

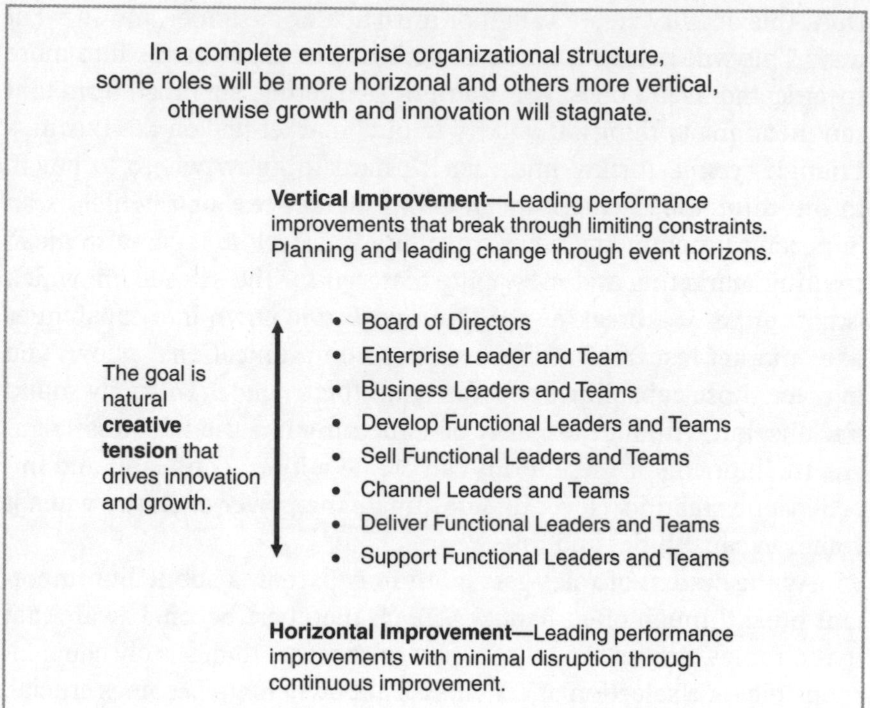

In a complete enterprise organizational structure,
some roles will be more horizonal and others more vertical,
otherwise growth and innovation will stagnate.

Vertical Improvement—Leading performance
improvements that break through limiting constraints.
Planning and leading change through event horizons.

The goal is
natural
**creative
tension** that
drives innovation
and growth.

- Board of Directors
- Enterprise Leader and Team
- Business Leaders and Teams
- Develop Functional Leaders and Teams
- Sell Functional Leaders and Teams
- Channel Leaders and Teams
- Deliver Functional Leaders and Teams
- Support Functional Leaders and Teams

Horizontal Improvement—Leading performance
improvements with minimal disruption through
continuous improvement.

FIGURE 16.1 Vertical and Horizontal Creative Tension in an Enterprise

the Business Triangle. They're responsible for the overall operating system of the company and for resolving constraints at the level of the organization. Whereas a team with a more horizontal perspective is involved in optimizing a specific business or function—making things operationally smoother and more efficient, translating strategic priorities into better and better outcomes. In each of these teams, circumstances may occasionally call for both orientations—at times resolving primary constraints that upgrade or shift the entire system (vertical) and at times optimizing for the efficiency of the existing system (horizontal). There are times when we are just trying to make the trains run on time, and then times when we are more focused on how to lay new tracks. And the job description of certain teams will naturally lean more toward vertical or horizontal. For example, a business support team, let's say accounting, will naturally have more of a horizontal perspective on the business or businesses they are supporting. It's the same with a sales team in one business. They're working to try to maximize the performance of that existing capability. A product development team, or an executive leadership team, however, has its sights on new potentials for the organization, and therefore leans more toward a vertical perspective. Everyone should know the distinction between a vertical orientation and a horizontal orientation, and both perspectives should be part of the toolkits of HPTs.

Again, trust will be tested as roles are restructured. This is where mini-kingdoms or power centers built in previous regimes may fall, or be radically altered, and that's never easy. Some will lose, or feel like they are losing, significant power. This is why it's important that everyone is fully engaged in this crucial conversation. Team members need to be at the table. It's critical that no one goes underground; no one shuts down; no one goes into sabotage mode. To that end, it's also important that this conversation is pursued in an iterative way (see "versioning" later). That helps keep this conversation from seeming as if it's a top-down solution being rolled out all at once that may put individuals in radically new roles that feel permanent and final. Team members need to be able to trust that everyone is trying to get the roles right, that nothing is set in stone, and that the first efforts at building this new system of roles will not be the last. Versioning works. It's also a reflection of humility on the part of leadership, an acknowledgment that they don't have every answer but that they recognize that together, as a team and an organization, they can get to a much better version. For team members, knowing that will help put those fears at ease.

Don't be surprised if your existing team or organizational maps don't fit together neatly at first. Complete systems of capabilities and roles don't emerge fully formed. If your system of roles has developed ad-hoc, it's likely you have key capabilities that are not owned by any particular role, or you might have roles or even whole teams that aren't clearly connected to any of your essential value-creating activities. The Business Triangle helps identify those types of problems. It's an essential tool as teams work to "straighten the spaghetti" of confusing and overlapping roles, capabilities, and strategies.

Remember that capabilities and roles don't map perfectly onto each other. After all, the one capability might break down into multiple roles. And one role might have oversight of many capabilities. This step is crucial for creating a shared language to describe your work, your skills, and how you do what you do. When you have the Business

Triangle as a simple, shared language in which to discuss what capabilities are needed and what roles are going to own those capabilities, it becomes so much easier to shorten the distance between a problem or a breakdown to elegant solution and resolution.

> The Agile concept of "**versioning**"—often used for project development—is helpful in Conversation 4 (and many others) as you redesign the system of capabilities and roles, allowing people to manage changes so that the implications of the change can ripple out to interdependent components, giving people and systems the time to respond, adapt, and align. This is an alternative to the big unveiling of a change initiative that has been worked out behind closed doors. Versioning or iterative change keeps people involved in the process of improvement that is flexible and ongoing, which you will ultimately need to develop versions that are truly high performing.

Another way of working that is essential in this conversation is leveraging creative tension. Mapping clear roles and capabilities and moving in the direction of a matrixed organization is akin to embracing creative tension as a foundational operating principle. Believe me, there will be a great deal of tension, and that's good. This approach purposefully designs conflict into your operating model, but it's the type of controlled, transparent conflict that is inherently productive and positive. Building the skill to leverage creative tension is essentially building intelligence directly into the social system. That is an important part of what allows leadership and power to be distributed in a stage 3 organization. It's not just going to individuals; it's being distributed to HPTs that are able to leverage creative tension to make healthy decisions. That process will provide needed checks and balances as well. No longer will the company be so dependent on key strategic thinkers or high-level executives. The social system itself, empowered by HPTs, will begin to express a higher level of strategic ability and decision-making capacity. Decisions will improve. Creativity will increase. Responsiveness will scale up and down. Creative tension, skillfully handled, becomes a forge for a type of collective intelligence that will bring immeasurable benefit to any company. *Healthy distributed leadership is impossible without it.*

CHAPTER 17

Conversation 5: Streamlining Interdependencies

> What other teams do we need to align with?
> Are the points of interdependence within and across teams explicit?
> Are shared processes and handoffs efficient?
> Do rewards and incentives support working as a team?

HPTs are not freestanding. They exist in a matrix, a larger social system, and inevitably they must optimize the business processes that are cross-functional, and pay attention to how they interact with multiple functional and business teams. In this conversation, we're still in the domain of Capabilities and Roles, but now we're seeking to manage the key intersection points where roles bump up against each other, inside or outside the team. We're seeking to understand how all the elements fit together, especially our team. Indeed, visualizing the Enterprise Map is a key way of working in this conversation that allows team members to see exactly how they fit within the whole organization. Any one team's ability to be high performing often depends on strategically aligning with other teams in the enterprise. When an HPT finds that it needs to advocate for its priorities up and down the enterprise hierarchy, a robust understanding of the connections and interdependencies across the organization will inform those conversations.

Analyzing the Performance System

HPTs need protocols and processes to begin to track their performance. Are there going to be reviews? What incentives will be put in place? What KPIs (key performance indicators) is the team going to work with? In this crucial conversation, one of the nitty-gritty ways of working involves the development of a performance system. Performance systems are too important to be overlooked in the development of HPTs. I've seen HR departments that had established systems that failed to update when HPTs were developed, and as a result, disincentivized people to participate fully in their teams. That needs to be guarded against, and more importantly, rewards and incentives need to be aligned with where the organization is going, not necessarily where it's been. If HPTs are truly important to your organization, that needs to be reflected in your performance system.

Incentives can be strange and subtle. Years ago, I was working with a major automotive company. The problem they were having involved cars coming off the assembly line every Friday with quality problems. When I examined more deeply what was occurring, an interesting pattern emerged. Managers of the plants were being asked to go to a Friday meeting with senior executives in the company. That pulled the managers of the plants off the production line. No surprise that they were having performance issues! But no one was keeping an eye on the consequences of those Friday meetings. The plant managers were essentially being punished, and losing bonuses, for doing what their senior leaders wanted them to do.

Always pay attention to incentives, explicit and implicit. As companies make the transition to stage 3, performance systems must evolve to support the new organizational structure, and to incentivize and reward the performance of teams, not just individuals. Some resistance may need to be overcome—first from individuals. Some people may resist having their own incentives and rewards partially intertwined with the performance of the team. It makes team members vulnerable, at least partially, to each other and to collective performance. But it also creates a powerful alignment and incentive for collective outperformance. Building those systems and getting them right is something that generally can't be done in the back office of HR. It needs to be worked out transparently and with input from team members. And that can present a second level of resistance—some HR departments are stuck in their ways. They may prefer to hoard the responsibility and be hesitant to innovate in a manner needed to build creative new performance systems. HR may need their own incentives for developing these new ways of working.

Aligning Between Teams

An important breakthrough in this conversation occurs as HPTs reach out beyond their own circles to engage the teams around them. They inevitably start to make compelling requests of those teams and work to establish a shared language around protocols and processes that is essential to streamlining those many points of interdependence. Little by little, instead of siloed workspaces with teams and departments who barely speak the same organizational language and have highly distinct processes and procedures, a grand sync-up starts to occur. It can seem miraculous. But it's not miraculous, it is simply the natural result of healthy HPTs having the right conversations with a shared language, and beginning to demand more of that same type of culture in the waters they swim in. And as they do so, organizational areas that once communicated like Mars and Venus find that they can actually talk to each other and enact the processes and procedures that need to happen to make things work. A level of unhealthy bureaucracy starts to fade away as a higher level of organizational interconnection emerges. This can happen at the level of teams in a business, or it can take place across an entire enterprise. That sync-up can even happen across an entire portfolio of companies, as HPTs start to align and influence the ecosystems they move in. Conversation 5, when it really comes online, is truly one of the most satisfying expressions of the Growth River methodology.

High-performing-team connectors are individuals who are members of more than one team. They can be team members of one team and leaders of another team. In that case, that individual is a link between the teams and their role is to advocate up and align down the hierarchy. These connectors are an essential element in the system.

They bring the technology of HPTs to the larger social dynamics that inform the entire organization. They connect and demonstrate best practices and effective ways of working up and down the organization. When the company is populated by high-performing teams, connectors model best practices, and the senior leadership adopts those standards, the whole organization will begin to align around upward evolutionary trajectory. See Figure 17.1.

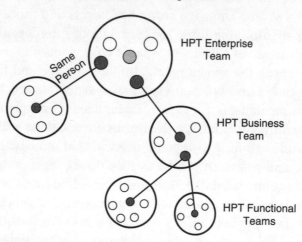

HPT Connections are members of different teams, who play important roles helping to scale ways of working across teams and organizations.

FIGURE 17.1

CHAPTER 18

Conversation 6: Aligning Strategies

Is there a strategy and a strategic planning process in place?
What is the role of the team in this process?
Is the path toward competitive advantage clear?

A s high-performing teams (HPTs) engage the third domain of change, moving into Conversation 6, important foundations have been laid. Ideally, leadership and culture conversations are robust and productive. The team has a clear focus and has built up a high level of trust and transparency. Conversations regarding capabilities and roles are productive and clear, including a shared understanding of how value is created in the business through the flow of capabilities. Creative tension between roles is being embraced. There is greater alignment across the enterprise, with ongoing attention being paid to points of interdependency. Next in our conversation cascade is a critical subject that is often (mistakenly) a starting point for change initiatives—strategy. Strategy, in its most basic sense, is simply a framework of choices designed to achieve a certain business or team goal that guides everyday work and decision-making. Notably, the placement of strategy so far down the cascade is not a reflection of its importance. In fact, it is hugely impactful. But for this conversation to take teams where they need to go, the foundations must be built to be able to surface and resolve strategic trade-offs. That's what the first five crucial conversations accomplish.

Strategy is not just something that happens at the top of an organization. Every key area of responsibility that falls under the ownership of the team needs a focused strategy, all the way from an entire enterprise strategy to a business strategy to a functional capability strategy. And the team or individuals on the team should naturally have the appropriate perspective, from the vantage point of their roles, to bring that strategy to life and to clearly advocate for it. They understand the unique visibility they have in the role (or roles) that they inhabit. In that sense, there is a symbiotic relationship among capabilities, roles, and strategies. Each one is closely connected with the others, and a change in any one of them naturally impacts the other two.

System of Strategies

There are seven types of strategies in a complete system of strategies, mirroring the roles in the system of roles in a mature, stage 3 Distributed Leadership company. They include:

1. Enterprise strategy
2. Business segment strategies
3. Develop functional capability strategies
4. Sell functional capability strategies
5. Channel strategies (for those companies that need them)
6. Deliver functional capability strategies
7. Support functional capability strategies

Four Metrics for Competitive Advantage

Strategy is not just about what you will do as a team, business, or an enterprise. It is also about what you choose not to do. That will naturally require mature conversations, good-faith disagreements, and tough decisions. Proposed strategies will come into conflict, either within the team or outside it. Again, that is a natural and desired creative tension. But HPTs need an unambiguous method for resolving these types of conflicts. And that's when two words cannot be emphasized enough—*competitive advantage*.

Why does understanding competitive advantage matter? Obviously, first and foremost, it matters because without it, you won't be in business for long. But it also matters because it can act as a North Star for everyday decision-making, strategic priorities, and team orientation. Where should we invest our money and our energy? Should we pursue this strategy or that? Should we hire this person or use the money to upgrade our backend technology? What investments do we make long-term in our business? What investments do we make in developing our people? These are the types of real-world questions that arise every day in any business. And well-meaning directives from the top leadership team don't necessarily solve them, which is a good thing, by the way.

As I described in Chapter 8: A Complete System of Roles, better decisions are often made when the decision-makers are closer to the action, so to speak. Business teams who are in the thick of a business every day often understand impactful decisions better than distant executives. They will also naturally feel more responsible and accountable for those decisions. But those teams still need an orienting focal point to help adjudicate and sort through the many various, sometimes-clashing perspectives that will inevitably be brought to bear on major decisions. As I keep reiterating, people tend to see the world through the perspectives of their own roles. To a salesperson, competitive advantage will look like more sales. To a developer, competitive advantage will look like more new products. To an IT person, competitive advantage may look like a tech upgrade. And they may all have a point! A business leader or business team needs a clear methodology for ascertaining competitive advantage whatever the specifics of the strategic question. That's why I've broken it down into four key metrics.

The **Four Metrics for Competitive Advantage** is a method for analyzing and aligning decisions toward competitive advantage. It works by defining competitive advantage as a desired end-state and as a cascade of key conditions (refer back to Transformational Journey Plan in Chapter 14.)

The challenge is that people in companies are naturally prone to advocate for strategies and priorities that elevate the roles that they play individually. These creative tensions can easily muddle strategy conversations. So how do you define competitive advantage in a way that it can be applied using Consultative Decision Making and Decision Analysis to break ties between alternatives?

The root question is—what ideal outcomes characterize an optimal business investment? There are four: (1) 100% share of a target market, (2) no constraints to meeting demand, (3) no significant business risks, and (4) above average returns.

The Four Metrics for Competitive Advantage are an application of that logic—competitive advantage means having the attributes of an optimal business investment. They include:

1. **Market potential:** team members prioritize choices that optimize demand for the company in its target market. The ideal is 100% potential share.

2. **Operational scalability:** team members prioritize choices that eliminate constraints to the company meeting demand in a target market. The ideal is no constraints.

3. **Business sustainability:** team members prioritize choices that minimize risks to the company's performance and to its key capabilities. The ideal is no significant business risks.

4. **Financial performance:** team members prioritize choices that best mitigate financial risks and optimize financial returns. The ideal is above average returns.

Decisions, investments, and changes will move either toward or away from this future state. Those that most move toward it should be prioritized. In practice, these four metrics can be translated into objectives in a Decision Analysis.

Imagine a situation where one team member wants to hire a new resource, while another wants to innovate a new product. The Four Metrics for Competitive Advantage provides a method for comparing these two very different vectors. The optimal choice will be the one expected to most contribute toward: (1) market potential, (2) operational scalability, (3) business model sustainability, and (4) financial performance. Decisions should be taken in the order of that cascade, because any other order will result in stagnation longer term. This robust logic cuts through inherent biases and enables teams to fly in formation toward overall competitive advantage. It is a powerful North Star for formulating and aligning a System of Strategies.

Market Potential

This is the first and most important measurement of competitive advantage. We live in the era of choice, more so than any other human beings in the history of the human race. Today's customers aren't just choosing between one or two brands or service providers that happen to be available locally. They have seemingly endless choices! Anyone seeking a product or service can select between numerous options, all made accessible in our increasingly connected and digital world. Choice is the name of the game, and to be successful, businesses need to win the game of choice. They need to stand out from the crowd and be chosen—by customers, first and foremost, but also by the other essential players in the business ecosystem.

Smart business leaders today recognize that their success depends not only on serving their customers and shareholders, but on serving a network of stakeholders that also includes their employees, their communities, and more. For each of these stakeholder groups, a business needs to be the preferred provider—the company of choice. We break this down into five key questions:

1. Am I the *provider of choice* for my customers?
2. Am I the *employer of choice*?
3. Am I the *channel partner of choice*?
4. Am I the *investment of choice*?
5. Am I the *community member of choice*?

In other words, am I achieving true excellence in my fundamental goal of serving all of my organization's key stakeholders?

Assessing market potential is the most important aspect of competitive advantage. It is also the highest risk part. It's the hardest area to get right, and the area in which so much can easily go wrong. That's why it's number one. If you prioritize any of the other metrics above this one, you will fundamentally undermine the business. Moreover, while each of these questions are critical, they are also presented in order of importance. Community may be the last stakeholder mentioned, but it still matters. It's very important that a business rigorously assess if it is a community member of choice for all kinds of reasons. Indeed, no companies today can afford to not concern itself with public image, whether that image is local or global. Positive or negative changes in public perception, from ESG (environmental, social, and governance) issues to DEI (diversity, equity, and inclusion) concerns, can ripple through a company, impacting everything from the stock price to the ability to attract talent. Regulatory issues, which fall under this purview, can make or break companies. Also, if there is an ethical or problematic gap between the larger organizational purpose of the company and activities on the ground or by leadership, that disconnect can be hugely consequential. Nevertheless, it's not first on the list for a reason. If you fail to have concern for being a provider-of-choice for your *customers*, it will eventually leave some of the other stakeholder assessments moot. Alternatively, if you are the provider of choice for your customers, but consistently fall short on the other four metrics, it will be hard to maintain that position in the market. But they all play a role. They all feed into each other and work together.

Operational Scalability

This is a mostly self-explanatory metric. How scalable is your business model? How far can it go? If you're selling high-end supercomputers, you might have an extremely limited market, with moderate potential for operational scalability. If you have a ridesharing business that consists of an app used by independent contractors, you can potentially scale your basic business model across the entire globe, at least in theory. Scalability determines a lot about the overall competitive advantage of any business. It's no accident that Wall Street's ideal investment moment is *after* a business has proven its market potential and right *before* it begins to operationally scale (while it still needs money to do it).

These days the term *TAM* (total addressable market) is a common way to speak about this metric. But this is more than simply the TAM. It also represents the reasonable or proven ability of the business to operationally scale into that market. Honest rigorous analysis of an organization's operational scalability is very informative when it comes to shining a light on the business decisions that will bring competitive advantage.

Business Model Sustainability

How sustainable is any given business? How long is your runway? Are there particular risks to your inputs or key capabilities? Are you in an industry like food or fashion where consumer tastes change rapidly? Or are you in technology, with the ever-present danger of a competitor making your business model obsolete? Do you have an effective moat or a near monopoly? Are you in the fossil fuel industry with political headwinds to consider? Or perhaps you're in the infrastructure business that is highly dependent on whichever political faction is in power? These are the types of questions you need to ask yourself about business model sustainability over the short and long term.

Financial Returns

No business will last long without financial returns. For public companies, this becomes a quarterly reality, but it's true for any business. It's worth noting that we've consciously put this metric as the last in this foursome. It's critical, but it's not the most important. Financial returns will naturally flow when we are increasing our metrics in the other three areas of competitive advantage. Leaders who think it works the other way around make a huge mistake. If you prioritize financial returns over market potential or operational scalability or business model sustainability, you may temporarily increase profits and returns, but you will compromise the business over the longer term. You may be extracting financial returns at the cost of market potential, scalability, or sustainability, and that is a dangerous path. Of course, financial returns must be part of the picture. But business leaders have to understand where they fall in the priorities of competitive advantage, or it's easy to get off course.

Interestingly, this can be especially difficult for public companies, because this last metric is often the most important to Wall Street investors. CEOs of public companies sometimes find themselves in the strange position of having to talk about metric number four as if it's number one. But for the sake of the company, in their everyday leadership decisions, they had better behave as if it's number four. I can't emphasize this point enough.

No business exists unless it has some degree of success in each of these metrics. Some will have great market potential, but lower financial returns. Some will have great opportunities for scalability but their timeline (sustainability) will be limited. Some may have a long runway and a sustainable business model, but are not that scalable. Any investor naturally wants to put money into a business that has all four in abundance—unlimited market potential, the ability to harvest that potential, the confidence it won't ever go out of business, and massive margins and huge profits. In the real world, such businesses don't really exist, or are exceedingly rare. But we can aim high.

Competitive advantage is a way of framing the choices of the moment so that we are choosing with an eye toward the optimal direction of growth. And it's not just a metric for business; I've applied it with nonprofits, educational institutions, and governmental organizations. The basic elements remain the same.

But whatever your specifics of the organization, these four metrics should exert a strong magnetic pull on its strategic compass. And strategies that most align with that magnetic pull should rise to the top level of consideration, in a team, in a business, or in an enterprise.

Alignment Is Required, Agreement Is Optional

A critical underlying mindset for distributed leadership is that when creative tensions are resolved in the direction of competitive advantage, team members choose to align with team or leadership decisions, even if they might not personally agree or would have done something differently on their own. Distributed leadership requires alignment, not agreement.

Alignment means a commitment to support and contribute to the collective effort. Of course, that alignment is in the context of the larger organizational purpose; it's not free floating. In contrast, **agreement** means sharing the same opinion or approach. You can align or commit to support and contribute, even when you don't agree, and vice versa— you can agree without necessarily supporting or contributing. It's important to note this difference in your daily interactions and decision-making with your team.

If the team operates on seeking agreement, major decisions will require a consensus. This means getting everyone to agree through persuading, convincing, alliances, or voting. In response, team members seek to satisfy their individual needs (essential conditions) and wants (desired but nonessential conditions) before they can fully endorse the decision.

On the other hand, the process for seeking alignment relies on team members' commitments to the shared purpose and having an effective, agreed-upon leadership mechanism. Alignment includes negotiating needs that are crucial for team members but doesn't necessarily accommodate individual wants. The negotiation is focused on reaching a decision that will lead the entire business in the direction of competitive advantage.

There will always be trade-offs when it comes to examining the competing interests that are expressed in various strategies. Resolution comes out of reconciling those trade-offs and choosing strategies that align toward competitive advantage. Everyone may not perfectly agree, but if they are able to strongly advocate for their own strategy and clearly appreciate the reasoning behind the choices made, clarity should prevail. And in that clarity is the opportunity for team alignment. That allows an HPT to move forward together without distraction. No one has had their perspective ignored or rejected without a fair hearing. The reasons for the decisions that have been made are clear and transparent. The right conversations are being engaged with the right people in the room to evaluate the best strategies that have been developed by those who truly understand the issues at stake. They are being held in a productive context with accountable, aligned people representing the key roles. Finally, a strategic direction is being chosen and pursued. That is the purpose of Conversation 6, and of the Four Metrics for Competitive Advantage. The strategic priority is shared and understood. And true alignment has one other benefit as well—it provides a massive boost to execution and implementation.

CHAPTER 19

Conversation 7: Implementing Initiatives

Do team members plan and manage programs and projects effectively?
Can the team forecast demand and budget their projects?
Are there sufficient dashboards for measuring and tracking performance?

You don't always know what's around the bend in the river until you get there. Will it be smooth flowing water, rushing rapids, or something else entirely? Will it be simple and straightforward, or immensely difficult? Will it require entirely new skills and capabilities, or simply make use of existing ones? Will it lead to surprising new opportunities, or present bigger challenges? Unless a team gets out of the endless eddies of the Swirl, they'll never know. The 7 Crucial Conversations are all about getting into the main current, and Conversation 7 is the culmination of that process. Indeed, if the first six conversations are active and engaged, something quite miraculous can happen. The team is liberated to focus its attention on implementation! The "get 'er done" power of the HPT ramps up enormously. The foundation has truly been laid for outperformance.

Conversation 7 allows an unusual freedom to focus with a laser-like attention on the quality and impact of the team's initiatives. After there is clarity around purpose and leadership, transparency around roles and accountabilities, and strategic alignment toward the path of maximum competitive advantage, the implementation questions come

185

to the fore. What is the method that will achieve the highest impact? How do we test and iterate? How do we minimize waste and maximize efficiency?

Of course, this crucial conversation is not without its important *ways of working*. Notably, there may be a high degree of project management required, and of course, skills like forecasting and budgeting and resource tracking will need to be employed. What's important is that the team has the knowledge and skillsets, or alternatively outsources the knowledge and skillsets, to achieve a high level of execution.

There is no point in reinventing perfectly good wheels. One core insight in this crucial conversation is recognition of the powerful principles of Agile design. In the past decade, the Agile revolution has transformed countless organizations' approaches when it comes to achieving effective implementation for projects and programs of all kinds, across most industries. From testing, iteration, and prototyping to designing a lean, flexible implementation process, the principles that flow out of Agile thinking have been revolutionary. Growth River places enormous emphasis on successful implementation, but this is territory already alive with new thinking and sometimes, the most relevant advice I can offer is to point the way toward many of these best-in-class solutions. Regardless, a high-performing team should have the built-in strength and intelligence to know what it needs to do, what it needs to learn, and where it needs to focus when it comes to the penultimate act in this ever-unfolding seven-part narrative.

CHAPTER 20

An Invitation to Transformation

We began this book with a description of organizational breakdown. The Swirl is quite capable, to again paraphrase Peter Drucker, of eating strategy for breakfast—and quite frankly, for lunch and dinner as well. The best laid plans seem to simply dissipate like smoke in the air when it comes to trying to force something through an organizational system that is caught up in that type of bureaucratic mess. But as teams become high performing, by engaging the Seven Crucial Conversations, the Swirl dissipates. A true HPT—confident, empowered, and intelligent—knows how to digest a business or enterprise strategy. It can understand its components, identify essential roles and responsibilities, connect them to the team's strategic purview, and implement and adjust where necessary. And it can even start to engage other teams around those issues and help encourage the smart adoption of a more effective approach throughout the organization. Ideally, the whole organization will begin to feel that energizing sense of being on a transformational journey.

A transformational journey in business is both a human journey and a shared journey. It may begin with a leader, but that person's leadership always involves a deeper degree of appreciation for those with whom they share the path, and an expanded sense that "we're in this together." It may sound like a cliché, but in a very direct and unambiguous way, it's true: you will succeed or fail together. And if you succeed, it will be in the discovery of greater creative powers and independent resourcefulness in the larger team rather than an elevation of one person or a small group of leaders. Leadership on this transformational journey is indispensable, but the fruits will be highly distributed.

What I have offered in these pages is an operating system for that journey and some initial directions. I've pointed out important signposts and milestones, and identified the rhythmic beats of the transformational narrative that you will be following. But make no mistake—this is still your team's journey, and no one can walk the path but you and those with whom you share your organization. Transformation, by definition, involves a step into unknown territory—a leap beyond an event horizon—and all of the insecurity that comes along with that step. No map, however accurate, can change that fact.

For some, that can be a cause of great anxiety. But it can also be a source of relief. We don't need to spend time and energy trying to figure out exactly how the future will unfold—because we can't know! We only need to embark on an authentic transformational journey, and engage with it wholeheartedly. And if you follow the guidelines for that journey that we've presented in these pages, I can promise you at least three things. First, the experience of being caught in the swirl will radically shift. Second, the potential of the organization will dramatically increase. And third, you'll have lots and lots of new problems— but much more interesting ones. Not the "groundhog day" problems of the swirl. No, you will be called to solve the types of problems whose resolution moves things forward, whose solutions effect real change and move the organization into the future.

I designed this book's trajectory to be a "slow zoom"—starting broad, ending deep. In Part I, we explored some of the biggest questions about the nature of organizations and businesses—what makes them tick, how they develop and evolve. Our focus zoomed in as we identified the patterns by which a business forms and scales, how it succeeds, where it gets trapped, and how it becomes dysfunctional. We pursued that dysfunction attentively until we were able to uncover its ultimate roots—not in a failure of grand strategy but in a social system of disempowered and misaligned individual agents and team. From there, we examined the principles of a different type of enterprise and explored how to evolve from the breakdown of stage 2 organizations to the breakthroughs of stage 3 and 4. Finally, we arrived at the ground unit of our social system—the team—and how to optimize the development of the organization through that lens. From Purpose to Focus to Mindset to Capabilities and Roles to Interdependencies to

Strategy to Implementation, the Seven Crucial Conversations constitute a transformational approach that is robust and comprehensive.
They set the individual, the team, the business, and the enterprise in
right relationship with one another, and it is my experience that such
synergy is inevitably the secret to good companies and great success.

There is never an end to transformation, but on that long and
winding journey of growth, there are certainly more favorable paths
and more desirable destinations. I hope this book helps you discover
the optimal route, and perhaps somewhere along that path, we will
meet and continue the conversation.

Closing Reflections

Thank you for getting this book. I have seen these ideas work power-
fully in the lives and work of others and in my own. I have seen them
work as a system of thought that naturally arises whenever business
teams purposefully engage in shared work. And I firmly believe that
these ideas will enable teams in businesses to rise up and contribute to
solving big complex challenges in a forwarding way.

I am also confident that I have only begun to discover some of
the many ways that transformational journeys will go terribly wrong.
Again, as Kurt Lewin is said to have declared "If you to want truly to
understand something, try to change it." So, from my experience what
do I think is the easiest way for you to mess up using the ideas in this
book? Let me share an insight from a kid.

When one of my daughters was about five years old, she brought
me a crayon drawing. It showed a line that started on the left side of
the paper, then it went up, around, down, and back, ending just next
to where it began. "Is it a bird I asked?" and she said "yes." "Oh, so this
must be the head" I said" and she said 'no, it's a bird." "So, this must
be a wing" I said" and she said 'no, it's a bird!" Getting frustrated she
put her hands on her hips and said "Daddy, why can't you see, the bird
starts here, goes there, and then there, and then it comes back to there,
almost next where it started. I just saw one do that." She had drawn
the flight path of a bird. And she was right, I couldn't see what she was

seeing because I was thinking about a bird as an object while she was thinking about birds in general as potential flight-paths. To her, "bird" was a verb and to me it was a noun. She was thinking from a non-dualistic perspective and I was not.

The easiest way to mess up using the ideas in this book is to think of them as nouns instead of as verbs. It is to look for birds instead of flight-paths. I am the author of this book, but Carter Phipps and Ellen Daly, and my team at Growth River helped me to write it. I did not simply invent the ideas in this book, they are the product of thousands of conversations and refinements. These relationships and conversations are the flight path. So, the easiest way to mess up would be for you to try and pin down the ideas in this book, like a 19th century butterfly collection. Conversely, the easiest way to succeed will be for you to courageously release these ideas into your team, business, and organizational social system, and watch how they fly.

Glossary

Learning a Language

Back in high school, I took a few years of foreign language classes but found them challenging. I didn't understand the payoff; memorizing words felt like unnecessary effort, and it was embarrassing to speak in front of others. Then, perhaps recklessly, I took a gap year as an exchange student, putting myself in a situation where I had no choice but to learn. If I wanted to make friends, order food, watch movies, blend in, etcetera, I had to do it in this foreign tongue. That reality provided the necessary motivation. I threw myself in entirely, starting with swear words because that made sense as a teenager, and moving on to food, and eventually, reading (spy novels). An important inflection point happened on this learning journey when suddenly it seemed like everyone started correcting me. The grandmother of my host family was particularly stern about my sloppy American ways. I didn't like people treating me like a wayward child, and it didn't feel good to be corrected, but it was a positive sign that others thought I was coachable. After that point, my learning accelerated. Today I see a lot of parallels between that experience and my experiences building high-performing teams and guiding business transformation journeys. Both involve learning new skills and new language. Both can seem, at first, like fumbling through a strange world of foreign meaning. But over time, the experience can be liberating; it can unlock new worlds. My point is that as you read the glossary of terms in the pages that follow, I hope you do it with a mindset of immersing yourself in a new language, one that will accelerate your learning and inspire more authentic and meaningful conversations.

Summary of the Seven Crucial Conversations

Crucial Conversations   are structured dialogues or multilogues that generate breakthrough insights, encourage continuous improvement, and lead to higher and higher levels of productivity and performance in a team.

The Seven Crucial Conversations (the 7CCs®) is a system of thought for building teams and growing and scaling companies toward competitive advantage through an optimal sequence of crucial conversations. This sequence aligns with the natural path of the Three Domains of Change. As such, the 7 Crucial Conversations are a roadmap for transforming teams and companies and for planning and implementing major change initatives.

Setting the Stage for the Seven Crucial Conversations

Guiding Questions	Terms That Tend to Cluster Together
• What is required to unleash the capacity of leaders and teams to grow and scale companies?	The Swirl, Social Systems Not Machines, Complex Adaptive Social Systems, Agency, the Art of Alignment, Transformational Change, Transformational Leadership, Three Domains of Change, Disruption
• How do businesses and companies naturally grow and scale? • Why to do they get struck? • What is required to get them unstuck?	The Business Triangle, Definition of a Business, Value Creation, Business Growth, Systems of Capabilities and Roles, Creative Tensions, Resolving Primary Constraints
	Enterprise Evolutionary Stages, Centralized Leadership, Decentralized Leadership, Independent Contributors, Directive Leadership, Distributed Leadership, Leaders Leading Leaders, Flat Agile Organizations
	The Seven Crucial Conversations, High-Performing Teams and Companies, Ways of Working, Growth River Operating System
	Change Teams, Leading the Transformational Journey, Leading Through Narratives, Challenge Statements, Influence Analysis, Guiding Coalitions

Change Domain 1: Leadership and Culture

Crucial Conversation 1, Activating Purpose

Guiding Questions	Ways of Working	Terms That Tend to Cluster Together
• Does this team have a leader who is willing and able to activate a shared team purpose? • How will decisions be made in this team? • What is the shared purpose of the team? • Are the needs of the customers and stakeholders whom we serve clear?	1.1 Law of the Lid 1.2 Effective Decision-Making 1.3 Customer and Stakeholder Analysis 1.4 Team Charter	Shared Purpose, Alignment, Agreement, Manifesting Team Purpose, Leadership Clearing, Single Journey Owners, Choice to Align, Decision-Making, Culture Team Charters, Team Types, Team Structures, Business Triangle Value Creation, Stakeholders and Customers, Customer Value, Customer Experience System of Meetings, Kairos and Chronos Balance, Vertical and Horizontal Improvement

Crucial Conversation 2, Driving Focus

Guiding Questions	Ways of Working	Terms That Tend to Cluster Together
• Are team members focused on a shared transformational journey? • Is the destination clear? • Have gaps and primary constraints been identified? • Are next steps and priorities clear?	2.1 Awareness of Focus 2.2 Transformational Journey Map 2.3 Primary Constraint Analysis 2.4 Visualizing Shared Work	Visualizing Shared Work, Business Triangle, Value Streams, Shared Work Bullseye Issue Action Lists, Decision Analysis Transformational Journey Maps, Ideal Future State, Gap Analysis, Event Horizons Choice Points, Breakthrough Experiences, Facilitation, Decision Analysis Primary Constraints, Continuous Improvement, Systems Thinking, Horizontal Improvement, Vertical Improvement, Innovation, Natural Paths, Cascades of Key Conditions, Five Pathways, Game Changers

Crucial Conversation 3, Shifting Mindset

Guiding Questions	Ways of Working	Terms That Tend to Cluster Together
• Are team members sober and honest about where they are on the journey and where the gaps are? • Are team members able to bring their best efforts to the team's success? • Are they accountable and coachable, giving and receiving feedback? • Do they resolve conflicts directly at the source? • Do they build dynamic interpersonal relationships?	3.1 Accountability for Leadership Impact 3.2 Giving and Receiving Feedback 3.3 Compelling Requests	Dynamic Interpersonal Relationships, Trust, Sensing, Active Listening, Solving Conflicts at the Source, Depersonalizing Conflicts Breakthrough Experiences, Limiting Stories and Beliefs, Coachability, Compelling Requests, Speech Acts, Toxic Rock Stars

Change Domain 2: Capabilities and Roles

Crucial Conversation 4, Specifying Capabilities and Roles

Guiding Questions	Ways of Working	Terms That Tend to Cluster Together
• Does every key capability and concern in the team's purview have an owner advocate? • Are the roles and responsibilities clear? • Are creative tensions leveraged?	4.1 Engaged Response 4.2 Leveraging Creative Tension 4.3 Aligning Between Roles 4.4 Analyzing Business Capabilities 4.5 Architecting Systems of Roles	Roles, Capabilities, Accountabilities, Responsibilities, Onboarding New Team Members Analyzing Business Capabilities, Organizational Structure Business Triangle, Enterprise Maps, Evolutionary Stages, Business Segmentation, Functions, Channels, Flat Agile Organizations, Straightening the Spaghetti Leveraging Creative Tensions, Innovation, Vertical and Horizontal Balance, Functionitis, Aligning Between Roles, Analyzing the Performance System

Crucial Conversation 5, Streamlining Interdependencies

Guiding Questions	Ways of Working	Terms That Tend to Cluster Together
• With which other teams do we need to align? • Are the points of interdependence within and across teams explicit? • Are shared processes and handoffs efficient? • Do rewards and incentives support working as a team?	5.1 Visualizing the Matrix 5.2 Aligning Between Teams 5.3 Cross-Functional Interdependencies 5.4 Analyzing the Performance System	Aligning Between Teams, Cross-Functional Interdependencies, High-Performing Team Connectors, Enterprise Change Teams, Home Team

Change Domain 3: Strategies and Implementation

Crucial Conversation 6, Aligning Strategies

Guiding Questions	Ways of Working	Terms That Tend to Cluster Together
• Is there a strategy and a strategic planning process in place? • What is the role of the team in this process? • Is the path toward competitive advantage clear?	6.1 System of Strategies 6.2 Enterprise Strategy 6.3 Business Segment Strategies 6.4 Functional-Capability Strategies	Aligning Competitive Advantage, Business Capabilities, Four Metrics for Competitive Advantage System of Strategies, Strategy Canvases, Business Segment Strategies, Enterprise Strategy Map, Basis for Competitive Advantage, Strategic Planning Process, Nirvana Meeting

Crucial Conversation 7, Implementing Initiatives

Guiding Questions	Ways of Working	Terms That Tend to Cluster Together
• Do team members plan and manage programs and projects effectively? • Can the team forecast demand and budget their projects? • Are there sufficient dashboards for measuring and tracking performance?	7.1 Project Management 7.2 Agile Innovation 7.3 Forecasting and Budgeting 7.4 Measuring Performance	Customer Value, Event Horizons, Agile Innovation, Design Thinking, Versioning, Grand Unveiling Versioning, Scrums

Glossary of Terms for the Growth River OS

About the Glossary

The following terms were identified and refined by facilitating the Seven Crucial Conversations in partnership with hundreds of teams across a wide range of industries and cultures. Every term has proven its value toward building high-performing teams and companies. Together these terms work as an integrated system of thought for growing and scaling companies.

The Glossary

Accountabilities are obligations to create outcomes or deliverables. There are nuanced differences between accountabilities and responsibilities. The objective is to have accountable and responsible team members. Accountabilities link to the Specifying Capabilities and Roles crucial conversation.

Accountability for Leadership Impact refers to team members being accountable for the impact that their leadership style creates. An "unintentional panicky" team leader creates an "unintentional and reactive" team, whereas an "intentional customer-focused leader" creates a team that is "intentional about creating value." Leadership impact links to intentional culture. It also relates to the Shifting Mindset crucial conversation. See Toxic **Rock Stars.**

Active Listening refers to team members listening in a way that creates clarity, confidence, and trust. Active listening requires fully concentrating on what is being said and the speaker's emotional cues to understand the speaker's message. This behavior is different from listening to respond, which comes from a transactional perspective, commonly an unconscious, default position. Active listening is essential for effective leadership and teamwork. It links to Accountability for Leadership Impact.

Agency refers to the power of individuals to choose their responses and actions. The goal is to align the agency of individuals with the purposes of teams and the purposes of teams with the organization's purpose. Supporting the agency of individuals and teams is core to the ideas of unleashing distributed leadership and leading Social Systems, Not Machines.

Agile Innovation refers to team members iteratively prototyping, testing, and validating products, services, and solutions in a customer-centric way. The core challenge is how to manage the uncertainty of Event Horizons by testing, validating, and Versioning in short iterations called sprints. You can't be sure that a technology, feature, design, or solution will have any real value until you have feedback and confirmation from actual customers, which means you must create dynamic interpersonal relationships with at least some representative customers. You start by analyzing needs using Stakeholder Customer Analysis. Then you try to fail fast and cheaply, making choices to pivot or continue, getting feedback, minimizing waste, and accelerating learning. Just as importantly, you avoid grand unveilings. Books and other materials about Agile innovation and its close cousin, design thinking, are generally available.

The Growth River Operating System supports these methods and the dynamic interpersonal relationships on which they depend. This links to the Implementing Initiatives crucial conversation.

Aligning Between Roles   refers to team members clarifying, negotiating, and structuring responsibilities and accountabilities. This way of working is essential to aligning systems of capabilities and roles. This links to the Specifying Capabilities and Roles crucial conversation.

Aligning Between Teams   refers to team members seeking to create alignment between the roles each team plays in delivering results across the enterprise. This way of working is part of Straightening the Spaghetti, which refers to the processes for analyzing capabilities, distributing roles, and delegating strategies in teams and companies. This links to the Streamlining Interdependencies crucial conversation.

Aligning Competitive Advantage   refers to team members planning and managing strategic tradeoffs or creative tensions between strategies and roles in the direction of competitive advantage. The Four Metrics for Competitive Advantage provides a formula to do this. This links to Decision Analysis. It also links to the Aligning Strategies crucial conversation.

Alignment   refers to the ideal arrangement of the parts in a system. In groups and teams, alignment depends on the Choice to Align. The objective of Primary Constraint Analysis is to create impactful alignment. The Seven Crucial Conversations are a roadmap of choice points for teams to align.

Alignment Is Required, Agreement Is Optional   refers to a critical underlying mindset for distributed leadership, where team members choose to align with team or leadership decisions, even if they might not personally agree or would have done something differently on their own. Distributed leadership requires alignment, not agreement. This links to Choice to Align.

Analysis   refers to the process of separating something into its constituent elements to understand it. The Growth River OS includes various kinds of analysis: Gap Analysis, Primary Constraint Analysis, and Decision Analysis. This links to the Driving Focus crucial conversation.

Analyzing Business Capabilities   refers to team members defining the essential factors for creating value in their roles and for the business, such as people, processes, tools, technologies or resources. Capabilities answer the question "What do we need to have in place to execute our strategy?" Capabilities represent sources of value at the intersection of customer and business, so how they are named profoundly impacts factors including culture, roles, influence, strategies, hiring, metrics, and rewards. Start with Stakeholder and Customer Analysis and then work backward to identify the most crucial business capabilities to value creation. Define business capabilities at the right level by being aware of the differences between business capabilities and value streams. Seek to assign every essential business capability as a responsibility to a single role or team. Apply the four types of business capabilities from around the Business Triangle to structure your analysis. Analyzing business capabilities is the first step in Straightening the Spaghetti. And it links to the Specifying Capabilities and Roles crucial conversation.

Analyzing the Performance System   refers to team members providing constructive feedback to the team and organizational leaders on performance system constraints or blockers (unclear roles, ineffective incentives, etc.). Team members will discuss: What policies, processes, incentives, or rewards block us from being high performing? This links to the Specifying Capabilities and Roles crucial conversation.

Architecting Systems of Roles   refers to team members structuring roles that enable distributed leadership and ensure ownership of critical decisions and activities. This way of working is the second step in Straightening the Spaghetti, the process of aligning capabilities, roles, and strategies. It is a Versioning process, and a healthy conversation, with no grand unveilings. It links to the Specifying Capabilities and Roles crucial conversation.

Art of Alignment   refers to leaders and teams becoming skilled at breaking complex issues into the key choice points required for people to engage, choose, and align toward higher performance as a collective (see Figure G.1). This relates to Setting the Stage for the 7 Crucial Conversations.

Awareness of Focus   refers to team members intentionally aligning perspectives toward priority outcomes. Issue Action Lists is a practice related to this way of working. This links to the Driving Focus crucial conversation.

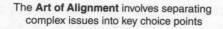

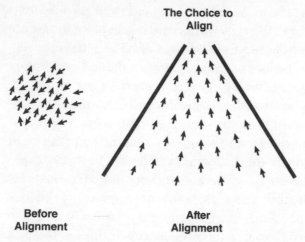

FIGURE G.1   The Art of Leading Alignment

Basis for Competitive Advantage   refers to team members planning the configuration of business capabilities most likely to enable business(es) to create competitive advantage. It is part of the Aligning Strategies crucial conversation. Key questions include: In which capabilities will we invest to be the standard-setter? Where will we seek parity? Where will we outsource? The four kinds of business capabilities around the Business Triangle and the Four Metrics for Competitive Advantage are helpful.

Breakthrough Experiences   refers to team members creating events that fundamentally change how things work, requiring the team to learn and adapt to new circumstances. Leaders must become skilled at breaking complex issues down to the vital choice points and breakthrough experiences, which is the purpose of the Seven Crucial Conversations. The premise is 'an experience always trumps an argument,' or 'seeing is believing.' A related concept is Breakthroughs in Systems, which relates to Primary Constraint Analysis. Willingness to create breakthroughs links to Transformational Journey Mindset. It also links to facilitation.

Breakthroughs in Systems   refers to an event in a system that resolves a primary constraint, creating the conditions for a higher-sustainable level of performance. It links to Primary Constraint Analysis.

Business refers to a system of capabilities and roles designed and managed to develop, sell, deliver, and support products and services to target customers toward competitive advantage. The Business Triangle is a way to visualize this definition. See **Business Triangle.**

Business Capabilities are strategic factors critical to creating value for a customer or in a business. Capabilities answer the question "What do we need to have in place to execute our strategy?" A capability can be almost any key factor or point of leverage, including people, processes, tools, technologies, and resources. In high-performing teams, members will actively discuss, "What are the essential capabilities to winning as a team or business? What are the capability gaps? Where are the primary constraints? Which roles are specifically responsible? And what are the next steps and priorities?" This links to Analyzing Business Capabilities. See **Business Triangle.**

Business Capabilities versus Value Streams: It can be easy to confuse business capabilities and value streams. Both are essential concepts for aligning teams and organizations to optimize customer value. However, they serve different purposes and operate at different altitudes. Business capabilities are more strategic, while value streams are more operational. Team members will usually not share the details of values streams with other team members unless these details impact points of interdependency or primary constraints. However, team members must share the details of business capabilities to make strategic tensions transparent and ensure strategic alignment. This links to the Aligning Strategies crucial conversation. See **Business Triangle.**

Business Leader or Business Team refers to the role responsible for leading and managing a business segment or Business Triangle toward competitive advantage in the enterprise. This links to the Specifying Capabilities and Roles and Streamlining Interdependencies crucial conversations. See **System of teams**.

Business Segment Strategies refers to team members formulating business strategies for one or more business segements. The Business Strategy Canvas is a way to summarize these strategies. This links to the Aligning Strategies crucial conversation. See **Business Triangle**.

Business Segmentation refers to identifying and separating Business Triangles to ensure customer focus and to elevate the business leader perspective. See **Business Triangle.** Differences in customers, products, services, sales processes, channels, delivery platform, geographies, and other factors create the need for segmenting business triangles and for separate and focused business teams and strategies for each business segment. Team members will discuss: What are the key differences that distinguish business triangles in terms of Develop, Sell, Deliver, and Support capabilities or value-streams? A stage 3 distributed leadership company will have an enterprise with multiple business segment leaders and teams. It will require a matrix of teams. See **System of Teams**. This links to the Capabilities and Roles crucial conversation. See **Enterprise Evolutionary Stages**.

Business Triangle   refers to a diagram for visualizing a business as a system that includes four business capability types: (1) Develop, (2) Sell, (3) Deliver, and (4) Support, as shown in Figure G.2. Team members apply this diagram to visualize business capabilities, analyze primary constraints, design systems of roles, leverage creative tensions, and accelerate value and throughput around the business

The **Business Triangle** envisions a business as
a social system in which the leadership challenge
is to structure and align Capabilities, Roles, and
Creative Tensions toward creating Customer Value
and Competitive Advantage

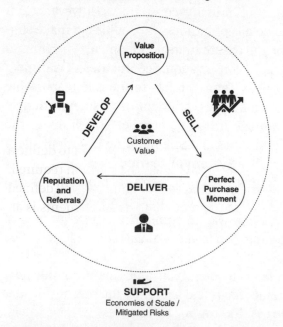

FIGURE G.2   The Business Triangle

triangle towards competitive advantage. It also links to the system of teams. See **Business**.

Capabilities and Roles refers to the second of the Three Domains of Change. See **Three Domains of Change.**

Cascades of Key Conditions refers to a powerful method for analyzing primary constraints in complex systems by testing against ideal operating conditions. This method works because changes in interdependent conditions are more likely to have impact than changes in independent ones. So, when a list of ideal operating conditions is sorted from most interdependent to most independent, the first condition is the most impactful, and the last one is the least impactful. This technique has been woven throughout the Growth River OS. Examples include the Three Domains of Change, the Seven Crucial Conversations, the Four Business Capability Types, the Four Metrics for Competitive Advantage, Systems of Teams, and Systems of Strategies. All of these models are based in explicit cascades of key conditions that can be applied through gap analysis with data to identify primary constraints. This links to the Driving Focus crucial conversation. See **Primary Constraint Analysis, and Game Changer**.

Centralized Leadership refers to a system of roles in which the decision-making powers are concentrated in a few leaders at the top of the organizational structure. Decisions are made at the top and communicated to lower-level managers for implementation. This links to the Specifying Capabilities and Roles crucial conversation.

Centralized versus Distributed Leadership refers to the relative strengths and weaknesses of two approaches to decision-making process and organizational structures (see Figure G.3). See **Centralized Leadership** and **Distributed Leadership**.

Challenge Statements refer to a statement that is written to define a critical gap or opportunity in a way that frames the solution required. A good challenge statement meets the adage "a challenge well defined is one half solved." Drafting and aligning challenge statements is an integral part of Leading Through Narratives. It is also important for aligning stakeholders and creating the conditions for distributed leadership to drive higher performance and for planning and leading transformational journeys. See **Leading Through Narratives**.

Change Team refers to a best practice for leading change in which a team leader forms a sub-team of close confidants to support in planning and managing the transformational journey of a team or

As complexity increases, teams and companies
need to learn **Distributed Leadership**.

Centralized Leadership—
decision-making
is centralized
among a few leaders.

Distributed Leadership—
decision-making
is delegated close
to where value is created.

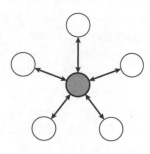 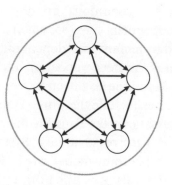

Capacity to manage complexity increases

FIGURE G.3 Centralized versus Distributed Leadership

company. Growth River consultants typically work with these change teams to design, customize, and co-lead transformational journeys for teams and companies. Ideally, there will be an enterprise change team that is responsible for tracking the company's overall journey as well as the developmental journeys of key leaders and teams across the organization. This book can be used as a primer for change teams.

Channels   refer to the capabilities or platforms where products and services are sold and delivered in a business. Channels encompass a subset of the Sell and Deliver capabilities and roles in a given Business Triangle. See **Business Triangle**. Channel leadership teams are a type of team that creates and aligns channel strategies. See **System of Teams.** This links to the Aligning Strategies crucial conversation.

Choice to Align   refers to team members choosing to align with team decisions to speak and act with a single intention. Alignment doesn't necessarily require agreement. Leaders must become skilled at breaking complex issues down to the key choice points and Breakthrough Experiences, which is the purpose of the Seven Crucial Conversations. See **Facilitation**. The Choice to Align is a behavior linked to the Law of the Lid and to Leadership Clearing. Both link to the Activating Purpose crucial conversation. See **Alignment Is Required, Agreement Is Optional**.

Chronos: See **Kairos and Chronos Balance.**

Coachability   refers to team members demonstrating a willingness and ability to receive and apply feedback in a way that creates high levels of trust and confidence for others. Coachability is a behavior linked to Accountability for Leadership Impact and to the Shifting Mindset crucial conversation.

Company   refers to a legal entity that represents an association of people dedicated to a shared business. See **Enterprise.**

Compelling Requests   refers to team members making time bound, specific, and actionable requests that compel others to engage. The objective is to set up a collaborative conversation. The method is to ask the other party to help you frame a request to that in a way that they will be compelled to reply with "yes" or "yes-if" instead of "no." Applying this method is key skill for Aligning Between Roles and Aligning Between Teams. This links to the Shifting Mindset crucial conversation. See **Speech Acts**.

Competitive Advantage   refers to a situation in which a company has superior business capabilities that give it a healthy lead over competitors. This links to the Aligning Strategies crucial conversation. Differential advantage is a related term. See **Four Metrics for Competitive Advantage**.

Complete System of Roles   refers to a system of roles in which every key issue, decisions, capability, creative tension, and strategy has a single capable owner and advocate driving resolution. This links to System of Roles, of Strategies, and of Teams. See **Leveraging Creative Tensions**.

Complex Adaptive Social System   refers to a network of individuals or a collective that exhibits purposeful, self-organizing, and adaptive behaviors. This links to Setting the Stage for the 7 Crucial Conversations. See **Three Domains of Change**.

Continuous Improvement   refers to team members identifying and resolving gaps in systems to create higher performance. There are two different paths towards continuous improvement (1) optimizing at the primary constraint or (2) resolving the primary constraint. This links to the Driving Focus crucial conversation. See **Horizontal versus Vertical Improvement**.

Creative Tensions refers to differences of opinion or perspective that naturally arise between roles or between teams. They exist in the system of roles in every team and in the system of teams in every company. In teams where team members are not intentional about how they work together, creative tensions can become sources of unhealthy conflict. This links to Leveraging Creative Tensions. See **Vertical and horizontal balance.**

Cross-Functional Interdependencies refers to team members planning and managing cross-functional processes to build knowledge, streamline work, share information, and drive alignment. Examples of this way of working include designing or implementing information systems or communications protocols. This links to the Streamlining Interdependencies crucial conversation.

Crucial Conversations refer to team members planning and implementing structured dialogues or multilogues that generate breakthrough insights, encourage continuous improvement, create alignment, and lead to higher and higher levels of productivity and performance in a team. Crucial conversations are how social systems evolve. Development in teams and companies happens at the speed of conversations, especially those that identify and resolve points of greatest impact or primary constraints. This links to Setting the Stage for the 7 Crucial Conversations.

Culture refers to how people think and act in groups. Natural culture is what people do when no one is telling them what to do. Natural culture refers to the natural flow of the social system when leadership is unintentional. In contrast, intentional culture is the ways of thinking and acting that are taught and reinforced in a group in the direction of leadership, hierarchy, and influence. Leadership and Culture are the first of the Three Domains of Change. This links to Setting the Stage for the 7 Crucial Conversations.

Customer refers to a role in the buying process. High-performing teams and companies create exceptional value by being customer-focused. The term *customer* can be applied with different levels of strategic sophistication. In less strategically mature organizations, a customer is a person who buys and uses products or services. In a more strategically mature organization, a customer is a system of roles, made up of different kinds of customers that influence each other to decide, buy, and consume products and services (channels, end-users, payers, gatekeepers, and influencers). The System of customers is in the center of the Business Triangle. See **System of Customers.**

Customer Analysis: See **Stakeholder and Customer Analysis.**

Customer Experience   refers to how customers experience and remember the interactions they have with a business. The develop, sell, and deliver business capabilities around the business triangle create the customer experience. The customer experience is part of the third domain in the Three Domains of Change, which describes how change unfolds in teams and companies.

Decision Analysis   refers to team members following a structured process to facilitate, document, and align complex decisions. The decision analysis process involves four steps for clarifying and aligning decisions by scoring alternatives against weighted decision objectives in a grid. This process is helpful with any of three main styles for Effective Decision-Making however it is most often part of consultative decision-making. It is a powerful facilitation tool that supports Leading Through Narratives. The steps include the following (see Figure G.4):

1. *State the Decision*: Use a short phrase that describes the decision to be taken. What is the purpose of the decision? Who is the decision-maker?

2. *List and Weight Objectives:* What are the "must" objectives? What are the "want" objectives? What are the relative weights (1–10) between these "wants"? "Must" objectives are initial threshold conditions for filtering alternatives.

Decision Analysis is a powerful tool
for facilitating complex decisions because it surfaces and clarifies logic.

Decision Statement:
To recommend changes to the enterprise leader for segmenting businesses by geography.

Type of Objective	Objective	Weight	Alternative One East and West		Alternative Two North, South, East, West	
			Score	Subtotal	Score	Subtotal
Must	Don't add new distributors		Passes		Passes	
Want	Focus on local competitive advantage	10	*7	=70	*10	=100
Want	Minimize complexity	5	*10	=50	*8	=40
	Total Scores		=120		**=140**	

This alternative has the highest total score
but what are the risks? Is it the best-balanced choice?

FIGURE G.4   Example Decision Analysis

3. *List and Score Alternatives:* What are the "alternatives" to be evaluated? How do the "wants" score for each "alternative"? What are the total scores (weight × scores)?

4. *Best Balanced Choice:* Are the risks for the highest-scoring "alternative" acceptable, and if not, is the next-highest scorer the best choice?

Decision Mechanism   refers to the process for driving a decision to closure in a team or organization. An Effective Decision-Making process requires an effective decision mechanism. See **Final Call.**

Depersonalizing Conflicts   refers to team members empathizing with the roles that others play and understanding the perspectives that they bring. This behavior relates to Leveraging Creative Tensions as well as Giving and Receiving Feedback.

Design Thinking   refers to an approach for being customer-centric by designing solutions and solving problems based on empathy and customer-needs analysis. Books and courses on Design Thinking are widely available. This process links to Customer and Stakeholder Analysis and to User stories.

Differential Advantage   is a term used mostly in not-for-profit organizations and institutions to describe the core principles of competitive advantage, but with a higher emphasis on value delivered than on profit generated. See **Four Metrics for Competitive Advantage**.

Directive Leadership Stage 2   refers to companies in the second of the four Enterprise Evolutionary Stages. In this stage, a single intact business leadership team leads the organization with the goal of nailing and scaling one business model. Functional capabilities are organized to support this business model. Aligned leadership is based on autocratic decision-making by the leader of the business and team, as required. See **Enterprise Evolutionary Stages**.

Disruption   refers to radical changes to circumstances that make new ways of working necessary. Event horizons are a way to think about the impact, experience, and leadership challenges of disruption. Teams that seek to identify and resolve primary constraints are in practice seeking to self-disrupt.

Distributed Leadership   refers to a system of roles in which decision-making powers are delegated across hierarchical levels and assigned to leaders closest to value creation. Leveraging distributed leadership is the key to creating flat agile organizations. It is an objective in stage 3 and 4 companies. This links to the Capabilities and Roles crucial conversation. See **Enterprise Evolutionary Stages**.

Distributed Leadership Stage 3 refers to companies in the third of the Four Enterprise Evolutionary Stages. In this stage, the organization is a portfolio of capabilities that serve multiple business models and segments. It has been restructured into a team-based matrix, based on intact high-performance teams (HPTs). Aligned leadership is driven mostly by consultative decision-making, direct conflict resolution, and other HPT ways of working. Decisions are only rarely escalated for autocratic decision-making by the enterprise leader. See **Enterprise Evolutionary Stages** and **Single Journey Owners**.

Dynamic Interpersonal Relationships refers to members building intentional relationships in which there is a dynamic back-and-forth conversation toward mutual success, learning, and leadership development. Such relationships are critical to building high-performing teams. This behavior links to Accountability for Leadership Impact. And it relates to Setting the Stage for the 7 Crucial Conversations. See **Sensing**.

Effective Decision-Making refers to team members practicing a transparent decision-making process that is informed by the minimum number of relevant perspectives. There are three main styles of decision-making:

1. *Autocratic*: One person, usually the leader, decides with minimal input from team members, who are expected to comply with the decision.

2. *Consultative*: With input from the team, and process support from a Single Journey owner, a call is made by a designated decision-maker and communicated with clear rationale. Although agreement may be desired, alignment will be expected. A decision analysis process may be used to structure this alignment conversation. To achieve alignment, it may be necessary to clarify a date or other conditions for when it will be okay for team members to revisit the decision.

3. *Consensus*: All team members are involved in agreeing on a course of action (majority rule). Individual team members may have veto power. Once the decision is reached, all team members are expected to comply.

Growth River's experience with many different teams shows that the decision-making style that allows a team to become high performing is somewhere between consultative and autocratic. Ideally, the team leader has the authority to make critical decisions but does so with input from team members—as it makes the logic and rationale for decisions transparent. See **Decision Analysis**. This links to the Activating Purpose crucial conversation.

Engaged Response refers to team members designing strategies and solutions by collaborating across business and functional roles. The objective is a healthy top-down and bottom-up conversation, which is especially critical in transformation where change impacts many stakeholders (e.g. Straightening the Spaghetti). This links to the Specifying Capabilities and Roles crucial conversation.

Enterprise refers to a matrix structure that includes functional capabilities supporting multiple business segments/business triangles. The Enterprise Map is a tool for visualizing an enterprise. A mature stage 3 enterprise will have a complete System of Teams. This links to the Specifying Capabilities and Roles crucial conversation. See **Enterprise Evolutionary Stages.**

Enterprise Change Team refers to a subteam that works closely with an enterprise leader to plan and guide the HPT transformational journey of an enterprise team. Enterprise change teams are essential for scaling and sustaining HPT ways of working in companies. See **Change Team.**

Enterprise Evolutionary Stages is a model that describes the natural journey that all companies go through as they grow and scale through stages. This links to Setting the Stage for the 7 Crucial Conversations. See Figure G.5 depicts the Enterprise Evolutionary Stages.

- *Stage 1, Independent Contributors:* A loose confederation of partners, each with its own business approach. Central leadership is based on achieving consensus among senior partners.

- *Stage 2, Directive Leadership:* A single intact business leadership team leads the organization to nail and scale one business model. Functional capabilities are organized to support this business model.

- *Stage 3, Distributed Leadership:* The organization is a portfolio of capabilities that serve multiple business models and segments. It has been restructured into a team-based matrix based on intact high-performing teams (HPTs). Aligned leadership is driven

The Evolutionary Stages Clock is a way to visualize the Four Stages
What time is it for your company?

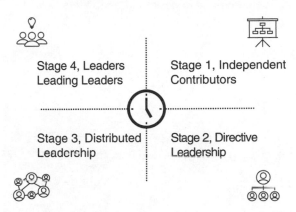

Stage 4, Leaders
Leading Leaders

Stage 1, Independent
Contributors

Stage 3, Distributed
Leadership

Stage 2, Directive
Leadership

FIGURE G.5   The Evolutionary Stages Clock

chiefly by consultative decision-making, direct conflict resolution, and other ways of working. The enterprise leader only rarely escalates decisions for autocratic decision-making.

- *Stage 4, Leaders Leading Leaders:* The enterprise has developed the capabilities to build and support self-managing teams. The organizational structure is a flat agile team matrix. Aligned leadership is driven by consultative decision-making, direct conflict resolution, and other HPT ways of working. Only rarely are decisions escalated to the enterprise leader.

Enterprise Journey Awareness   refers to team members being clear about how the company creates value and governs itself and what needs to change to grow and scale. Pragmatically, to effectively engage and align teams toward business transformation, leaders need to create enterprise journey awareness. This way of working relates to Enterprise Evolutionary Stages and Primary Constraint Analysis. It links to Setting the Stage for the 7 Crucial Conversations.

Enterprise Maps   are a way to visualize a matrix of business triangles and functional capabilities. The various business segments will be on one axis and the four types of capabilities on the other, and it will show the intersection points between them (see Figures G.6 and G.15).

Enterprise Strategy Map   refers to a system of strategy documents that captures the critical dimensions and objectives of a company's enterprise strategy. Businesses segments and functional

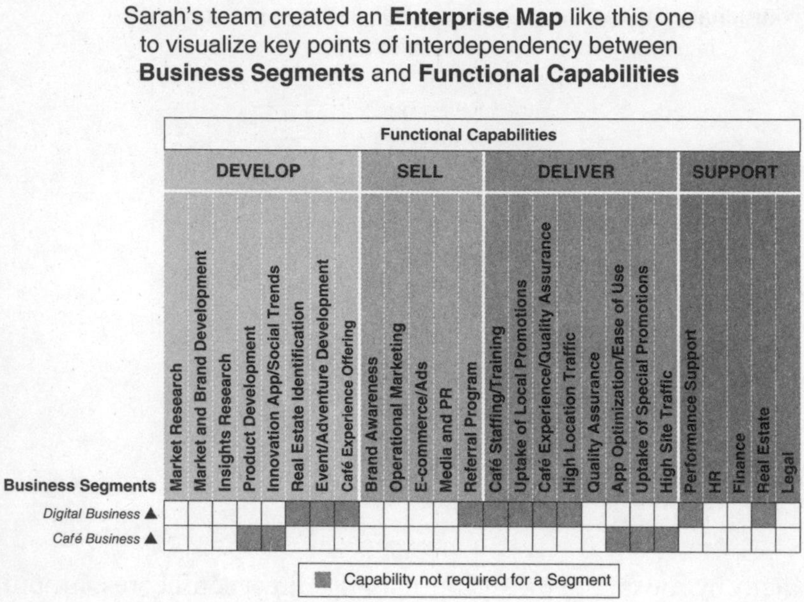

Sarah's team created an **Enterprise Map** like this one to visualize key points of interdependency between **Business Segments** and **Functional Capabilities**

Functional Capabilities																									
DEVELOP								SELL					DELIVER								SUPPORT				
Market Research	Market and Brand Development	Insights Research	Product Development	Innovation App/Social Trends	Real Estate Identification	Event/Adventure Development	Café Experience Offering	Brand Awareness	Operational Marketing	E-commerce/Ads	Media and PR	Referral Program	Café Staffing/Training	Uptake of Local Promotions	Café Experience/Quality Assurance	High Location Traffic	Quality Assurance	App Optimization/Ease of Use	Uptake of Special Promotions	High Site Traffic	Performance Support	HR	Finance	Real Estate	Legal

Business Segments — Digital Business ▲ — Café Business ▲

Capability not required for a Segment

FIGURE G.6 Example Enterprise Map

capabilities strategies should align with enterprise objectives. This cascade of strategy documents may include:

1. Enterprise Purpose
2. Enterprise Culture
3. Enterprise Brand Promise
4. Enterprise Value Promise
5. Target Market Scope
6. Business Segment Scope
7. Product and Service Scope
8. Enterprise Capabilities and Basis for Competitive Advantage
9. Enterprise Operating Model/Organizational Structure

Enterprise Strategy refers to team members being clear about the overall enterprise strategy and any impact it should have on the team's strategy. Enterprise Strategy Maps are used to summarize enterprise strategies. This links to the Aligning Strategies crucial conversation.

Managing the uncertainty before and after **Event Horizons** is a core part of leading transformational change.

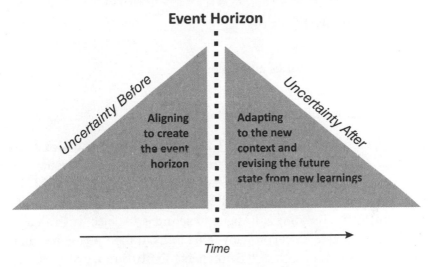

FIGURE G.7   Uncertainty Before and After an Event Horizon

Event Horizons   refers to team members accounting for moments in time beyond which they cannot plan and, as such, calibrating energy and time invested in speculation in order to stay focused on actionable conversations. Managing the uncertainty before and after event horizons is a fundamental leadership challenge, which is critical to controlling the speed of change (see Figure G.7). Event horizons often relate to primary constraints being resolved. This behavior links to Transformational Journey Mindset and Agile Innovation.

Facilitation   refers to the skills, methods, and tools that a facilitator uses to guide a group through crucial conversations to adopt new ways of working and behaviors, to align decisions, and take actions to achieve a common goal. The Seven Crucial Conversations is a powerful framework for facilitation.

Final Call   refers to the mechanism or process for driving a decision to closure in a team or organization. See **Effective Decision-Making**.

Five Pathways   refers to a process for analyzing the optimal focus for a company on its unfolding transformational journey. The approach is for team members to discuss and analyze the pattern of primary constraints in the following five pathways and then to align roles and priorities accordingly. The five pathways include:

1. Leadership Effectiveness
2. Team Effectiveness
3. Systems of Capabilities and Roles
4. System of Strategies
5. Metrics for Competitive Advantage

This is a type of Stack Analysis. See **Cascades of Key Conditions.**

Flat Agile Organizations refers to a team matrix organization in which the top team is a high-performing transformational leadership team. The subteams reporting into it are high-performing teams or self-managing teams. Building a flat agile structure is an objective in a stage 4 leaders leading leaders company. This links to the Capabilities and Roles crucial conversation. See **Enterprise Evolutionary Stages.**

Forecasting and Budgeting Resources refers to team members planning and forecasting capacity to deliver. This way of working links to the Implementing Initiatives crucial conversation.

Four Business Capability Types refers to team members distinguishing between four fundamental capabilities around the business triangle. Each type has a different purpose, as shown in Figure G.8.

Four Metrics for Competitive Advantage refers to a method for aligning decisions and strategies toward competitive advantage. The

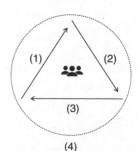

The Business Triangle in Action

Four types of capabilities...

△ (1) **Develop** winning products, services, and value propositions

◁ (2) **Sell** to create perfect purchase moments

△ (3) **Deliver** value and generate positive referrals

△ (4) **Support** economies of scale

...are executed through a system of roles...

(1)　(2)

(3)

(4)

...to create competitive advantage...

✓ Market potential
✓ Operational scalability
✓ Business model sustainability
✓ Financial performance

FIGURE G.8 The Business Triangle in Action

root question is—what ideal outcomes characterize an optimal business investment? There are four: (1) 100% share of a target market, (2) no constraints to meeting demand, (3) no significant business risks, and (4) above average returns. The Four Metrics for Competitive Advantage are an application of that logic—competitive advantage means having the attributes of an optimal business investment. They include:

1. Market Potential—team members prioritize choices that optimize demand for the company in its target market. The ideal is 100% share. It is to be "the alternative of choice" for all key stakeholders, including:

   a. Provider of choice

   b. Employer of choice

   c. Channel partner of choice

   d. Investment of choice

   e. Community member of choice

2. Operational Scalability—team members prioritize choices that eliminate constraints to the company meeting demand in a target market. The ideal is no constraints.

3. Business Model Sustainability—team members prioritize choices that minimize risks to the company's performance and to its key capabilities. The ideal is no significant business risks.

4. Financial Returns—team members prioritize choices that best mitigate financial risks and optimize financial returns. The ideal is above average returns.

Between strategic trade-offs or between competing investment opportunities, the optimal choice will be the one expected to most contribute toward these four metrics in the order of the cascade. This robust logic cuts through inherent biases, enabling all members in a team and all teams in a company to fly in formation toward overall competitive advantage. See **Decision Analysis** and **Cascades of Key Conditions**.

Function refers to a type of role that is responsible for execution in a business or enterprise. The term can be applied with different levels of strategic sophistication. In less strategically mature organizations, *function* is simply a moniker for a nonexecutive role, job, or team with an area of expertise, such as marketing, sales, or quality. However, in companies with greater strategic sophistication, in which teams Analyze Capabilities, a *function* is a label for a cluster of closely related capabilities. So, for example, the marketing function will be responsible for managing and improving capabilities that include market research, customer experience, market messaging, and so forth. Functions are responsible for formulating and aligning functional capability strategies. See **System of Teams**.

Functional-Capability Strategies refers to team members creating and aligning functional-capability strategies. The objective is for these functional strategies to align with business segment strategies and enterprise strategy. This links to the Aligning Strategies crucial conversation. See **System of Strategies**.

Functional leader refers to the leader of a function, a functional team, or a capabilities leadership team. This links to the Capabilities and Roles crucial conversation. See **Business Triangle**.

Functionitis refers to problematic situations in which functional-capability teams override the business or enterprise perspective, causing growth to stagnate or stop. It is often a situation in which horizontal improvement is being achieved at the expense of vertical improvement. See **Vertical and Horizontal Balance**. Functionitis is a system-of-roles problem that relates to the Specifying Capabilities and Roles crucial conversation. The solution is a complete System of Roles and System of Teams enabled to leverage creative tensions.

Gap Analysis refers to a method of analysis. A checklist of conditions or criteria of success is created (these are the "shoulds"). Data is applied to identify performance gaps in these conditions (which are called the "actuals"). Then priorities and plans are created to resolve the performance gaps in the "actuals." See **Transformational Journey Map**.

Game-changer refers to an event that resolves one or more primary constraints across a stack of subsystems. When radical transformation occurs in companies or industries, it is the result of game-changers. An example is an innovative product, service, or organizational change that resolves constraints in marketing, sales, and delivery. See **Stack Analysis.**

Giving and Receiving Feedback refers to a way of working in which team members demonstrate being responsible for the success of others through giving and receiving feedback. This way of working is vital to creating and restoring trust and therefore fundamental to developing high-performing teams. It links to the Shifting Mindset crucial conversation.

Grand Unveiling   refers to a situation in which a plan or solution is presented as a done deal without creating sufficient input and buy-in from key stakeholders or customers. See **Agile Innovation**.

Growth River   refers to a company that is dedicated to unleashing the potential of leaders and teams to grow and scale businesses through proven ways of working. See **Growth River OS**.

Growth River Operating System (OS)   refers to the system of thought presented in this glossary. The objective is to systematically build high-performing teams that grow and scale companies toward competitive advantage. See **Setting the Stage for the 7 Crucial Conversations.**

Guiding Coalitions   refers to change leadership approach. The challenge is for team members to structure and manage guiding coalitions that create two-way collaborative relationships with larger target audiences with the goal of creating adoption of change. This links to Setting the Stage for the 7 Crucial Conversations.

High Performing Company   refers to a company in which high-performing teams come together and align to create business competitive advantage. High-performing companies are a natural result of applying the 7 Crucial Conversations with the top leadership teams in a company over time.

High-performing Company Journey   refers to the sequence of event horizons, milestones, and breakthrough experiences that comprise a company's optimal journey toward higher performance. The purpose of the Seven Crucial Conversations is to build high-performing teams that lead and manage high-performing company journeys.

High-performing Team Journey   refers to the sequence of event horizons, milestones, and breakthrough experiences that comprise a team's journey toward higher performance. The purpose of the Seven Crucial Conversations is to accelerate high-performing team journeys that, effectively navigate the swirl, and ultimately create high-performing companies.

High-performing team (HPT)   refers to an intact team with a single team leader developed toward higher performance through intentional ways of working. The purpose of the Seven Crucial Conversations is to build and sustain high-performing teams. See **Team Structures.**

High-performing Team Connectors   refer to individuals who are members of more than one team. They can be leaders of one team

HPT Connectors are members of different teams, who play important roles helping to scale ways of working across teams and organizations.

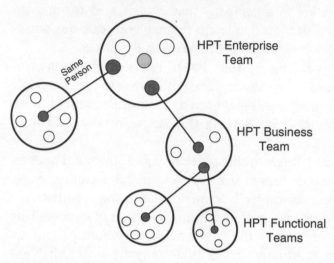

FIGURE G.9 HPT Connectors

and members of another. Connectors help to align teams, and they also model best practices across the system of teams (see Figure G.9).

Home team refers to a team in which a given member is peer but is not the the team leader. For example, the home team for a marketing executive is the senior leadership team, where she is expected to give and receive peer-to-peer feedback. In contrast, the marketing team for which she is the team leader is not her home team. Home teams can be a powerful distinction for developing and leveraging strong dynamic peer-to-peer relationships and creating accountable organizations. A common misinterpretation of this idea is that your home team is one that you lead or a place where you spend most of your time; this may or may not be the case.

Horizontal Improvement refers to improving the performance of a system by managing or optimizing conditions at the present limiting constraint while not resolving the constraint itself.

Horizontal versus Vertical Improvement refers to two fundamental approaches towards continuous improvement (see Figure G.10). See **Vertical and Horizontal Balance**.

Independent Contributors Stage 1 refers to companies in the first of the four Enterprise Evolutionary Stages. In this stage, a loose

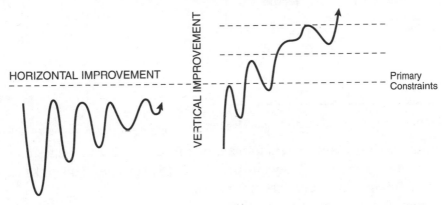

Horizontal Improvement is about keeping the trains running on time, whereas **Vertical Improvement** is about adding new track. The Creative Tension between these two perspectives drives innovation and people development.

FIGURE G.10   Vertical and Horizontal Improvement

confederation of allies has joined forces, and a nascent business is born. The goal of the group is to pool resources, but it is not necessarily to align as a single business. Aligned leadership in the group is based on consensus. See **Enterprise Evolutionary Stages.**

Influence Analysis   refers to assessing the levels of influence in a Stakeholder and Customer Analysis as a basis for planning how to best lead change. Influence can be of two kinds. Power to promote: some roles will have the power to promote your purpose and solutions. These will be the target partners in your coalition who you will need to assist you in selling or advocating internally or externally. Power to block: some roles will have the power to block your purpose and solutions. These will be a target audience for your change narrative and to influence through your guiding coalition. The roles with the most influence will have both the power to promote and block. These will be your target customers. This links to Setting the Stage for the 7 Crucial Conversations.

Innovation   refers to a process for creating better solutions to meet new requirements, unarticulated customer needs, or existing needs. See **Vertical and Horizontal Improvement.**

Interdependencies   refer to team members managing and improving the points of intersection between roles or teams. This links to the Streamlining Interdependencies crucial conversation.

Two Conceptions of Time
that drive different meeting agendas

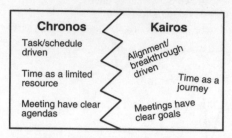

Chronos

Task/schedule driven

Time as a limited resource

Meeting have clear agendas

Kairos

Alignment/ breakthrough driven

Time as a journey

Meetings have clear goals

FIGURE G.11 Chronos versus Kairos Meetings

Issue Action Lists refers to team members prioritizing issues and concerns to routinely review, track, and drive closure. This links to the Driving Focus crucial conversation.

Intact Teams refers teams that have a single team leader who is responsible for team performance, dynamics, accountability, and continuous improvement. See **Leadership Mechanism**.

Kairos and Chronos Balance refers to two Greek words for time and to two types of meeting agendas. *Chronos* refers to thinking about time as a limited resource allocated to tasks and constrained by resources. Chronos meetings have clear agendas and a tight schedule. *Kairos,* on the other hand, is what happens when we immerse ourselves in crucial conversations around goals and realities. (See Figure G.11.) Participants work together to process complex topics— studying, listening, sensing, designing, choosing, and aligning. This links to the Driving Focus crucial conversation.

Law of the Lid refers to team members recognizing when their leadership is the lid on team or company performance. The principle is that a team or company can never sustain performance at a higher level than its leader(s). John Maxwell initially proposed it. This law links to the Activating Purpose crucial conversation.

Leaders Leading Leaders Stage 4 refers to companies in the fourth of the four Enterprise Evolutionary Stages. In this stage, the enterprise has developed the systems needed to charter and support agile self-managing teams, at the level below intact teams that are required at senior enterprise, business, and functional capability levels. The organizational structure is flat, with the fewest required intact teams at the top and self-managing teams reporting into those teams. Aligned leadership is driven by consultative decision-making, direct conflict resolution, and other HPT ways of working. Decisions are only rarely escalated for autocratic decision-making by the enterprise leader. See **Enterprise Evolutionary Stages.**

Leadership refers to the art and the science of building relationships that inspire, guide, and develop people to align and navigate the uncertainty of change. Leadership is critical to the Activating Purpose crucial conversation.

Leadership and Culture refers to the first of the Three Domains of Change. See **Three Domains of Change.**

Leadership Clearing refers to team leaders having the license to address factors that undermine team purpose. This license includes removing toxic rock stars and resolving other dysfunctions. This behavior links to Team Charter. See **Intact Teams**.

Leadership Mechanism refers to the idea that teams require an effective mechanism for defining purpose, clarifying roles, setting goals, taking decisions, and ensuring alignment. In an intact team that mechanism is a single leader who is responsible for team performance, member development, and strategic alignment. See **Team Structures**.

Leading Through Narratives refers to team members framing challenges in writing to clarify logic, test thinking, and drive alignment. Narratives are an essential tool for leading change, creating alignment, and building Guiding Coalitions. The key to a good narrative is clear, concise communication, focusing on articulating the Challenge Statement first. This links to Setting the Stage for the 7 Crucial Conversations.

Leveraging Creative Tensions refers to team members leveraging creative tensions between different perspectives and roles as sources of accountability, insight, learning, and innovation. There are Natural Creative Tensions between: the roles of team members and team leaders, the roles responsible for the Four Business Capability Types around the business triangle (Develop, Sell, Deliver, and Support), and the Operational Purposes of different types of teams in a System of Teams. At times, these tensions might be personalized as conflict, or viewed as blockers to innovation rather than supporting it. However, creative tensions can and should be leveraged as a source of insight and innovation under the right conditions. This way of working depends on Depersonalizing Conflicts. (See Figure G.12.) This links to the Specifying Capabilities and Roles crucial conversation.

The objective is to design in **Creative Tensions** as sources of innovation and people development.

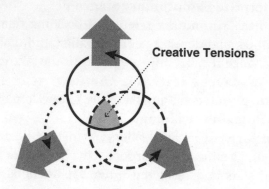

Creative Tensions

- Creative Tensions are the natural result of opposing values, roles, or perspectives.

- The objective is to design in all the roles and perspectives needed for a successful outcome.

- Ongoing creativity and innovation is the result, because no single idea or solution will perfectly satisfy all roles and perspectives.

FIGURE G.12 Creative Tensions

Limiting Stories and Beliefs   refers to team members managing stories and beliefs that negatively impact perceptions and performance. Examples include: "My teammates don't respect my skills and expertise because I'm new on this team." "My team leader gives all the best projects to the teammates who are loud and ask for it. I'm not like that, so I have no chance here." Often, we are so habituated by our self-talk that we have become unconscious that these limiting beliefs and stories are blockers. It cannot be overstated how important it is for team members to become aware of their own limiting stories and beliefs and manage them. This links to the Shifting Mindset conversation.

Manifesting Team Purpose   refers to putting a purpose or intention into physical reality through thought, feelings, and beliefs. It means that whatever you focus on is what you are bringing into your reality. The 7 Crucial Conversations are a cascade of conditions for teams to manifest their purposes. See **Cascades of Key Conditions.**

Measuring Performance   refers to team members assessing progress against people, process, and business metrics. This links to the Implementing Initiatives crucial conversation.

Natural Path (or Natural Development Path) refers to the order in which transformation naturally unfolds in a complex adaptive social system, like a team or company. It comprises the best sequence for you to drive performance improvements in a complex system for maximum impact, and minimum resistance. See the **Three Domains of Change.**

Natural Creative Tensions see Creative Tensions. Nirvana Meeting refers to an optimal strategic alignment process. In this ideal process, business segment leaders will present their business strategies, then functional capability leaders will respond with their functional strategies; natural creative tensions and conflicts will surface key strategic trade-offs, which will be resolved by the enterprise team, toward overall competitive advantage. See **Strategic Planning Process.**

Onboarding Team Members refers to team members orienting new members to the team's purpose, priorities, behaviors, and ways of working. The objective is to acclimate new team members to the team's leadership mindset and shared ways of working. This links to the Aligning between roles way of working.

Operational Purpose Statements refers to statements in team charters that describe a team's shared value streams. Types of teams in the system of teams will have different operational purposes. This links to the Activating Purpose crucial conversation. See Figure G16.

Optimal Path refers to the ideal sequence of interventions or event horizons for evolving a complex system toward higher performance. The Three Domains of Change are a natural path that helps to reveal the optimal paths for leading social systems to higher performance. Primary constraint analysis reveals optimal paths. See **Primary Constraint.**

Organizational Structure refers to how organizations divide roles, authority, and reporting relationships. This links to the Specifying Capabilities and Roles crucial conversation.

Organizational Swirl (the Swirl) refers to a state of inertia in which teams and companies become so absorbed in the whirl of everyday problems, dramas, and turf battles that they don't feel motivated to think more clearly about a shared journey toward higher performance. The Seven Crucial Conversations are designed to enable teams and companies to break free of the Swirl. See **Seven Crucial Conversations.**

Primary Constraint refers to the one key condition that currently most limits higher sustainable throughput or performance in the system. All systems will have a single primary constraint. Once you identify the primary constraint, you have two choices. You can choose to resolve it, and then the new one will emerge to take its place, requiring you to plan and manage any related event horizons. This process is called Vertical Performance Improvement. Alternatively, you can choose to optimize at the constraint, meaning that you intend to keep it where it is and use it as a single point of control for managing the system. This process is called Horizontal Performance Improvement. See **Cascades of Key Conditions.**

Primary Constraint Analysis refers to team members analyzing those blockers that will have the most significant impact on performance when managed or resolved. See **Cascades of Key Conditions.**

Project management refers to the process of planning and leading the work of a team to achieve all project goals within the given constraints. This links to the Implementing Initiatives crucial conversation.

Responsibilities are duties to act. These duties relate to the Specifying Capabilities and Roles crucial conversation. See **Accountabilities.**

Role refers to the function, responsibilities, and accountabilities assumed by a person or a team in a particular situation, scenario, or system. Roles are the building blocks of organizational structures. Roles may be defined by their title; however, they are much more than the title itself. A role definition should include a variety of aspects of daily work, including responsibilities, accountabilities, interdependencies, and business capabilities. This links to Architecting Systems of Roles.

Scrum refers to an agile development methodology for teams to design, validate, and test solutions in an iterative and adaptive way. See **Agile Innovation** and **Versioning.**

Sensing refers to a way of working in which leaders intentionally create and apply dynamic learning relationships with other leaders to clarify shared intentions, surface intuitions, and creatively follow a gut sense to anticipate and define risks and create opportunities. What is the ideal future state for the company? What are the gaps in the current state? What are the target milestones and breakthroughs for the company, as an adaptive social system? Ideally, the top leadership team is a sensing team, operating from a strategic purpose-driven perspective. See **Dynamic Interpersonal Relationships.**

Setting the Stage for the 7 Crucial Conversations   refers to the conversation that creates understanding and buy-in to the Seven Crucial Conversations as a basis for building high-performing teams. This book is designed to help with that.

Seven Crucial Conversations   (the 7CCs®) is a system of thought for building teams and growing and scaling companies toward competitive advantage through an optimal sequence of crucial conversations. This sequence aligns with the natural path of the three domains of change. As such, the 7 Crucial Conversations are a roadmap for transforming teams and companies. They include:

1. Activating Purpose
2. Driving Focus
3. Shifting Mindset
4. Specifying Capabilities and Roles
5. Streamlining Interdependencies
6. Aligning Strategies
7. Implementing Initiatives

These Seven Crucial Conversations play several roles in the journey of a team and organization. They establish the key conditions that a transformational template is based on. Each conversation includes specific ways of working that outline the basic ways in which the team is are going to interact and work together, becoming a shared language for a team's performance and growth.

Seven Crucial Conversations and the Three Domains of Change. See **Three Domains of Change.**

Shared Purpose   refers to the reason a team or company aligns to create value and for which it exists. See **Team Charter**.

Single Journey Owners   refers to team members assigning each important topic to a "single journey owner" with clear accountability for resolution. This practice is an essential element in Effective Decision-Making, and it relates to the Activating Purpose crucial conversation.

Social Systems, Not Machines   refers to team members envisioning and leading teams and companies as systems of evolving relationships between people. They recognize that teams and companies are complex adaptive social systems, not mechanistic systems and that these systems evolve through crucial conversations, which require building dynamic interpersonal relationships. The Three Domains of Change describe how change naturally unfolds in these systems. This links to Setting the Stage for the 7 Crucial Conversations.

Socialware refers to a system for working together in a social system that enables higher performance through shared ways of working. It is an upgrade for the human system in the same way that software can be an upgrade for a computer system. See **Social Systems, Not Machines** and **Seven Crucial Conversations**.

Solving Conflicts at the Source refers to team members resolving conflicts directly, crossing hierarchical and functional lines as needed. This behavior is critical to giving and receiving feedback. It is also essential to Leveraging Creative Tensions, Aligning between roles, and Aligning Between Teams.

Speech Acts refers to how some words and phrases are most pivotal to conversations, changing and aligning shared understanding around situations, relationships, and probable outcomes—for example, "you're fired," "I'm sorry," and "I'd like your help on this project." Speech Acts links to Compelling Requests.

Stack Analysis refers to team members applying an approach to analyze primary constraints for each level in a stack and then using the pattern to surface game-changers. A stack is a visualization of the set of components or subsystems needed for a complete platform or solution. See **Five Pathways.**

Stakeholder and Customer Analysis refers to team members validating the perspectives and needs of customers and stakeholders as a basis to define value. It involves identifying the customer and stakeholder groups for which the team creates value and then drafting and validating user stories. This way of working links to the Activating Purpose crucial conversation. See **Influence Analysis** and **User Stories.**

Straightening the Spaghetti refers to team members versioning and aligning capabilities, roles, and strategies to resolve redundancy and duplication toward higher performance. The challenge is that the circular interdependencies between strategies, capabilities, and roles make it necessary to iterate solutions. Each iteration must be thoughtfully led. An objective for high-performing teams is to navigate these iterations and event horizons with grace and style. (See Figure G.13.) This links to the Capabilities and Roles crucial conversation.

Straightening the Spaghetti means versioning and aligning Capabilities, Roles, and Strategies.

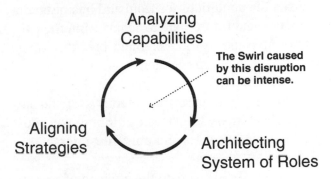

FIGURE G.13 Straightening the Spaghetti

Strategic Planning Process   refers to the activities and meetings by which strategies are formulated, advocated, and aligned in a system of strategies. See **Nirvana Meeting**.

Strategies and Customer Experience   refers to the third of the three domains of change. See **Three Domains of Change.**

Strategy Canvases   refer to one- or two-page documents used to summarize, discuss, and align strategies. The Business Triangle is applied in the Growth River OS to structure business strategy canvases. See Figure G.14.

The Business Triangle is applied to structure Strategy Canvases.

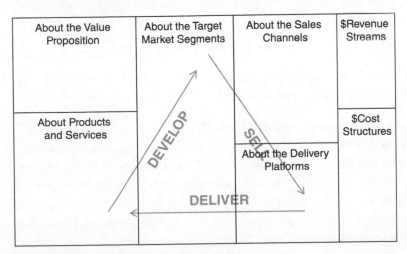

FIGURE G.14   The Business Strategy Canvas

Strategy refers to a framework of choices designed to achieve a particular goal. Ideally, these choices guide everyday work and decision-making to create the conditions for team and business success. Strategies outline the ideal future state to achieve and the path forward, including current priorities and planned breakthroughs. See the Aligning Strategies crucial conversation.

Swirl. See **Organizational Swirl**.

System refers to a group of things or parts that interact to create outputs or outcomes. To apply Primary Constraint Thinking you must visualize the system, describing its parts and how they interact. See **Systems Thinking**.

System of Capabilities and Roles refers to the division of responsibilities and authority between roles for managing and improving specific capabilities. This links to the Capabilities and Roles crucial conversation. See **Straightening the Spaghetti**.

System of Customers refers to the roles that different customers play at the center of the business triangle. Types of customers in this system include:

- Channels/Channel Partners: Resell or deliver your products and services.

- Clients/End Users: Use your products and services.

- Payers/Buyers: Pay for your products and services. It could be the same as clients/end users, but not necessarily.

- Gatekeepers: Control access to channels, clients/end-users, and payers.

- Influencers: Influence the choices of other roles.

- Markets/Personas: Types of customers that are grouped by similar attributes for focus and influence.

See **Stakeholder and Customer Analysis.**

System of Meetings refers to team members organizing meetings to cover the full scope of their shared work. This planning process includes team members setting aside time to work both *in* and *on* the business, with Chronos and Kairos agendas that balance vertical and horizontal improvement. This links to the Awareness of Focus. See **Kairos and Chronos Balance**.

System of Roles refers to the division of roles within a team or organization. For a team, the system of roles depends on the purpose and the type of team and the capabilities to be managed. In a complete system of roles, every key issue, concern, capability, creative tension, and strategy has a capable owner and advocate. See **Architecting Systems of Roles**. See Figure G.19.

System of Strategies refers to team members being clear about how the team's strategy aligns with and contributes to business and functional strategies. This way of working links to the Aligning Strategies crucial conversation. The seven types of strategies provide an excellent taxonomy for the different kinds of strategies in a complete enterprise system of strategies:

1. Enterprise Strategy

2. Business Segment Strategies

3. Develop Functional Capability Strategies

4. Sell Functional Capability Strategies

5. Channel Strategies (for those companies that need them)

6. Deliver Functional Capability Strategies

7. Support Functional Capability Strategies

System of teams refers to the different types of teams in a mature enterprise (see Figures G.15 and G.16). These types follow the logic of the Business Triangle. They are a helpful template for writing Team Charters as part of the Activating Purpose crucial conversation.

Systems Thinking refers to team members identifying, modeling, and analyzing systems. A system is a group of things or parts that interact to create outputs or outcomes. Analyzing a system begins with identifying its purpose, parts, critical interdependencies, and outcomes. See **Primary Constraint Analysis.**

Team refers to a group of people who work together to achieve a shared purpose. Teams are the building blocks for scaling companies for creating effective cultures in companies.

Team Charter refers to team members clarifying the team's purpose, outcomes, and in-team commitments. Different types of teams in a company's System of Teams will have different purposes. To truly activate purpose, team leaders must be licensed to create effective

What type is your team?

System of Teams
in an Enterprise Team Matrix

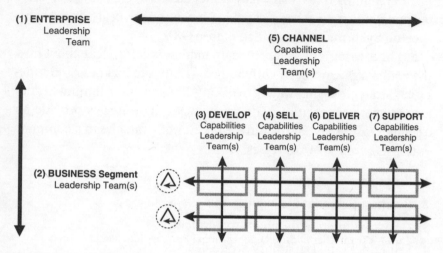

(1) ENTERPRISE Leadership Team

(5) CHANNEL Capabilities Leadership Team(s)

(3) DEVELOP Capabilities Leadership Team(s)

(4) SELL Capabilities Leadership Team(s)

(6) DELIVER Capabilities Leadership Team(s)

(7) SUPPORT Capabilities Leadership Team(s)

(2) BUSINESS Segment Leadership Team(s)

FIGURE G.15 System of Teams in an Enterprise Team Matrix

What is its **Operational Purpose**?

	Team Types	Operational Purpose Statements by Team Type (part of a Team Charter)
1	Enterprise Leadership Team	The purpose of an Enterprise Leadership Team is to lead, manage, and continuously improve a company's portfolio of businesses and functional capabilities toward overall competitive advantage.
2	Business Segment Leadership Team(s)	The purpose of a Business Segment Leadership Team is to lead and align Develop, Sell, Deliver, and Support capabilities to provide products and services to target customers in a way that creates targeted competitive advantage.
3	Develop Capability Leadership Team(s)	The purpose of a Develop Capability Leadership Team is to develop winning value propositions (including technologies, products, and services) for target end-users, channels, and buyers.
4	Channel Capability Leadership Teams(s)	The purpose of a Channel Capability Leadership Team is to lead and align Sell and Deliver capabilities to create perfect purchase moments with target channel partners in target markets for target buyers and target end-users and to provide a winning experience for all key stakeholders.
5	Sell Capability Leadership Team(s)	The purpose of a Sell Capability Leadership Team is to gain access to target markets and to create perfect purchase moments in target channels for target buyers.
6	Deliver Capability Leadership Team(s)	The purpose of a Deliver Capability Leadership Team is to deliver products and services through target channels to target end-users as promised and as a result to generate positive referrals.
7	Support Capability Team(s)	The purpose of a Support Capability Leadership Team is to provide support services and capabilities that create economies of scale or mitigate business risks for internal customers and stakeholders.

FIGURE G.16 Operational Purpose Statements by Team Type

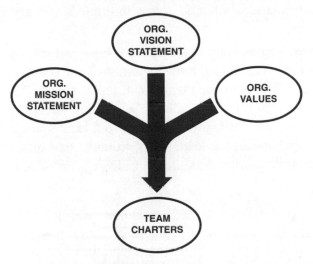

FIGURE G.17   Team Charters and Organizational Purpose Statements

Leadership Clearings. Naturally, team charters need to align with organizational purpose (see Figure G.17). This links to the Activating Purpose crucial conversation. See **System of Teams.**

Team   Structures refers to the different ways in which teams can be organized and led. Capabilities to build and sustain these different team structures roughly correspond to the four Enterprise Evolutionary Stages.

1. **Workgroups or Natural Teams** are a group working together to achieve common interests. The key point is that workgroups or natural teams are not led, designed, or developed intentionally as is the case with high-performing and self-managed teams.

2. **Intact Teams** are teams with a single team leader responsible for team performance, dynamics, accountability, and continuous improvement. The team leader is fully in it with the team, doing the work of the team.

3. **High-Performing Teams (HPTs)** are intact teams designed and developed intentionally by the team leader and by implementing specific ways of working, using an approach like the 7 Crucial Conversations.

4. **High-Performing Transformational Leadership Teams** are high-performing teams that are top leadership teams responsible for leading transformational change across multiple teams and stakeholder groups.

5. **High-Performing Self-Managed Teams** are high-performing teams that are not intact teams but have been trained and coached to be self-managing. Self-managing teams will report to a leader, but they will not necessarily have all the leadership strengths of intact teams. This kind of team will report to a leader, but it will not necessarily have all the leadership strengths that intact teams will have. Agile work teams are typically a form of self-managed teams.

Throughput   refers to the flow through rate and capacity of a system to create intended value in a given time frame. See **Systems Thinking.**

Three Domains of Change   refer to the Natural Path by which transformation unfolds in social systems, including teams and companies.

Toxic Rock Star   refers to an individual who plays a critical role in the success of a team, business, or organization and has a negative impact on the effectiveness of others and organizational culture. Managing toxic rock stars and other sources of resistance is critical to leading change. See **Leadership Clearing.**

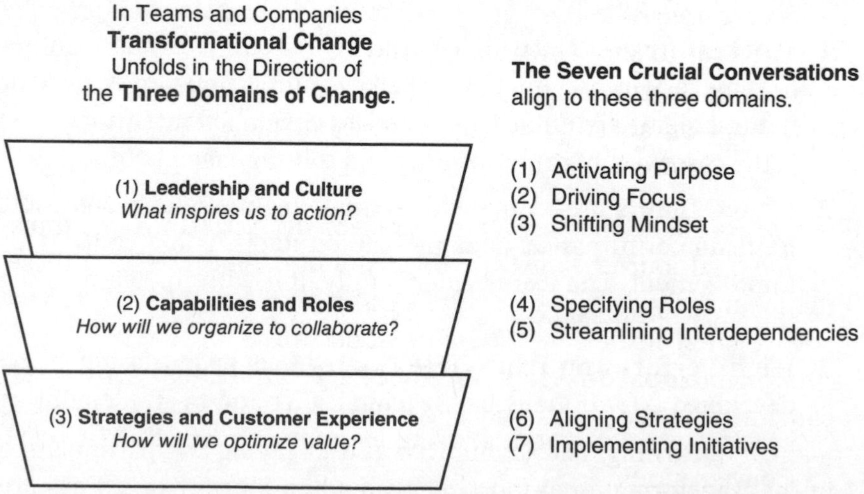

In Teams and Companies
Transformational Change
Unfolds in the Direction of
the **Three Domains of Change**.

The Seven Crucial Conversations
align to these three domains.

(1) **Leadership and Culture**
What inspires us to action?

(1) Activating Purpose
(2) Driving Focus
(3) Shifting Mindset

(2) **Capabilities and Roles**
How will we organize to collaborate?

(4) Specifying Roles
(5) Streamlining Interdependencies

(3) **Strategies and Customer Experience**
How will we optimize value?

(6) Aligning Strategies
(7) Implementing Initiatives

FIGURE G.18   The Seven Crucial Conversations and Three Domains of Change

Transformational Change refers to a shift in how something works that is significant, fundamental, and irreversible. In living systems, like teams or organizations, transformational change is a shift in leadership mindset or business culture, leading to profound changes in the organization's ways of being and working.

Transformational Change Leadership refers to the art and the science of planning and leading transformational change and transformational journeys.

Transformational Journey Map refers to team members mapping the team's journey from the current state to the ideal future state and planning steps on the journey. This links to the Driving Focus crucial conversation. Envisioning that "ideal future state" is the first step in being on a transformational journey together. The following is a four-step process for mapping out a shared transformational journey for a team, business, or organization.

1. *A Vision for a Better Future:* What is the ideal future state you're working toward?

2. *The Urgent Need for Change:* What is the current state, including the gaps and constraints?

3. *Priorities for Tomorrow:* Given those gaps and that ideal, what are your priorities from today to tomorrow? How can you get your immediate needs met? What initiatives will drive horizontal optimization of your current state?

4. *Breakthroughs to the Future:* What are the breakthroughs you're targeting to move from tomorrow to the future? What do we need to learn? What skills do we need to master? What initiatives or ahead-of-the-curve investments will drive vertical transformation?

If you're not aligned around these four elements, you're not on a transformational journey together. Once you are aligned around these, the team truly comes into focus. And it removes the anxiety that change often creates. See **Primary Constraints**.

Transformational Journey Mindset refers to team members recognizing that the path of change will reveal itself through engagement and learning. They commit to fully engaging and participating in the transformational journey; even when journey outcomes are unknown, there are event horizons to manage and breakthrough experiences to facilitate. This links to Setting the Stage for the 7 Crucial Conversations.

Trust   refers to a belief or an experience that something is reliable, dependable, and true. In leadership, trust is a belief bestowed to unleash human potential. In relationships, trust is the residue of kept commitments. Broken trust is restored through giving and receiving feedback.

User Stories   refers to a format for representing and validating customer needs. The format is: in my role as ____, I need ____, so that ___. This approach is commonly used in Agile Innovation and Design Thinking methodologies. See **Stakeholder and Customer Analysis.**

Value Streams   are operational processes optimized for customers. Using the term *value streams* instead of similar terms like *process* or *activity* is a way for team members to signal the importance of remembering the customer. SIPOC (Supplier, Input, Process, Output, Customer) is an acronym for value streams from the worlds of Six Sigma and Lean Manufacturing.

Versioning   refers to managing the interdependencies, ripples, and speed of change by ensuring a structured process for versioning releases and updates. Matrix organizations and companies are like big spider webs, where each strand is connected to countless others. Touching one strand will vibrate through the whole network. The challenge is to manage changes to these interdependencies, relationships, and ways of working, while each strand continues its work. This links to Engaged Response and Agile Innovation.

Vertical and Horizontal Balance   refers to team members intentionally leveraging the natural creative tension between roles focused on vertical versus horizontal performance improvement. Figure G.19 shows a complete system of roles in an enterprise team matrix. This balance is especially critical in stage 3 Distributed Leadership companies. See **Vertical and horizontal improvement, Creative tensions,** and **Enterprise Evolutionary Stages.**

Vertical Improvement   refers to improving the performance of a system by resolving and removing the limiting constraint, leading to a breakthrough that allows the team to attain a higher sustainable level of performance, awareness of focus, creative tensions, and disruption. See **Horizontal Improvement.**

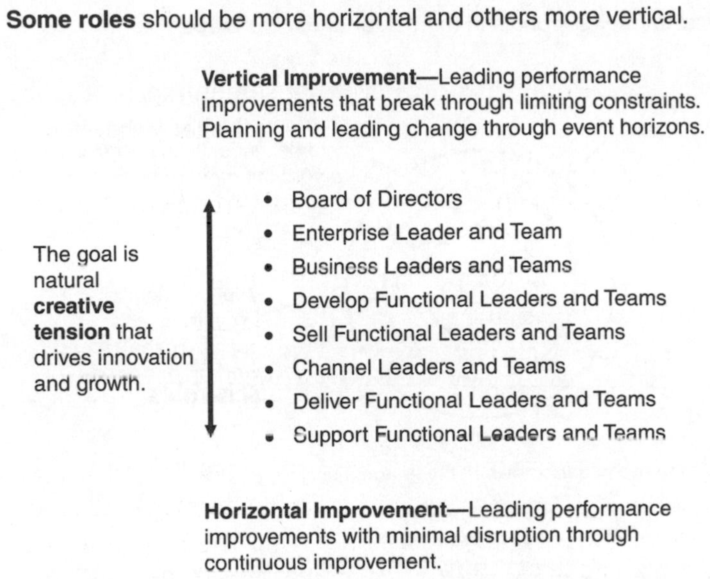

Some roles should be more horizontal and others more vertical.

Vertical Improvement—Leading performance improvements that break through limiting constraints. Planning and leading change through event horizons.

The goal is natural **creative tension** that drives innovation and growth.

- Board of Directors
- Enterprise Leader and Team
- Business Leaders and Teams
- Develop Functional Leaders and Teams
- Sell Functional Leaders and Teams
- Channel Leaders and Teams
- Deliver Functional Leaders and Teams
- Support Functional Leaders and Teams

Horizontal Improvement—Leading performance improvements with minimal disruption through continuous improvement.

FIGURE G.19   Vertical and Horizontal in an Enterprise

Visualizing Shared Work   refers to team members visualizing workflows, processes, and systems as a basis for continuous improvement. We human beings are visual creatures. If we can see it and accurately name it, we can align to engage with it, whatever it is, together. Envisioning the processes and systems around us is the first step toward creating a shared language, defining accurate challenge statements, defining shared work, and aligning solutions. This links to the Driving Focus crucial conversation. Figure G.20 shows one method for teams to visualize shared work as a bullseye.

Visualizing the Matrix   refers to team members mapping the systems teams across the enterprise. See **System of Teams** and **Enterprise Maps.**

Ways of Working   refers to impactful agreements, deliverables, processes that enable teams to achieve higher performance. Artifacts of these ways of working serve as tangible evidence of a team's progress and continued commitment to higher performance. The ways of working in the Growth River OS are organized according to the Seven Crucial Conversations.

The most impactful work is in the center of the **Bullseye**.

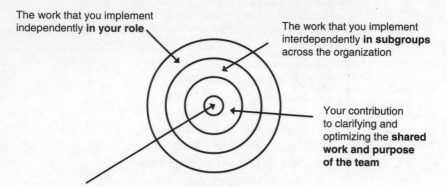

The work that you implement independently **in your role**

The work that you implement interdependently **in subgroups** across the organization

Your contribution to clarifying and optimizing the **shared work and purpose of the team**

Your contribution to **the organization** in these domains:

(1) Leadership and Culture Key Behaviors
(2) Team Effectiveness Ways of Working
(3) Systems of Capabilities and Roles for Creating Value
(4) System of Strategies for Winning
(5) Metrics for Competitive Advantage

FIGURE G.20   The Bullseye for Shared Work

Index

NOTE: Page references in *italics* refer to figures.